T0283663

Additional praise for *Super Deciders*

Besides providing an invaluable tool for decision-making in dynamic and uncertain times, the *Super Deciders* explores the role of personal inclinations, emotions, and values in decision-making. In doing so, it helps build self-awareness, empowering decision-makers make choices that align with their values and goals.

—**Alain Bejjani**, *former Chief Executive Officer of Majid al Futtaim*

The *Super Deciders* is a guide that blends the latest research with practical tools to chart your course wisely. It should be considered by every leader and strategist looking to thrive in an unpredictable world.

—**André Wyss**, *Chief Executive Officer of Implenia*

In times of permacrisis in business, as in life uncertainty abounds. Success heads of this volatile reality by embracing the notion of probability. In two instances in the past I had to face such challenges: first by defining the entry strategy in totally new markets of Central Europe after the fall of the Berlin Wall for ABB and secondly by ensuring a resilient supply chain and substantial impact on profitability during the financial crisis in 2008 for Siemens. The newly issued decision navigator is based on recent findings in neurology, management, and psychology. It is a comprehensive and useful model for thriving in today's ambiguous, volatile and fast-changing markets.

—**Barbara Kux**, *Multiple Board Director*

This book brilliantly develops a powerful framework of the decision-making process and integrates scientific principles, hypotheses testing, and real-world applications while offering approaches for leaders to work on themselves to become better decision-makers in the complexities of our dynamically evolving world. Making important decisions under uncertainty is a quite frequent reality in the business, public administration, and academic world, but an insufficiently researched topic with limited insightful practical advice. This book fills the gap making it an essential read for all present and future leaders.

—**Bruno Pfister**, *Corporate Director and Private Investor,*
former CEO of Swiss Life Group

This book is a compass for decision-makers in a fast-paced world. It expertly combines the science of decision making with practical insights, ensuring that leaders are well-prepared to succeed in today's dynamic and uncertain times.

—**F. Michael Ball**, *Chairman of Alcon*

Just thinking about if you should be getting another coffee or not is a grind? Then this book's for you. Isabelle Dubois, the book's main character will take you thru the newest decision-making techniques. And prepare you for the VUCA world we live in. The story will draw you in in not time.

—**Fabian Unteregger**, *Comedian, Entrepreneur, and Author.*

Making decisions is fun and making the right decisions even more so!! However, the luxury of having choices in our professional and private lives may become a burden when being concerned about the risks of wrong decisions. Assuming that there is no wrong decision at the time it was made—because it was made with the best of knowledge, tools, intuition and at the right speed—is hence liberating. This book is giving us the tools to feel that way and, if in hindsight we did not make this expected "super decision", the book helps us to understand that we are on a journey and learning from the wrong decisions will turn the multiple decision-making paths into inspiration and success.

—Jean-Christophe Deslarzes,
Chair of the Adecco Group and Chair of Constellium

Super Deciders is a must-read for decision-makers in today's fast-changing environment. The decision model that the book outlines, combines intuition and experience with experimentation. It not only leads to better decision making, it also helps to build agile, learning organizations that will thrive in today's markets.

—Joe Jimenez,
former Chief Executive Officer of Novartis

Decisions have a lot to do with us, with our feelings, our emotions, our values, and our personalities. This book explains how all these factors shape the decisions we make and how–working on ourselves – we can learn to make better decisions.

—Kathrin Amacker, *Board President Max Havelaar Foundation,*
Board Member Basel University,
former Member Executive Board Swisscom and SBB

There is a growing gap for senior leader teams to make critical decisions that will determine the future of their organizations. *Super Deciders* book gives leaders a scientific approach to improving their decision-making capability by cultivating an experimentation-based, learning-oriented, and adaptive approach to decision-making. This book is a must-read for any leader who works in a fast-changing environment where their decisions impact their companies and society. After reading this book leaders will have the tools needed to enhance their decision-making and increase their ability to take well-founded, calculated risks.

—Lisa Danels, *Executive Director of Human Edge Management*
and author of The Human Edge Advantage

Today's volatile and fast-changing markets and changing consumer needs make planning ahead challenging. Companies are required to use their collective intelligence to build flexible strategies and to learn and adapt as they progress. *Super Deciders* is an indispensable read for leaders that want to build flexible strategies and agile organizations.

—**Michele Rodoni**, *Chief Executive Officer of Mobiliar*

Super Deciders is a true gem for those who crave both knowledge and entertainment. This book seamlessly merges the thrill of a fiction novel with the depth of serious science, offering a refreshing and enlightening perspective on decision-making in our fast-paced, uncertain world.

—**Peter Olson**, *former Chairman and Chief Executive Officer of Random House*

In *Super Deciders* the authors brilliantly explore the complex terrain of decision-making in uncertain times. Grounded in science and the principles of humility and self-awareness, the proposed framework for decision-making offers a practical approach to steer organizations in today's dynamic markets.

—**Pierre Gurdjian**, *Chair of Board of Directors of Solvay*

Super Deciders delivers profound and practical insights on understanding and resolving many dilemmas we face in today's world.

—**Pietro Supino**, *Publisher & Chairman of TX Group*

Super Deciders is an indispensable resource for anyone looking to improve their decision-making skills, especially in situations involving difficult, high-stakes outcomes where no obvious, right choice is immediately available or easy to see. Feser, Laureiro-Martinez, Frankenberger, and Brusoni introduce the highly-original Decision-Navigator model, which serves as a complement—not a substitute—to intuition and experience when making difficult decisions. The authors propose an experimentation-based approach that seeks to elicit relevant and helpful feedback to build intuition and to add to experience, thus aiding effective decision making. The model nudges decision makers into developing adaptive mindsets based on progressive and cumulative evidence-based learning, which is essential to effectively tackle tough decisions in complex and ambiguous environments, and to become "Super Deciders".

—**Ramon Casadesus-Masanell**,
Herman C. Krannert Professor of Business Administration
at the Harvard Business School,
and co-editor of the Journal of Economics & Management Strategy

Making Super Decisions is about teams, about critical thinking, and about staying humble. But it also about going onto a journey of introspection and self-leadership.

—**Roberto Paganoni**, *Managing Partner,*
Chief Executive Officer and co-founder of LGT Capital Partners

In *Super Deciders*, the authors deliver a compelling exploration of the science and practice of decision-making. They unveil the secrets of navigating through uncertainty by understanding the importance of building flexibility into each choice. This book is a compass for anyone on a journey of informed decision-making.

—**Stefan Asenkerschbaumer**,
Chair of the Supervisory Board, Bosch

This book is about making the best decisions for yourself and your business. It contains no magic formulas, but rather insightful advice drawn from experience, research and psychology to find the best ingredients for effective decision-making. A useful and impactful read for all managers in these uncertain times.

—**Thomas Buberl**, *Chief Executive Officer of AXA Group*

Super Deciders describes a structured approach on how to make and implement difficult and complex decisions in a fact-based, agile, and adaptive way. The book provides the ultimate resource for steering organizations in volatile and uncertain markets in the perma-crisis age.

—**Vassilios Psaltis**, *Chief Executive Officer of Alpha Bank*

The authors have masterfully distilled the essence of decision-making in a dynamic and uncertain world. *Super Deciders* is a must-read for anyone looking to enhance their ability to make informed choices, backed by rigorous research and practical advice.

—*Winfried Ruigrok*, *Former Dean of the Executive School of Management, Technology and Law, University of St. Gallen and Professor for International Management at the University of St. Gallen*

Super Deciders

Super Deciders

*The Science and
Practice of Making Decisions
in Dynamic and Uncertain
Times*

Claudio Feser,
Daniella Laureiro-Martinez,
Karolin Frankenberger,
and Stefano Brusoni

WILEY

Registered Office(s)
John Wiley & Sons, Inc., 111 River Street, Hoboken, NJ 07030, USA
John Wiley & Sons Ltd, The Atrium, Southern Gate, Chichester, West Sussex, PO19 8SQ, UK

Editorial Office
The Atrium, Southern Gate, Chichester, West Sussex, PO19 8SQ, UK

For details of our global editorial offices, customer services, and more information about Wiley products visit us at www.wiley.com.

Wiley also publishes its books in a variety of electronic formats and by print-on-demand. Some content that appears in standard print versions of this book may not be available in other formats.

Library of Congress Cataloging-in-Publication Data is Available:

ISBN 9781394239771 (Hardback)
ISBN 9781394238842 (ePDF)
ISBN 9781394238835 (ePub)

Cover Design and Image: Wiley

SKY10066026_012924

Contents

Foreword by Mario Greco   xiii

Introduction   xix

Prologue   xxvii

Part One: Understanding Decisions
Under Uncertainty

Chapter 1: Making Great Predictions   3
Chapter 2: Case 1: Making People Decisions   19
Chapter 3: Developing Options to Approximate
               the Right Decision   29

Part Two: Making Decisions
Under Uncertainty

Chapter 4: Case 2: Making Strategic Decisions   57
Chapter 5: Identifying Assumptions and Testing Them   69

Chapter 6: Case 3: Making Decisions About
Company Growth 95
Chapter 7: Developing Better Options 107

**Part Three: Managing the Tensions
Created by Decisions Under Uncertainty**

Chapter 8: Case 4: Implementing Decisions 129
Chapter 9: Managing Change 135

Part Four: Becoming Super Deciders

Chapter 10: Case 5: Making Work-Life Balance Decisions 157
Chapter 11: Becoming Better at Making Decisions 165
Chapter 12: Case 6: Making "Tough" Decisions 185
Chapter 13: Preparing to Be Wrong 195

Part Five: Conclusions

Chapter 14: Epilogue 211
Chapter 15: Conclusions 215

Notes 225
Appendixes 227
References 249
About the Authors 267
Index 271

Foreword

I have been Chief Executive Officer of insurance companies for more than ten years of my professional life. Decision-making is the constant and defining aspect of my daily routine and it is what colleagues expect from me. I have learned a lot during my career, from the intricacies of the products to the nuances of the markets and to the subjective preferences of very different individuals. Especially, I have learned how to make decisions in uncertain conditions, facing different emergency situations.

This knowledge and experience have equipped me with the ability to make – I believe – informed and sound decisions in today's industry.

However, the insurance industry – like many other industries – is now changing rapidly. What once was considered a mature, highly regulated, and relatively stable industry is now experiencing rapid and fundamental changes due to technology, changing customer needs, and changing stakeholder expectations.

The advent of emerging technologies, particularly digital connectivity, big data and artificial intelligence (AI) has brought forth innovative competitors and has created new opportunities for the leaders of the industry. For instance, digital connectivity is allowing us today to provide valuable, needed services to customers and is making access to insurance easy and fast. Big data are allowing us to carefully price risks, rewarding good risk customers and properly managing capital exposures. AI offers immense opportunities to improve services and can be harnessed to develop more accurate risk assessment models, among others.

The rapid shifts in customer preferences and expectations are not solely a result of technological advances but also of demographic changes. The rise of Gen Z, the generation born between the mid-1990s and the early 2010s, has brought forward a new set of expectations. Gen Z is characterized by their digital fluency, their desire for personalized and convenient services, and, importantly, for their environmental consciousness. Customers are increasingly interested in insurance products that align with their sustainability goals. For instance, they seek policies that provide coverage for eco-friendly initiatives, green technologies, and climate change-related risks.

Sustainability isn't changing the expectations of only customers, but also those of many other stakeholders. Stakeholders in the insurance sector encompass a broad spectrum, including investors, regulatory bodies, advocacy groups, and the general public. These stakeholders increasingly demand that insurance companies take an active role in addressing environmental and social issues. This includes the insurance industry's commitment to sustainable practices, such as reducing its carbon footprint, supporting renewable energy, and providing insurance products that promote sustainability, like policies for green businesses or renewable energy projects. It also includes a heightened emphasis on transparency and ethical conduct. Stakeholders expect insurance companies to disclose their environmental, social, and governance performance, that is, reporting on carbon emissions, diversity and inclusion efforts, and responsible investment practices, among others. Investors, in particular, are increasingly evaluating insurance companies based on their approach to sustainability. Firms that embrace sustainability are seen as more resilient in the face of environmental and social disruptions, making them attractive to investors seeking sustainable returns.

These changes demand agility and responsiveness from organizations and leaders alike.

But agility isn't only about dealing with those changes. It is also about dealing with heightened uncertainty. The unpredictability introduced by new technologies, shifting customer behaviors, and evolving stakeholder expectations is accentuated by geopolitical developments and by emerging new risks such as pandemic diseases. In a volatile environment characterized by wars, geopolitical crises, and new health crises, the insurance industry – like many other industries – faces uncertainty and risk. Geopolitical shifts can lead to economic instability, changing regulations, and increased concerns about security.

Nobody can really predict how all these changes will pan out, where this all will lead us, and how the insurance industry will look at the end of this decade.

While knowledge and experience worked well in the past, they may not be sufficient to lead large organizations in our industry into the future the same way we used to lead them a decade ago. On the contrary, knowledge and experience, while a cornerstone of effective decision-making, can today inadvertently blind us to new challenges and opportunities in this fast-paced, rapidly changing, and uncertain world.

This book, which I wholeheartedly recommend, serves as a guide to augmenting our knowledge and experience with a multi-faceted approach in uncertain scenarios. It highlights an approach that builds on team collaboration, critical thinking, data and facts, humility, and values.

Team collaboration means using teams across the organization to encourage diverse perspectives, ideas, and points of view, thus fostering a richer, more informed decision-making process.

Critical thinking means advocating for the practice of asking questions rather than asserting answers, emphasizing the importance of taking time and "digging deeper" with questions such as "Why do I believe what I believe? What assumptions I am making?" or "Why do you believe what you believe? What are your hypotheses?"

Data and facts suggest a shift in our approach from asserting beliefs to acknowledging hypotheses and assumptions that can be tested and validated. It is about changing the way we think and speak about what we believe. It is changing the narrative from "I believe it is" to "my hypothesis is" or "my assumption is." Beliefs are personal, rigid, and are difficult to challenge. Challenging someone's beliefs often means challenging someone's identity or character. Hypotheses and assumptions are not personal. They are just what they are: hypotheses and assumptions that can be tested and validated. They are flexible and change as new facts emerge. This flexibility allows for learning as new evidence emerges, reducing rigidity in thinking and decision-making.

Humility means recognizing the importance of humility in leadership, acknowledging that we don't have all the answers and can learn from others.

Values means making decisions using an inner compass. Sometimes when making decisions in dynamic situations we face dilemmas, a situation in which no available option is desirable. Sometimes we can't or don't have the time to search for an "optimal" option to choose, and we need to make a decision that may turn out to be the wrong choice of option. In these situations, values – our inner compass – matter. In these situations, when the environment changes rapidly and not in our favor, we may end up having chosen the wrong option. But at least we made "the right" decision creating inspiration and followership that will help leaders when making the next decision. Making decisions based on values may differentiate great leaders from mediocre leaders.

The approach outlined in this book fosters a culture of continuous learning. It encourages organizations to experiment, study, learn, and adapt as they evolve.

But it's not solely about adaptation in a rapidly changing environment; it's about actively shaping the course of developments.

Firms are often likened to living organisms, responsive to environmental changes. However, firms are not biological entities; they are shaped by the decisions and actions of their leaders.

This book champions the concept of "super decisions," highlighting the power of effective leadership in shaping organizations. It's an invitation to embrace an approach to decision-making that can make a substantial difference in shaping the development of organizations, and because organizations are composed of people, in the development of people's lives and of society.

Making "Super Decisions" can help shape our future.

Mario Greco
Chief Executive Officer
Zurich Insurance Group

Introduction

**Claudio Feser, Daniella Laureiro-Martinez,
Karolin Frankenberger, and Stefano Brusoni**

Should we improve our internal combustion engine or switch to electric engines? Should we upgrade our organization or change it? Should we optimize our branch network or launch a digital channel? Should we build our new business organically, or buy a competitor to accelerate our development?

These are all examples of "either/or" decisions that executives face day in, day out. Deciding on and resolving such dilemmas constitute much of what executives do. According to a recent study by the consultancy firm McKinsey & Company, executives spend nearly 40% of their time making decisions (De Smet et al., 2019). Management guru Peter Drucker wrote that whatever managers do, they do it through making decisions (Drucker, 1967).

The performance of executives is to a large extent the result of the quality of their decisions (Harrison, 1996). In fact, research suggests that, of all leadership skills, decision-making is the one most strongly associated with leadership effectiveness (Hoffman et al., 2011).

In business, making good decisions matters and making bad ones can be fatal.

In the late 2000s, major automotive companies largely overlooked the demand for fully electric cars and were reluctant to invest in electric vehicle technology. Tesla, a newcomer in the industry, seized upon this opportunity and disrupted the market to become the world's most valuable automotive company in July 2020. In 2008, Yahoo rejected a takeover bid of nearly USD 45 billion from Microsoft. In 2012, the Instagram founders agreed to a USD 1 billion sale to Facebook. They may regret it. Instagram is now arguably one of the hottest social networks on the planet. As of 2023, it generated over USD 50 billion in revenues for Meta (formely the Facebook company) and analysts estimate it to be worth over USD 100 billion. Until late 2022, Google decided not to launch new services based on their LLM technology, paving the way for OpenAI's ChatGPT to dominate the generative artificial intelligence market.

The importance of making good decisions isn't limited to the realm of important business decisions. It comes up in every walk of life. Who should I marry? Should I marry my current partner or continue searching for my perfect match? Should we stay as a couple, or should we have kids? What is the best next step in my career? Should I stay and build my career at my current company, or change company or even career?

Making good decisions isn't easy. We make most decisions in dynamic situations, and they are dynamic in two ways. First, externally, meaning that often, when we need to make decisions, we're missing relevant information. Time is tight, we're facing uncertainty, and the environment is constantly changing. Second, internally, our objectives, preferences, and inclinations are not stable, they evolve and depend on the context.

This book is about making great decisions – or what we call super-decisions – in dynamic, ambiguous, and uncertain environments. No general rule or mathematical formula will tell you how to make such decisions exactly or perfectly. However, understanding what drives decisions under uncertainty can help leaders make better decisions.

This book explores the factors that drive effective decision-making as reported in research in neuroscience, psychology, and management. It explains the scientific foundations of decision-making and adaptation in volatile, fluid environments.

It introduces a model of decision-making, which we call the Decision Navigator. An evidence-based model, the Decision Navigator significantly improves decision-making performance in uncertain and dynamic situations. It improves the quality of decisions of both individuals and organizations as it helps creating learning environments and cultures where people perceive decisions as experiments and do not stigmatize failing initiatives, but rather understand them as steps on a journey toward new knowledge, insights, and progress.

Making great decisions does not depend solely on the situation. They are also a result from our objectives, our preferences, and our inclinations. Importantly, the model we put forward in this book fosters introspection and contributes to self-knowledge.

Structure of the Book

The book is divided into five Parts.

In Part I, "Understanding Decisions Under Uncertainty," it discusses decisions under uncertainty as "either/or" dilemmas – specifically, as exploit/explore dilemmas. Our brain has the tendency to present decisions in complex situations as a challenge of choosing either stability (exploit) or change (explore). The choice is not obvious. Stability has many advantages. It builds on experience. But experience may not be sufficient when the environment changes, and when change might be the right approach.

Part II, "Making Decisions Under Uncertainty," builds on advances in neuroscience, management, and psychology to outline the Decision Navigator model. The model transforms high stakes "either/or" decisions into a step-by-step process of developing options, testing assumptions, and refining decisions. The model combines the advantages of two alternative problem-solving approaches, the inductive and the deductive, and creates innovative, creative, and possibly less biased decisions. It also recognizes that cognition and emotions are not two separate entities, but always interact, and should do so to achieve good decisions.

We make most of our daily decisions efficiently and fast, leveraging intuition and experience. The Decision Navigator model is a slow approach to decision-making. It is a model of decision-making that fits high-stakes, important decisions in unfamiliar situations, where relying solely on intuition and experience may not be sufficient. The Decision Navigator model cultivates an experimentation-based, learning-oriented, and adaptive approach to decision-making that matches the complex, environment in which we operate.

In Part III, "Managing the Tensions Created by Decisions Under Uncertainty," the book explores venues for managing tensions in organizations. Such tensions arise from addressing exploration/exploitation dilemmas of organizations and from pursuing several, often contradictory strategies simultaneously. While reviewing approaches to handling these tensions, the book discusses a framework for effectively managing corporate adaptation and change.

Part IV, "Becoming Super Deciders," illustrates approaches leaders can use to become superior decision-makers. Some leaders may be better than others at making decisions, but everyone can become better at it. The book explores how leaders can work on themselves – managing their cognitive states, furthering their cognitive skills, and better knowing what they stand for and what drives them – to improve their decision-making under uncertainty, that is, to become "Super Deciders."

Part V, "Conclusions," summarizes the book's key concepts and derives implications for both individual decision-makers and organizations.

This book is intended for leaders and potential leaders in organizations, individuals who frequently make or will make far-reaching decisions in dynamic situations. But we hope it is not only for leaders.

Following the launch of ChatGPT, the public discussion about the opportunities and dangers of AI has gained considerable momentum. Historian Yuval Noah Harari, for instance, argues that AI has the potential to destroy democracy (*The Economist*, 2023). He argues that democracy is a conversation, and conversations rely on language. When AI can manipulate language, he argues, it could destroy our ability to have meaningful conversations, thereby destroying democracy. AI has developed a remarkable ability to manipulate and generate reality, whether with words, sounds or images. For instance, in June 2022, several mayors of European capitals were deceived by an AI-generated deepfake of Vitali Klitschko, the mayor of Kyiv. The deepfake argued against arming the Ukrainian army and highlighted the risk of migration in Europe of a prolonged war in the Ukraine.

The benefits of the proposed concepts of decision-making may go well beyond improving the effectiveness of decisions in organizations. By augmenting intuition and experience through a "scientific experimentation" approach, the concepts presented in this book may foster critical thinking and help people to effectively function in a world where AI can exploit our brain's predisposition to use experience and stereotypes, and where AI can distort our perceptions and influence our thinking. This book may prove to be useful for everyone.

To make the concept of Super Deciders specific and practical, the book illustrates it with a narrative that unfolds through the experiences of Isabelle Dubois, a fictional CEO of an equally fictional international travel operator. Unlike prior work of researchers who often think of decisions as "discrete," isolated events, we describe making decisions as journeys of navigating an ever-changing environment. Decisions are path-dependent: all decisions we make are connected, each a step leading to another step. Also, we do not travel alone: we do not make decisions by isolating ourselves from everything and everyone. We need interactions to reflect and frame problems. The cases that we describe unfold as a journey and are meant to generate a reflection also about how Isabelle interacts with other people, and how these interactions help her make sense of the situation she finds herself in.

Isabelle will undertake a journey of discovering, step-by-step, the science of making decisions in uncertain and dynamic situations. She will also discover much about herself. We hope that this book will also spark some reflections about yourself.

The story is composed of six separate cases, Cases 1–6, which build on one another. The cases transport you into real-life situations of making difficult, high-stakes decisions. They include people-related decisions, decisions about company's strategy and expansion, how to manage organizational change and work-life balance. We also discuss the so-called "tough decisions", dilemmas for which there seems to exist no good solution. The six cases are currently in use as teaching cases in the Executive MBA programs of the Swiss Federal Institute of Technology (ETH Zurich) and the University of St. Gallen. The story also includes dialogues between Isabelle and Eve, an equally fictional young academic. These dialogues are intended to help the reader to connect the different decisions that Isabelle makes to relevant scientific research. The dialogues are intended to fill the gap between practice and research. They also provide, to those who are interested, additional material to explore selected topics more fully.

We would like to emphasize that the cases and the overall narrative are pure fiction. The cases are exemplary of situations that we have encountered many times in our consulting and research experience. While fictional, they capture – we believe – in a realistic way the fundamental features of many relevant decisions made under uncertainty.

Any resemblance to any existing persons, firms, or events is purely coincidental.

Now, let's meet the main character in our story, Isabelle Dubois, the CEO of ATG. Like you, she is about to go on a journey.

Prologue

**Claudio Feser, David Redaschi,
and Karolin Frankenberger**

It was an unusually sunny and chilly day in November when Franziska stood nervously at the entrance to the CEO's office, waiting to meet the new CEO. Franziska was the assistant to the CEO of Alpina Travel Group, ATG for short, a large tour operator based in Zurich, Switzerland. The last CEO, Jack Mayer, had been quite strict and unapproachable. He always kept his distance and never cracked even a tiny smile. For this reason, Franziska was quite surprised when Isabelle Dubois arrived. The woman with the warm expression and dark hair had to be ATG's new CEO. She came straight up to Franziska.

Franziska gulped, "Good morning, Mrs. Dubois, I am Franziska Knecht, your assistant."

"Pleased to meet you, but call me Isabelle," Isabelle said, extending her hand.

Franziska then reached for Isabelle's beautiful but worn bag. Isabelle immediately picked it up herself. "That's fine, thank you,

you do not have to carry the bag for me," she said firmly, but pleasantly. "Is this my new office?"

Franziska nodded, though she was quite confused by Isabelle's self-confident yet inclusive, non-hierarchical appearance, that starkly contrasted with that of Isabelle's predecessor.

"Thank you for welcoming me," Isabelle said. "Have you been with the company long?"

"For about three years, Ms. Dubois," Franziska said as they entered the CEO's office. "I worked with your predecessor, Dr. Mayer."

"Please call me Isabelle," the new CEO said again in a calm but firm voice.

"Yes, Mrs. Dubois, ahh. Sorry, I meant Mrs. Isabelle, uh, Isabelle."

"That's okay. Is it alright if I call you Franziska?" asked Isabelle.

"Yes, of course! Thank you!"

"How are things going at ATG? Do you like the company?" Isabelle continued.

Shocked at Isabelle's interest and still feeling the nervous anticipation of the last few weeks, Franziska found herself practically babbling, "Working at ATG is a great honor and joy for me. I love traveling. It opens new horizons, new perspectives. It makes people more empathetic and understanding of each other's cultures. It brings people closer together."

"Working for ATG is an honor for me too, Franziska. Could you please ask if the GET members have time to meet me? I would like to meet them, individually," said Isabelle.

"Sure. I'll call immediately and see who is available. . ."

Franziska's voice trailed off as she walked almost backward out of Isabelle's office.

Isabelle smiled faintly and leaned back in her executive chair and enjoyed the view. Her new office was on the top floor of a high-rise in Zurich. The large windows offered a fantastic view of the skyline with the Alps in the distance. There was almost no snow on the peaks even though it was the end of November. Proud to be back home in Switzerland and in her new executive office, Isabelle let her thoughts drift to the events of the last few months.

Since the late Alpine explorer Manfred Lohner founded Alpina Travel Group, or ATG, more than 80 years ago, the company had been a tour operator active in the "vacation travel" sector. ATG's great strengths included its customer base and its expertise in destinations. ATG specialized in planning, designing, and coordinating trips for all sizes of groups and all kinds of purpose. Overall, the company had a history of constant profitable growth.[1]

In the last years, however, it had come under increasing pressure. Changing customer needs and the emergence of digital travel companies, such as Booken.com, had caused ATG's market share to dwindle. For this reason, the board had appointed a new CEO, Jack F. Mayer, or as he liked to be called, Dr. Mayer. An accomplished and experienced executive in the travel industry, Jack Mayer came to ATG with strong opinions, and a directive leadership style. His pretentiousness, his arrogance, his assumption that he was always right, proved to be his downfall. His mission had been to align ATG with the industry's changing conditions and to put it back on the road to success. Unfortunately, he did not succeed, and he shredded internal morale. ATG's negative market situation continued to worsen, and sales plummeted.

ATG was still a leading player in the industry, but not the shining star it had been when Isabelle had left her job there as a rising executive eight years earlier. As ATG's position continued to deteriorate, the board spent nearly a year discussing Mayer's possible successors, though his dismissal took him by surprise. During that time, the board considered several internal and external candidates. In the end, however, they all appeared unsuitable.

Last spring, Carlo Proconi, chairman of ATG's board of directors in the last years of Mayer's tenure, had contacted Isabelle. He planned to be in Denmark and wanted to see her. She had started her career at ATG and had been on a strong upward trajectory before leaving for The Travel Group, a smaller Danish tour operator which hired her as Head of Marketing, a higher executive position. Two years later, she became Vice President of Sales and Marketing.

When she heard from Carlo, Isabelle was an integral member of The Travel Group's Executive Board. Leaving had not crossed her mind. The Travel Group, a niche-focused, fast-growing, Copenhagen-based tour operator owned by a European private equity firm, had a strong market position, providing high-end personalized travel experiences across Europe. Industry insiders saw clearly that Isabelle was the executive behind the company's growth with internal influence that extended far beyond her role in sales and marketing.

Carlo visited her in Copenhagen "to talk about the trends in the industry," as he put it. He was a tall man in his early sixties and, like Isabelle, a Swiss citizen, but from the Italian-speaking part of Switzerland. He was punctual, unassuming, thoughtful, and very experienced. He'd spent an impressive career in the financial industry and enjoyed the respect of the wider Swiss business community for his enterprising acumen, judgment, and integrity.

When Carlo and Isabelle sat down together, they didn't talk much about business. They spent most of their dinner talking about their families and personal interests. She was somewhat surprised, since they hadn't met before. But Isabelle immediately felt at ease. At the end of the day, just before Carlo left to catch his flight back to Zurich, he asked – casually, at least so it appeared, "Isabelle, would you consider coming back to Switzerland and to ATG?" Carlo told her about an opportunity to run a new ATG unit focused on business travel and the B2B market. Always ambitious, Isabelle was obviously very interested, because ATG was five times larger than The Travel Group company.

"Well," she told him, "I would consider it. In fact, I'm honored. I'd have to talk to Marco and the girls, but I think it would be great to join the executive team at ATG. Keep me posted."

For months, Isabelle heard nothing more. She thought Carlo had probably changed his mind. Then, six months later, when she had almost forgotten the conversation, Carlo called, "Isabelle, we are considering you for the position of CEO of ATG. Could you come to Zurich to meet some of our board members in the next few weeks?"

"Wow," Isabelle said. Being considered as a CEO candidate exceeded her wildest expectations. All sorts of thoughts flashed through her mind, and she worked to keep her emotions under control. "I need to think about this, and I need to discuss it with my family. When do I need to give you an answer?" she asked.

"Is 24 hours enough?" Carlo answered.

Isabelle took a few hours off. She took a walk through the nearby park where she usually ran in the early morning. She needed to sort out her thoughts and think things through. That evening, she and her husband Marco talked about the opportunity to return to ATG for several hours. Eight years earlier, when she was an up-and-comer at ATG, the offer to join The Travel Group had seemed very risky, but Isabelle saw it as a big opportunity to accelerate her career.

At the time, Marco had accepted the change, albeit reluctantly. Since he had already established good working relationships with publishers in Zurich, moving to Denmark didn't seem ideal for his career as a novelist. Marco was making a transition from his more serious earlier works, including the Booker-nominated *Mann & Mankind*, to a fledgling series of historical detective mysteries, already known for both authenticity and wit. He and his publisher both hoped his *Charlemagne's Secrets* series would be a hit. As it was – and continued to be.

Now, after eight years, he had come to enjoy writing clever mysteries and living in Copenhagen. He and Isabelle had many friends, and their daughters, Marie and Annelies, were happy, doing well in school, and developing splendidly.

But Marco knew what her role as CEO at ATG meant to Isabelle, and he was ready, though certainly not immediately happy, to move his family back to Zurich. Marie, 15, belonged to a student group dedicated to the environment and all things related to Greta Thunberg, and Annelies, 12, was a rising star on her school's tennis team. He and Isabelle hoped that the girls could replicate those opportunities in Zurich.

For as long as she could remember, Isabelle had worked hard, really hard, for this chance. Isabelle was the last child born into a family of six. The family was poor. The father, sometimes working as a carpenter, but often unemployed, was a heavy drinker. When drunk, he would become violent and hurt Isabelle's mom and the children. Her mom was just trying to survive. She was trying to make ends meet to provide the necessities for the kids. But beyond that, she didn't have much to give to the children, neither time nor affection.

The experiences of her childhood left wounds. Isabelle often felt sad and irritated. She continuously longed for recognition, but she couldn't say why. She always felt under pressure to prove to the world and to herself that she could do whatever she set her mind to, but few people other than Marco knew the depth of her wounds and her feelings. She had a hard time trusting other people, other than her husband and the girls. She didn't have any friend that she could discuss matters in confidence with. Although her siblings shared the same childhood, they didn't trust each other either. If anything, they were competing, in the past, for the little attention their mother was able to give, now for anything. Her perfectly polished exterior projecting self-confidence revealed little of her insecurities. Isabelle was a lonely ranger who had learned to hide her emotions.

But despite the experiences in her childhood, she had managed to develop strengths in many areas. She had learned to fight. She was smart, tough, and combative. She set ambitious targets for herself, and she worked hard, really hard, to achieve them. She built assets that served her well: her ambition, her drive, and her work ethic earned her a full scholarship at the University of Zurich, an Executive MBA, and now the role of the CEO of ATG.

For her, being appointed CEO of ATG was the pinnacle of an impressive career and the ultimate confirmation of her abilities. For a woman who constantly sought affirmation, recognition, and admiration, the opportunity felt like the ultimate triumph. "After all these years and sacrifices, I now have the chance to become the CEO of ATG. This is incredible," she thought.

The next morning, Isabelle called Carlo: "I would be very happy to apply for the job. It is a great honor for me to be given a chance. Thank you for your confidence in my abilities. When should I fly down to meet the board members?"

"Can you come next week?" asked Carlo.

Two months later, the board announced the appointment of Isabelle Dubois as CEO of ATG.

Despite her success at The Travel Group, Isabelle's appointment as CEO was a surprise to everyone. The Swiss business media covered her appointment extensively. Some newspapers questioned the decision of the board to appoint her. They reported on it as if ATG's board had entrusted one of the country's leading, best-known companies to an inexperienced, young woman. In her mid-forties, Isabelle was indeed young. Most of the members of ATG's executive team were in their mid-fifties. Although Isabelle had held important positions in finance and marketing at both ATG and The Travel Group, she had never been a CEO.

Isabelle's start at ATG was rocky. On day one, after a series of brief introductory meetings with the members of the executive team, also known as the Group Executive Team and a town-hall with hundreds of employees in the large auditor-ium of the Zurich headquarters, Isabelle sat down for a longer session with the CFO, Hugo Werner, to discuss ATG's upcoming third-quarter results.

Hugo was a German, from Munich's suburbs which gave him a strong Bavarian accent. He was highly respected in the investment community. He had been one of the two internal candidates for the chief executive position, but he didn't seem to resent the board's decision to select Isabelle. His short, precise way of speaking – he never said an extra word, even to explain himself – and his stiff, formal suits showed his seriousness and competence. While he faced change reluctantly, Hugo was a capable, resolute executive.

"Estimates of third-quarter profit show a 38% year-over-year decline," Hugo told Isabelle flatly, soon after she took office. "This is due to unfavorable exchange rate movements with the Swiss franc. Our fundamental position and momentum remain strong. Our investors will see through this, and they'll understand."

They didn't.

Following the release of the third-quarter results in mid-November, ATG's share price fell 11%. But the results were not the only problem.

As she learned more about ATG, Isabelle quickly discovered some of the reasons why the organization no longer held the leadership position it had enjoyed when she had left for The Travel Group. ATG had lost its edge. It had missed the opportunity to digitize its business model just when digitization – that is online marketplaces, digital enablement of travel, and gaming, among others – increased the number and heft of its competitors – both large companies and small niche players.

Struggling to keep abreast of its rivals, ATG was shrinking and losing market share, and its profitability was depressed.

But the lack of digitization and the depressed profitability weren't the only concerns she had. The economy was cooling down and tour operators started to experience a more general slow-down in demand. Further, a number of new trends beyond digitization – ecotourism, personalization, Bleisure travel (the combination of business and leisure travel), among others – started to emerge and it was unclear how this would impact not only the performance, but also the strategic outlook of the travel industry.

But the outlook wasn't only uncertain for the industry, it was particularly uncertain for ATG.

Its investors were wondering what's next. They seemed nervous. Even before the earnings release, the volatility of ATG's share price had been increasing, and significantly so in recent months.

The morning after the earnings release, Isabelle flew to London to meet and pacify some of the investors, including its main investor, LHF, a large hedge fund.

Isabelle felt irritated and alone. ATG's current performance was poor, and the strategic outlook very uncertain. And it seemed that she could not expect much help from her GET colleagues. The welcome that the new CEO – the "whiz kid," as she was cynically but not overtly called – received from her top management team colleagues was icy, to say the least.

Life had taught her that it was more advantageous to appear self-contained and inclusive when making decisions, but now she wasn't so sure. She wondered whether she should become more directive with the GET members.

She boarded the plane and was greeted by name by the crew. Being the CEO of a well-known company in the travel industry makes one visible, she thought. She enjoyed the recognition. As the plane took off, her thoughts quickly went back to the situation of ATG.

Isabelle was so immersed in her thoughts that she didn't notice the young woman who had sat down next to her. The woman, who must have been in her mid-thirties was immersed in reading and making corrections to the stapled pages of a paper titled, "Making Decisions in Dynamic and Uncertain Situations."

She caught Isabelle's eye, and Isabelle couldn't help but say, "That paper has an interesting title."

"Thanks, I wrote it. I'm just proofreading it for the last time before it I submit it. It's part of my postdoctoral work."

"I'm Isabelle Dubois. I'm the CEO of ATG, the Swiss tour operator based in Zurich. Making decisions under uncertainty is important in my job."

"I am Dr. Eve Redoni, but please call me Eve. Pleased to meet you," Eve said with smile.

"Are you a professor, Eve?"

"Me? I wish!" she said with a laughter. "Hopefully, one day. I have written my habilitation, my postdoctoral thesis, to qualify as a professor, but I am not there yet. I started a career in management consulting but discovered that I enjoy doing research and teaching more than I do consulting. I research decision-making processes in practice, in particular, in situations of high uncertainty."

Eve was short and puny. She wore huge, horn-rimmed, thick spectacles on her tiny nose. The spectacles made her look like a nerd who had just escaped from a dusty library. But her voice was all but puny. She spoke fast, energetically, and enthusiastically, always with a big smile on her face.

"It is an interesting topic to me, but why did you decide to study it?" asked Isabelle.

"Decision-making has always been a passion, or rather a challenge that I have. I don't enjoy and I am not very good at making decisions. I tend to procrastinate when I need to make even the simplest decisions. Even when I need to decide on a restaurant for dinner, I struggle. I am helpless! It drives my boyfriend crazy. So, I thought by studying it, maybe I can improve," Eve said with a big smile on her face. Her openness and wit were disarming. They made Isabelle immediately feel at ease.

"I hope you do. I am also interested in the topic, because in my job I must make lots of decisions, and in the current environment it's really difficult. . . ."

"Well," said Eve, settling back in her seat, "shall I tell you a bit about my work?"

Unknowingly, Isabelle had started a conversation with a consultant turned academic, who was widely renowned for her work on the study of uncertainty and decision-making. It would turn out to be a wonderful and illuminating discussion. . .

Super Deciders

Part One

UNDERSTANDING DECISIONS UNDER UNCERTAINTY

Chapter 1

Making Great Predictions

**Claudio Feser, Daniella Laureiro-Martinez,
and Stefano Brusoni**

It is not enough to possess a good mind; the most important
thing is to apply it correctly.
—René Descartes, *Discourse on the Method* (2018)

During their flight to London, Isabelle shared with Eve some, but given confidentiality, not all aspects of her situation.

"The situation the company is facing is very challenging," she said, "I expected to be taking the helm of a well-performing, 'lighthouse firm' and I found myself in a situation where ATG is challenged on two fronts. One, poor results. In fact, I am flying to London to pacify some of our investors after the last earnings release. And, two, the market outlook is very uncertain. Like all our traditional competitors, we must make difficult decisions: should we digitize? Should we specialize on smaller niches? Should we merge with a competitor? But also, what changes should I make to the organization?"

"You seem to be facing uncertainty. A very dynamic situation with many unknowns. You probably wonder what is the right thing to do," commented Eve.

"Yes, I do. In this situation, and as a new CEO, the investors and the board are expecting me to address the situation, to analyze the situation, and to make important strategic and operational decisions," answered Isabelle.

"OK, you need to make lots of decisions under uncertainty," confirmed Eve.

"You have studied making decisions under uncertainty, I know. What are those?" asked Isabelle.

"Well, decisions can be categorized into one of three types. First, decisions under certainty. With decisions under certainty, you know all possible options and the consequences of each option. The outcomes of each option are certain. There is no risk, or if there is, it is minimal. Signing a rental contract for your apartment is a decision under certainty. You have only two options: you can sign it, or not. The outcome of signing is clear. You will have the right to use the apartment, and you will be bound by the provisions of the lease, including paying the rent. That's for sure," said Eve.

"OK, got it. What are the other two categories?"

"The second category is decisions under risk. As with decisions under certainty, you know all possible options and their outcomes. The outcomes are only probable, but you know the probabilities. These are situations for which the statistician Leonard Savage, who is generally regarded as the founder of probabilistic or Bayesian decision theory, coined the expression 'small worlds.' According to Savage, 'small worlds' are the situations in which Bayesian theory – in essence, probabilistic thinking – provides the best answer (Savage, 1954). Examples are the games of poker or blackjack. In those games, players know all possible card combinations and their payouts. Further, for each combination, which changes as the game unfolds, they know the probability of winning," added Eve.

"And the third?" asked Isabelle eagerly.

"The third category are decisions under uncertainty. With decisions under uncertainty, all possible options, outcomes, and probabilities are unknown. For such situations, Savage coined the term 'large worlds' (Savage, 1954). Examples of large worlds are decisions about when to plan a picnic, where to go on vacation, where to eat tonight, or whom to marry (Volz and Gigerenzer, 2012)."

"Well, aren't most of the decisions made under uncertainty?" asked Isabelle.

"Yes, that's right. Decisions under uncertainty come up in every realm of life: from simple decisions such as where to eat tonight (Shall we go to the usual place and order what we like and usually eat, or shall we order something different, or even try another restaurant?) to potentially life-changing decisions (What is the best next step in my career? Should I stay and build my career at my current company, or change companies or even careers?), all these decisions are decisions under uncertainty. We make such decisions most of the time, while we relatively seldom must make decisions under certainty or under known risk. What's interesting is that classical approaches of decision theory aren't sufficient to make decisions in such situations. Approaches such as scenario planning, decisions trees, and statistics are not sufficient because new branches in a decision tree continuously pop up, payouts aren't stable, nor are probabilities. To make decisions amid uncertainty, we need strategies beyond Bayes' rules."

"That is?" asked Isabelle.

Eve continued: "When making decisions under uncertainty we – consciously or unconsciously – make predictions about the future. We make a guess about the return of an investment, about the need for surgery of an unusual tumor, or about the behaviors of a competitor or an adversary (Satopää et al., 2021). And then, we apply heuristics, or general rules, to make decisions (Volz and Gigerenzer, 2012)."

"Predictions and heuristics? That sounds interesting. Can you tell me more?" asked Isabelle.

When making decisions under uncertainty we – consciously or unconsciously – make predictions about the future. And then, we apply heuristics, or general rules, to make decisions.

The Crystal Ball in Your Head: Wired to Make Predictions

Our brain's ability to make predictions may have been a key aspect of the development of the human species. Throughout the intricate tapestry of human evolution, the capacity of our ancestors to anticipate and prepare for potential future events provided a substantial survival advantage. In the primordial landscapes, being able to predict the movement of prey or anticipate the lurking of predators was paramount for survival. Over successive generations, individuals endowed with heightened predictive faculties were more likely to evade danger, secure sustenance, and subsequently reproduce. As such, natural selection favored these predictive neural circuits, leading to the gradual entrenchment of this ability within our brain's architecture (Figure 1.1). The advanced predictive capabilities we observe today in modern humans can be understood as a sophisticated manifestation of these primordial neural adaptations.

The brain's predictive wiring has also a crucial role in optimizing cognitive resources. As we will discuss later in the book, the human brain, while remarkably powerful, is also "chemically" expensive to operate. By constantly forecasting upcoming stimuli, the brain can effectively reduce the amount of information it needs to process at any given moment. Instead of reacting to every new piece of data as a unique and isolated event, the brain leverages past experiences to

Figure 1.1 Our brains are wired to make predictions.

set up expectations, allowing for quicker and more efficient responses to familiar stimuli. This not only reduces cognitive load and fatigue but also facilitates rapid decision-making in dynamic environments. Thus, the brain's predisposition to make predictions is not merely a relic of our evolutionary past, but a vital component of our cognitive economy.

"Sure," said Eve, who continued, "let me start with predictions. For example, there is a very interesting line of research that was started in 2011 by two psychologists teaching at the University of Pennsylvania: Philip Tetlock and Barbara Mellers. In that year, they launched the Good Judgment Project (GJP), a series of tournaments on predictions. Their goals were to understand whether some people are better at making guesses than others, and whether people doing forecasts could learn something from them and enhance their prediction performance. The GJP initiative, which ran from 2011 to 2015, asked forecasters to answer the types of questions that US intelligence agencies would pose to their analysts: would Greece exit the Eurozone? Would Russia see a leadership change? To what extent would China experience a financial panic? (Schoemaker and Tetlock, 2016). The tournaments run for long stretches of time, so that forecasters could gain more information, learn, and revise their predictions as they got closer to the event they were forecasting."

"Interesting approach!" said Isabelle.

Eve continued: "Indeed. The competition ignited a whole series of research papers. In a recent one, researchers studied the effect of different strategies – they called them 'treatments' – to improve forecasters' prediction accuracy (Satopää et al., 2021). They randomly assigned some forecasters to undergo three types of treatments. The first group of forecasters had to complete a tutorial on probabilistic reasoning. The tutorial trained forecasters in the basics of statistics and to avoid judgmental biases, such as overconfidence or confirmation biases, using data. The second group was asked to debate forecasts in teams. In this group, forecasters, whether they had received 'treatment one' or not, worked in teams in which they debated each other's predictions."

"And the third group?" asked Isabelle.

Eve continued: "The third group was called Track performance. Researchers tracked forecasters' results over time. Periodically, the researchers identified the top 2% of forecasters, which they called superforecasters, and gave them the chance to work with each other."

"So, the third strategy or treatment was to form groups of so-called superforecasters?"

"Yes, that's right," and Eve continued, "The researchers then analyzed and compared the accuracy of predictions made by people who received treatment and those who did not, calculating their individual and group performance. This may sound a bit technical, but they used Brier scores to measure the accuracy of the forecasters' predictions. Brier scores range between 0 and 1. A Brier score of 0 means that the forecaster always correctly predicts the future, and a score of 1 means that the forecaster never correctly predicts the future[1] (Schoemaker and Tetlock, 2016)."

"So, if it is a range, then the closer the score is to zero, the better the forecast or prediction?" asked Isabelle.

"Yes, that's exactly right. An average individual would typically get a score, a prediction accuracy, of 0.2–0.25," said Eve, who started to flip through the pages of her folder as she appeared to be looking for something.

"I found it! Here it is," said Eve holding up a page depicting a table for Isabelle to see (Figure 1.2).

Eve explained, "This analysis shows groups that received the different treatments, or combinations of treatments, and their respective Brier scores (Satopää et al., 2021)."

And she continued: "The analysis suggests that attending a tutorial in probabilistic thinking reduces the Brier score from 0.21 to 0.19, that is, it improves individual forecasters' prediction accuracy by 10%."

"10%? That's not insignificant, but also not a lot," said Isabelle.

Eve continued: "Well, the effect is much bigger when trained forecasters can debate their predictions with other people working in a team. Then the teams' prediction accuracy increases by another 26%, or by 33% compared to untrained individuals."

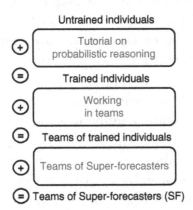

Figure 1.2:   Impact of selected interventions on prediction performance.
Source: Adapted from Satopää et al. (2021).

"That is quite a bit. So, teams overperform individuals. Does this imply that all decisions should be taken by teams?" asked Isabelle.

"Well, no, that's not the right conclusion. Teams aren't always the best solution," answered Eve. "While, in general, when making predictions in situations of uncertainty, teams outperform individuals, teams are not a panacea. Sometimes teams add little value, when, for instance, a decision-maker is surrounded by team members who clearly lack the necessary capabilities or willingness to contribute. Poor team dynamics can make teamwork and collaboration painful."

"Hmm. . . sounds familiar," mumbled Isabelle.

Eve continued: "Also, working in teams takes time. Issues sometimes need debating and that can be time-consuming. Team members need time to work together. They need to agree on common objectives, on the problems they are trying to solve, and on the approach forward, on how to solve the problems. It's not worth it for simple decisions, say, renewing a short-term lease in the office, or enhancing a product. Studies on team performance suggest that teams are not ideal when the tasks are simple. In such cases, teams just add complexity and time."

"So, when should I debate my predictions with others or use teams?" asked Isabelle.

"Let me show you another graph," answered Eve as she leafed through her papers looking for the graph. "Here it is. This comes from a study done by a group of researchers at University of Pennsylvania, MIT, and Purdue University. They compared the performance of 1,200 individuals working in teams and alone in solving tasks of varying complexity (Figure 1.3)."

Eve continued: "The graph shows that teams are not efficient for simple tasks, but clearly outperform individuals on complex tasks (Almaatouq et al., 2021)."

"That means that difficult decisions – the strategy of ATG, for instance – should be taken by a team. But also, that I should make sure that all team members are contributing constructively to the making of such a decision, that is, that we have good team dynamics," said Isabelle.

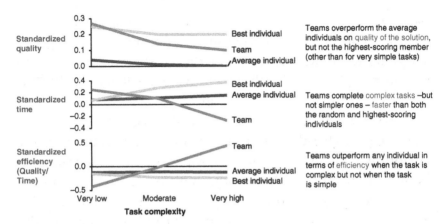

Figure 1.3: When do teams outperform?

Source: Almaatouq et al. (2021).

> Teams outperform individuals on complex tasks.

"That's exactly right," confirmed Eve.

"But tell me about the third intervention. Teams of superforecasters have even lower Brier scores. 0.08, that's very close to perfect predictions. That's massive!" affirmed Isabelle.

"Yes, if you put the 2% best forecasters in teams to debate their predictions, the teams' prediction accuracy increases by another 43% compared to individual forecasters who have received a tutorial in probabilistic thinking and who are working as a team," said Eve.

"Wow, that's impressive. What makes someone a great forecaster or a superforecaster? Are great forecasters just born with that gift or are they using specific prediction strategies or techniques that can be learned?" asked Isabelle.

"Well, it is a bit of both, but I'd dare say a lot of it can be learned," answered Eve. "In two studies published in 2015, Barbara Mellers and her colleagues tried to answer this very question (Mellers et al., 2015a; Mellers et al., 2015b). To understand what drives forecast accuracy, they looked at 15 or so different variables that can be broadly grouped into three categories. One, traits, that is, characteristics that individuals are born with and that are rather hard to change. Two, situational factors, such as, for instance, being placed in a group to debate forecasts. And, three, behavioral patterns that forecasters displayed during the tournaments (Mellers et al., 2015b)."

"What did they find?" asked Isabelle.

"Let's start with traits, which they called cognitive abilities and styles. The variable that most predicted forecast accuracy in this category was intelligence. The best forecasters, the superforecasters, were quite smart. They scored high on several measures of intelligence. They scored one standard deviation or more, higher than the general population on both fluid and crystallized intelligence. Fluid intelligence is the ability to quickly solve novel problems without any previously acquired knowledge. It is related to several important abilities, such as grasping new ideas, problem-solving, and learning (Unsworth et al., 2014). Crystallized intelligence is the ability to solve problems using knowledge acquired in the past. It is the ability to connect the dots and to develop new abstractions, new theories, based on experience (Cattell, 1987)," answered Eve.

"At least one standard deviation? That means that superforecasters were in the top 15–20% in terms of intelligence," said Isabelle.

Eve confirmed, "Yes, that's right. They were. Intelligence was the single most important driver in the category of cognitive abilities and styles, but there were a few more drivers that mattered: superforecasters tended to be competitive, they liked thinking, and they tended to be open-minded. They also did not seem to have a very 'deterministic' view of things (Tetlock and Gardner, 2016). They do not assume that what happens is meant to be. For them, faith doesn't play a big role. They preferred taking a scientific worldview (Mellers et al., 2015b)."

"OK, these traits are rather given. What about the second category, the situational factors?" asked Isabelle.

"Situational factors are interventions performed ahead of the start of the tournaments and included training forecasters in probabilistic thinking and forming groups to allow the forecasters to debate their predictions with others. In this category, working in teams was the most important driver of prediction accuracy," answered Eve.

"And the third category?" asked Isabelle.

"The third category included abilities and thinking styles exercised by great forecasters during the tournaments," responded Eve, and continued, "The category included behaviors such as how often forecasters gathered information, how frequently they updated their predictions, and how much time and effort they put into making predictions. While it turned out that all these behaviors mattered, the single most important predictor of forecast accuracy in this category was the frequency of updating forecasts. In fact, it wasn't only the most important factor in the behavioral category, it was the most important factor across all three categories. Superforecasters updated their estimates more frequently when new information became available, than the others (Mellers et al., 2015b). Great forecasters behaved like scientists. As more facts became available, they took the time to study them and to revise their estimates accordingly. Like scientists that revise their hypotheses when new evidence emerges."

"Interesting. Superforecasters work like scientists!"

"Yes, very much so. It is not so much who the forecasters were, but how they thought and, therefore, what they did. Their behaviors mattered more than other factors. Behaviors predicted forecast accuracy to a greater extent than dispositional traits or situational factors (Mellers et al., 2015a)," responded Eve, sharing another slide (Figure 1.4).

Eve continued: "This is good news, because behaviors can be trained and turned into skills."

"Hmmm. . . lots of insights," said Isabelle, and continued, "Let me summarize. First, most of the decisions we make every day are decisions under uncertainty. With decisions under uncertainty, all possible options, outcomes, and probabilities are unknown. Second, when making decisions, we – consciously or not – make predictions about outcomes and use heuristics to guide our decisions.

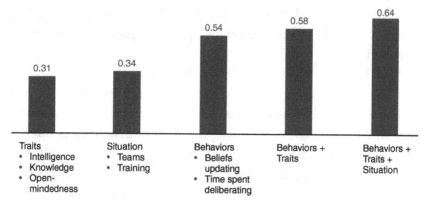

Figure 1.4: Predicting overall forecasting accuracy (Multiple R).
Source: Mellers et al. (2015a).

Third, debating predictions with others helps. Individuals who work with others make better predictions, and hence better decisions. Fourth, the ability to make predictions differs among people. Those who are best at it, the superforecasters, tend to be smart. But more importantly, they approach predictions like scientists. They continuously update their predictions when new evidence or data becomes available."

Do You Need to Be Super-Smart to Make Great Decisions?

General intelligence is generally considered to be fixed. Therefore, at this point of the discussion you may wonder whether – if you score average on intelligence tests – you are doomed to making poor predictions, and hence bad decisions.

You aren't.

There are several strategies that can help you increase your ability to make more accurate predictions. The most important ones are:

1. Build great teams. In two studies with 699 individuals working in groups of two to five, Anita Wooley from Carnegie Mellon University and colleagues showed that when diverse individuals collaborate effectively in groups, these groups develop a form of group intelligence called collective intelligence (CI), and that collective intelligence outperforms individual intelligence on a wide range of tasks. Interestingly, collective intelligence is neither strongly correlated with the average individual intelligence of group members, nor the maximum individual intelligence of group members. Collective intelligence relies on the average social sensitivity of group members (empathy), the equality in distribution of conversational turn-taking (equal share of voice), and the diversity (proportion of females) represented in the group (Wooley et al., 2010).

2. Surround yourself with smart people. Being together with intelligent people will not make you automatically smarter. But it will give you more to think about, as you are exposed to other points of view, differing perspectives, and opinions. That will help you make better predictions.

3. Take care of yourself. Several studies suggest that eating a healthy diet, exercising regularly, and getting enough sleep among others, will improve your cognitive abilities. More on this later in the book.

4. Possibly, adopt a growth mindset. The term growth mindset was coined by Carol Dweck, a psychologist teaching at Stanford University. In her work, including her important book, *Mindset: The New Psychology of Success*, she found that people doing better in life and at work are convinced that one can improve, that skills can be learned, and are

(continued)

16   Super Deciders

(continued)

not fixed or given (Dweck, 2006). For instance, in a 2019 study, 300 students who were taught to have a growth mindset achieved higher grades in advanced math classes than students who did not adopt a growth mindset. However, the size effect of adopting a growth mindset is a matter of debate currently. A recent study suggests that the positive effect of adopting a growth mindset on academic achievements might have been overestimated and that it might be rather small (Macnamara and Burgoyne, 2023).

But let's also add a note of caution on intelligence. Unlike decision-making skills, intelligence is not strongly correlated with leadership effectiveness (Hoffman et al., 2011). Also, above-average intelligence might be a blessing for predictions but a curse for decision-making. Studies suggest that while smart individuals may make better predictions, they may also be more vulnerable to cognitive biases than average intelligence individuals. For instance, a recent study revealed that the higher your IQ score, the higher the probability that you fall for stereotypes, a form of cognitive biases (Lick et al., 2018). As we will review later in the book, cognitive biases can lead to poor decisions, especially in volatile, unfamiliar environments.

"A perfect summary! That's a better synthesis than what I had in mind," said Eve.

"Yes, but hang on, what about the heuristics, the decisions rules, you mentioned earlier?" asked Isabelle, as the plane landed in London.

Eve, who was excited about Isabelle's interest in her thesis, started to speak faster, as if she was concerned she would not have enough time to share all her work. "Making good predictions is important, but not sufficient to make great decisions. Making the wrong decisions at work and, for that matter, in life, isn't the same as making predictions. Think of your own decisions. When advising a friend, say, on buying a house, you give excellent advice. But when making that decision for yourself, you struggle. All sorts of questions pop up in your mind. For instance, you may ask yourself, 'What will people think of me, if I buy a house in this area?', 'What if the sellers didn't give me all information? Will there be some work to do?', 'What if I am wrong in my assessment about the value of the house? Will I have overpaid?', and so forth. Your emotions get in your way."

"Sounds familiar," affirmed Isabelle.

"Yes. Not much happens when you make a wrong prediction. Unlike making a prediction such as a hypothetical forecast in a prediction tournament, wrong decisions in organizations – and life, actually – come at a cost. There is a difference between analyzing and taking risks. After all, not all great financial analysts are good investors, not all great consultants make great CEOs, not all great management professors make good businessmen or good businesswomen."

"Is that when heuristics come in?" asked Isabelle as passengers in the front rows started to stand up and leave the plane.

"Yes, exactly. When making decisions under uncertainty, a lot goes on in our brain. The brain uses – sometimes consciously, sometimes unconsciously – decision rules, sort of 'what-if' rules of thumb. I call them heuristics," answered Eve.

"Eve, I have to dash now," said Isabelle, who was in a hurry to make it to her first meeting in London. "I found this conversation incredibly insightful. It has given me a lot of food for thought. Is there a chance we could meet or even do a video call in the coming weeks? I'd love to understand what heuristics are and how they work!"

"Yes, of course. I love discussing and debating my work! It also helps me in making it more succinct. I like how you summarized it!" said Eve smiling as she stretched out her hand to shake Isabelle's. Isabelle, who felt satisfied and empowered by the conversation they just had, shook Eve's hand, and said goodbye.

Key Takeaways

- You spend a significant part of your day – at work and beyond – making decisions.
- Most of the decisions you make every day are decisions under uncertainty, where possible options, outcomes, and probabilities are unknown.
- When you make decisions, you – consciously or not – make predictions about outcomes and use heuristics to guide your decisions.
- When you debate our decisions with others, your predictions get better.

The ability to make predictions differs among people. Those who are best at it tend to be smart. That said, the most important factor that sets them apart is their scientific approach to forecasting: they put in the time and effort to reflect and revise their predictions with an open mind whenever new information becomes available.

Chapter 2

Case 1: Making People Decisions

Claudio Feser, David Redaschi,
and Karolin Frankenberger

In London, Isabelle was able to pacify ATG's main investors. That said, they asked a lot of questions about ATG's strategy, about ATG's organization, and about the company's top team; questions that she couldn't answer. She agreed to come back once she had found the answers.

In the following weeks and back in Zurich, Isabelle spent a lot of time familiarizing herself with all facets of ATG's situation. Above all, she wanted to understand how, as its new CEO, she could strategically develop the company. She asked ATG's strategy officer, Konstantinos "Kosta" Georgiades – a creative young Greek who had completed his master's degree at St. Gallen just a couple of years earlier – to develop a perspective on the travel market and ATG's position. He didn't have much time in the trenches, but he understood ATG remarkably well.

But while she waited for Konstantinos' report and her other research to come to fruition, ATG's overall situation continued to worsen. The economic environment was rapidly deteriorating, and therefore demand for leisure travel was plummeting (see Appendices 3 and 4). Isabelle needed to understand the financial implications of this new development as fast as possible. She asked Hugo to develop a financial outlook for the rest of the year and for the following 24 months. She specifically requested his estimate of how revenues, profits, the equity, and the cash flow would develop in the coming year. While Isabelle – after the events of the third quarter – had learned not to entirely trust Hugo's judgment, she trusted his numbers. Hugo was conscientious and precise, if sometimes a bit conservative in his estimates. And he delivered the goods on time (see Appendix 5).

The results showed a devastating picture. Apart from a projected 8% slump in revenues in the following 12 months, ATG's efforts to build up its B2B business – a campaign Dr. Mayer had initiated in what seemed like a sensible strategic decision at the time – was swallowing enormous amounts of money, significantly more than expected. Hiring business travel experts and building relationships with business buyers proved expensive and more time-consuming than expected. Without drastic action, ATG would soon slide into the red. Moreover, return on equity (ROE), which had stood at 14% the year before Isabelle's appointment, would collapse to -6%. Isabelle, who had worked for an acquisitive private equity (PE) firm in her last role, feared that ATG could become a takeover target for PE investors and competitors. She could be ATG's last CEO.

The following weekend was not a good one for Isabelle. She was tense and irritable. On Saturday, she got into an argument with her daughter Marie, which ended with Marie crying and spending the rest of the afternoon in her room texting her friends and surfing social media. Her husband, Marco, sensed that Isabelle was not able to enjoy family time while she so badly needed the space to think about ATG. On Sunday, he took the two girls, Marie and Annelies, snowboarding.

On Monday, Isabelle called an urgent meeting of the GET, the executive team she had inherited from Dr. Mayer. Her board of directors held all the GET members in high esteem, and Carlo, the chair of the board, specifically expected Isabelle to work with this team and not to make any personnel changes – at least not in the short term. The GET members seemed well qualified and experienced. In addition to Hugo, four other people were on the executive team:

Frank de Vries was an extroverted, jovial, tall, and bald Dutchman who ran foreign sales subsidiaries. He had been in the travel business for nearly three decades and was considered an open book. Everyone knew his point of view. A former cruise ship captain out of Rotterdam, and then an international cruise industry executive, he had been everywhere and knew everyone. Frank was straightforward and deeply informed but confrontational and accustomed to getting his own way.

Constance Keller, a Swiss economist, headed ATG's Swiss sales and marketing department (including the B2B business the company was building). Introverted and terse, she was quite atypical for a commercial executive. While Isabelle respected Conny's knowledge and practicality, she found it hard to read her or figure out what she really thought about the company's situation or, in fact, anything at all, beyond her routine cut-and-dried reports. Interestingly, despite her strictly business manner and uniform dark suits, Conny had a strong following in her own department and was well respected by both the unions and outside observers. Isabelle hoped to get to know Conny better, but the Swiss sales head seemed to save most of her confidences for her elderly mother, her dogs, and her chess club.

Italian Alessandro Rossi managed ATG's entire backbone – operations and IT – as well as central services. Originally from Milan, he had moved to Zurich in the late 1980s to study computer science at ETH. After his studies, he worked for ExecUnited, a consulting firm, before joining ATG. He rose rapidly through the ranks. He was well-spoken, well-dressed, analytical, and ambitious.

Alessandro was long thought of as a hot contender for the CEO position. The board considered him, given his broad skills, but found him self-centered, a poor motivator, and too narrowly focused on his area of responsibility.

He behaved in a rather passive-aggressive manner toward Isabelle, who realized that he most likely resented her for being appointed CEO over him. As a result, while she tried to exercise her usual calm professionalism, a level of clear tension emerged between them. Seeing how he bristled as she quietly ratcheted up her projection of authority, Isabelle wondered if he would quit.

And, finally, Isabelle found an ally in Alison Brown, a British expat. It was somewhat surprising that an English-speaking executive would head the Human Resources (HR) department of a predominantly German-speaking company, but Alison's German was good enough to follow any work-related conversations, though she preferred to speak English in meetings and other professional settings. She had come to ATG after an impressive career in the human resources department of a large consumer goods company. With her tied-back silver hair and steady gaze, Alison looked like an Oxbridge professor, and Isabelle trusted her. Other than her assistant Franziska, Allison was the only one who had welcomed Isabelle warmly and opened up to her.

But, although the GET members all seemed experienced and qualified, they strongly disagreed about the challenges ATG faced and the underlying strategies it should pursue.

Isabelle gave a brief welcome to start the GET meeting, and then Hugo presented the forecast he had shared with her on Friday. As soon as he had finished his presentation, the discussions began. Frank led the way: "I have always said that we should not have invested in the B2B business. We have some advantages, but the market is far too competitive, and we are too late. I always said we were spending too much money on it. We have spent millions to build a business that produces losses of nearly two million yearly. It might be strategic, but this looks like bad strategy to me."

Conny, chattier than usual, defended the B2B business: "The discussion about the B2B business is a red herring! Our profits are collapsing by 29 million francs. Closing the B2B business will save us a few million, but not make a big difference. And B2B is indeed a strategic priority. Business travel is an important growth area, and it matches our competencies. There are other options out there for us to grow, such as new technology-based business models, but we may not be the best owner in those fields because we lack digital capabilities. We aren't good even in digitizing our own business, let alone venturing into new business models."

"You want me to digitize our business?" defended Alessandro, who, as head of IT, took Conny's comment as criticism – not without justification. "Before we do that, we should rethink our distribution network in Switzerland and Europe. We have way too many sales agencies. You and Frank have expanded too much. While the older agencies generate most of our sales and the largest contributions to our margins, by and large, our newer agencies do not make a positive contribution to covering central costs. Why should I digitize agencies that you will soon be closing anyway?"

Frank was visibly upset by Alessandro's comments. "Opening more agencies was not my decision. That's what Dr. Mayer directed us to do. Despite that, closing recently opened agencies is not a good idea – and it would damage our reputation and undermine our future growth." For Isabelle's benefit, he added, "We know that a new agency needs four to five years to reach its target contribution margin."

Alessandro was about to answer when Isabelle held up her palm and shook her head. "Thank you, Frank. Overall, I think that's enough for now," she said. "We're going round in circles. Pointing fingers at one another and taking apart our business piece by piece is not helping." Isabelle was frustrated, and although she didn't trust Hugo's judgment, she turned to him first for an opinion: "Hugo, you know the numbers best, what would you suggest?"

"I can't judge the merits of the B2B business. But I know we need to cut costs quickly. Sales are collapsing. It's drastic, but I'm

proposing a 25% reduction in headcount. We might lose more revenue, but we could restore a high-single digit, positive ROE." He
offered a brief report from KPS, the accounting firm which had
helped him prepare the financial plan, to support his assessment. In
addition, Hugo suggested spreading the 25% staff reduction evenly
across all divisions and departments, because he feared long nego-
tiations with individual members of management and the unions.
He was afraid ATG didn't have enough time for that.

"A 25% cut? No way," Alison replied, "That will destroy morale,
which is already weak. We'll lose our best people. We'd lose our
skills and institutional knowledge. And, besides, I'm not sure how
the unions would react."

This dangerous choice was a thorn in Isabelle's side. She wanted
to address short-term profitability challenges so she could protect
the firm from a potential acquisition. She knew the market was
cooling, and she felt she needed to act quickly. At the same time,
she didn't want to start her tenure as CEO with a reduction in staff.
She also feared the reactions of ATG's employees and unions – not
to mention the stockholders and the business press. Moreover, she
doubted she would get the OK from the board of directors to
take such drastic measures. She knew that Carlo, the board chair,
believed that executives should not get distracted by the short-
term cooling of the market. He believed in the future of the travel
industry, in the B2B business, in the opportunities that came with
new technologies, and in ATG's agency-based business model.

Like Conny, Carlo saw many opportunities for growth in the
travel industry. He thought ATG should build on its competitive
edge and take advantage of positive long-term trends. Thanks to
technology and changing customer needs, many new business models were emerging. The guidance she received from the chairman of
the board was clear: don't just look beyond the crisis – use depressed
valuations of technology-based start-ups to make acquisitions.

Isabelle considered the GET members calmly. She didn't let
them see that she felt irritated by the discussion and the team's lack
of decisiveness. The options they were debating made her head

spin. Should she launch an aggressive cost-cutting program and discontinue the B2B business to stop the cash outflow and restore profitability, as the CFO was suggesting? Or should she continue to invest in the potential of the B2B business, plus make some additional investments to take advantage of the more optimistic long-term trends in the industry?

Isabelle had invited Konstantinos to join the meeting to present his strategic assessment, and she was pleased when he unexpectedly spoke up and offered a surprising, creative alternative approach: "Why don't we raise capital and acquire a competitor? We could achieve cost savings through synergy. We could migrate their data to our platform, close their platform, and keep their agencies open only in cities we don't cover. That would solve the cost problem. We're not the only ones struggling. Booken.com and TripAdmiror are hurting all of our competitors. I'm sure their executive committees are discussing these issues as well."

The idea seemed interesting, but Conny immediately threw cold water on it: "Kosta, this is a good option. However, it is theoretical. I don't know of any concrete evidence in the market that similar travel operators are looking for buyers."

The team was ready to start going in circles again, but Isabelle was running out of patience. She decided to adjourn the meeting.

She was used to making decisions on her own and fast. But in her conversation with Eve, she had learned about the importance of making decisions in a team, and she really wanted to try it. She was wondering how to make it work in the GET, however. There was no alignment among the members about which strategy to choose. Even worse, it was becoming increasingly clear to her that the dynamics among the GET members were so poor that she had to be cautious about deciding at all. Alessandro's behavior in particular wasn't helping. She feared that whatever choice she made, not only he but also half of the GET wouldn't support her. She was very aware of the shifting alliances around each issue.

That evening, she arrived home late, as always. The girls were already asleep. Marco sat with her at the dining table while she hastily ate a dish of leftover cannelloni heated up in the microwave. "It is incredibly frustrating. We are heading into a crisis, and I need all hands on deck, but the top team is dysfunctional, mainly – I think – because of Alessandro. There is tension between me and him, but also between him and the other GET members," she said, "and I can't tell anyone except you how torn I feel about the choices ahead of me. We are facing difficult decisions and I want to make them together with the team."

"Let's look at one thing at a time," Marco suggested gently. "Why do you think Alessandro is being so combative, Isabelle? Do you think he still resents not being chosen as Mayer's successor?"

"I think so, but that's not the only thing. I mean, Alessandro seems well versed in technical issues. He runs the IT department impeccably, though not innovatively, and he always delivers what he is asked to do. At the same time, he is over-sensitive and defensive when anyone touches on his areas of responsibility. Also, he isn't proactively engaging in the discussion and development of a new strategic direction. Alessandro seems to have a will issue, not a skill issue. Maybe I should manage him more forcefully and perhaps coach him – after all, that's one of my strengths. But it will take a lot of my time."

"So, what do you plan to do?" her husband asked.

"I am inclined to let him go and look for someone who would add a more positive dynamic to the team. I know it sounds drastic, but it is not uncommon for new CEOs to make management changes early in their tenure. Maybe I should do it too. What do you think?"

"Well, that sound like the right decision," Marco responded.

"Yes. But there are some repercussions. I'd first have to find someone who could replace him," she said.

"Anyone in mind?" Marco asked.

"I was thinking about Jakob," Isabelle answered.

"Jakob Berman, the Chief Digital Officer of your previous employer, The Travel Group?" asked Marco.

"Yes, him. He's very collaborative. I worked well with him in Denmark. He is also good in IT and understands the digitization of business processes. He would add a lot to the team and ATG. But I am not sure about it," added Isabelle.

"Sounds good. But you seem hesitant. Why?"

"Alessandro's behavior is irritating, but I am somewhat reluctant about taking a capable person away from The Travel Group, when we need all the help we can take. And, candidly, I'm not sure Jakob would integrate well at ATG. It would take some time for him to get to know its IT systems. I don't know how Alessandro's people would feel about it and whether they would support the transition from Alessandro to Jakob. Importantly, and besides the fact that the chairman doesn't want me to make changes now, I don't want firing Alessandro to be my first major decision at ATG. That may give the wrong signal to the organization. It doesn't feel right."

"Maybe it would be the right signal though," said Marco. "After all, you want to signal to the organization that you don't accept people who are not willing to collaborate for the good of the company."

She finished her pasta, looked up at Marco and took a deep breath. "You might be right. What shall I do?" she asked.

Questions for Reflection

Based on what you know about ATG's situation now, what should Isabelle do? In particular,

- Should she continue working with Alessandro, manage him in a more directive manner and perhaps coach him?
- Should she let Alessandro go?

You may want to write down your answer before continuing.

Chapter 3

Developing Options to Approximate the Right Decision

Claudio Feser, Daniella Laureiro-Martinez, and Stefano Brusoni

All things carry yin yet embrace yang. They blend their life breaths in order to produce harmony.
—Lao Tzu, *Tao Te Ching* (2016)

Isabelle was looking forward to the conversation with Eve scheduled in the morning following the conversation with her husband.

"Hi, Eve, nice seeing you again. And thanks for taking the time to do this video call with me. Our last conversation was very helpful. It made me think a lot, especially about the importance of having a well-functioning top team at ATG. Also, we didn't finish the conversation about heuristics. I would love to know more about these decisions rules," said Isabelle.

"Thank you! Our last conversation was helpful to me as well. It helped me synthesize my work," said Eve with her typical smile. "I sometimes get lost in my own research. Amidst all the trees, I don't see the forest anymore, so to speak. Talking about my research helps me clarify my thinking."

Eve's humility was disarming. Isabelle felt again immediately at ease with her, as she did when they had first met on the plane.

Isabelle continued: "Thank you. I'd be interested to learn more about heuristics. In fact, I am facing a decision that I don't know how to make. More than a decision, it is a dilemma. I am confronted with two choices, and, to be honest, I don't like either of them. Can I tell you about it in confidence?" asked Isabelle.

"Absolutely!" said Eve.

Isabelle then explained the situation, careful to not mention specific names of her team members to protect confidentiality. She changed the team members' names but shared the essence of the situation with Eve. Isabelle wondered whether she should continue to work with A (she used "A," not to mention Alessandro's name). She knew that he was capable and that he knew ATG well, but he was passive-aggressive and had not integrated well with the rest of the team. She shared that she didn't know whether he would be open to her coaching. Alternatively, she could let him go. Maybe B (Jakob Berman) would be a much better fit with the rest of the ATG GET. He was very qualified, but, still, Isabelle didn't feel comfortable firing A. Also, it wasn't clear that whatever she decided to do would work out as she planned. How would A react? Would she able to convince B to move to Switzerland? Would B be able to integrate at ATG?

"Dilemmas such as the one you are facing are typical for decisions under uncertainty," said Eve. "Under uncertainty, we often must choose between continuing to do what we are doing or changing the approach. We must choose between a known alternative with a known reward – in this case, A – and an unknown one with unknown but potentially higher reward – in this case,

B (Kayser et al., 2015). We call choosing the known alternative exploit, while choosing the unknown alternative is called explore. Under uncertainty, our brain naturally seeks optimization of exploit-explore dilemmas when making decisions. That is, we ask ourselves if we should play it safe and keep doing what we know and try to make the most of it, that is, exploit. Or if should we try something different, venturing into new, possibly more fruitful, pastures, that is, explore."

"Let me understand. Is exploiting the optimization of the current state, while exploring is dropping the current state and looking for a novel solution?" asked Isabelle.

"Yes, that's exactly right!" answered Eve. "Exploitation is the optimization of performance. It usually results in high-level engagement, refinement, and efficiency (Laureiro-Martínez, 2014; Laureiro-Martínez et al., 2015). It is the safe option. Exploration, on the other hand, involves disengagement from an ongoing task to discover novel opportunities and enable experimentation and innovation. It can lead to new discoveries, but it is not certain it will (Laureiro-Martínez, 2014; Laureiro-Martínez et al., 2015). It could lead to nothing."

"Got it. But how do I decide to choose between A, that is exploitation, and B, that is, exploration? What is the right answer? Is there any rule I can apply?" asked Isabelle.

"Hmmm. . . there are seven heuristics, but before discussing them we need to recognize that while a dilemma looks like a choice between two options, it isn't. Our brain has the tendency to simplify a complex situation into two categories. Psychologists call this the binary bias (Fisher and Keil, 2018). We seem to be evolutionarily wired to categorize and interpret information into dichotomous, or two-part, divisions. When we think that we are confronted with a dilemma, we are in fact facing a choice between an unlimited number of options" answered Eve.

"Unlimited?," said Isabelle who seemed surprised.

Wired to Think in "Either/Or" Categories

The "binary bias" is a deeply entrenched cognitive predilection, an outcome of the evolutionary imperatives and neural processing mechanisms inherent to the human brain (Figure 3.1). At its core, the binary bias refers to the human brain's propensity to categorize and interpret information into dichotomous, or two-part, divisions. This inclination can be traced back to the primal survival needs of our ancestors. When faced with complex and multifaceted environmental stimuli, the ability to rapidly segregate information into simple "safe" vs. "dangerous" or "friend" vs. "foe" categories offered a survival advantage. Rapid decision-making in the face of potential threats, even if it occasionally led to oversimplification, favored those who could avoid immediate dangers.

Figure 3.1   Our brains are wired to think in "either-or" categories.

On a neurobiological level, the binary bias can be attributed to the way our brain processes and encodes information. The human neural architecture, specifically the synaptic organization, thrives on patterns and contrasts. Neurotransmitter systems, particularly those that involve dopamine, are known to respond robustly to binary reward systems, reinforcing behaviors that align with perceived positive outcomes and discouraging those associated with negative ones. Furthermore, the brain's inherent preference for cognitive ease means that it naturally gravitates toward simpler models of understanding, hence frequently opting for dichotomous interpretations over nuanced ones. This dualistic cognitive shortcut, while efficient, can at times oversimplify the complexities of the world, but it underscores the balance the brain strikes between accuracy and expediency.

"Yes," responded Eve, and continued: "Let's take one simple dilemma as an example: the choice of a vacation destination. You and your family may need to make that decision this year. Do you decide to go to your favorite place in the Swiss mountains? Or do you opt for trying out somewhere new? While the dilemma looks like a choice between two options, going to the favorite place (exploit) or trying out a new place (explore), it is in fact a choice between many options (Figure 3.2): you could do both – mountains and something new – and split your vacation time of, say, three weeks and go to your favorite place in the mountains for one week, and somewhere

Exploit ←◯─◯─◯─◯─◯─◯─◯→ **Explore**

"Going to the
favorite place in
the mountains"

"Trying out a
new destination"

Figure 3.2   There is an infinite number of options along the exploit-explore continuum.

to a seaside destination, perhaps in Italy, for the remaining two weeks. Or you go to your favorite place, and then after, say, two weeks, you add a trip to a city destination you have not yet visited in Europe. Or perhaps you could try out some destinations in Asia, maybe Thailand or Bali. Or maybe you could go to Sub-Saharan Africa. You've never been there. 'Africa would be an adventure,' you think. And so on. The only factor that limits the number of possible options is your imagination. The Rubik's cube is a good analogy for a dilemma. The original 3*3*3 Rubik's cube has only six colored faces, but it is possible to produce more than 43,000,000,000,000,000,000 or 43 quintillion combinations."

> The only factor that limits the number of possible options is your imagination.

"So, the two options are just two points on a continuum of an infinitive number of options?" asked Isabelle.

"Yes, that's exactly right. We often frame decisions as 'either-or decisions': 'should I stay at my employer or quit and find another job?,' 'should we optimize the current technology or invest in a new one?,' 'should we reduce costs or invest in new businesses?,' for example. But the two options we often consider are no more than two points on a continuum between exploitation-oriented and exploration-oriented options," confirmed Eve. "It isn't about 'either-or,' but more about 'and, and.' Going back to the vacation example, some of the options are more exploit-oriented, that is, they allocate more time spent in your favorite mountain place, while some others are more explorative, that is, allocate more time to exploring new places. Some of those new places in turn are more explorative (Africa, Asia) than others (seaside destination in Italy, or city destinations in Europe)."

> It isn't about "either-or," but more about "and, and."

"OK, got it. When I face a dilemma, it probably isn't. There are potentially many other options for me to explore, some might be a bit more exploit-oriented and some more explore-oriented," said Isabelle.

"Yes, correct," said Eve, "Decisions that combine exploit and explore initiatives create flexibility. I optimize what I am already doing, but I add variability. I add exploration that allows me to discover new opportunities for the future. Every decision that combines exploit and explore ensures some degree of optimization of the current state, while adding flexibility and creating options for the future."

> Every decision that combines exploit and explore ensures some degree of optimization of the current state, while adding flexibility and creating options for the future.

"I understand. But what is the right balance between explore and exploit activities? Should I devote 90% of my energy on optimization, i.e., exploit, and 10% on exploration? Say, should I stay in my favorite place in the mountains 90% of the time, and spend 10% trying out something new? Or should I focus my energy on exploration? Say, should I stay in my usual place only a few days and try out lots of new destination and new hotels? What is the correct balance between exploit and explore?"

"Making a perfect decision under uncertainty is not possible," said Eve. "Some researchers have tried to develop mathematical models to do so, but their models rely on assumptions that seldom hold."

"What do you mean?" asked Isabelle.

"Gittins and Jones (Gittins and Jones, 1974; Gittins, 1979) developed an approach for finding optimal answers to such questions," replied Eve. "They suggest a general rule – the Gittins index – for optimally making decisions to resolve exploit–explore dilemmas. The Gittins index assumes that you're making choices from a finite number of options for which the rewards are delivered with unknown but fixed probabilities. It also assumes that the decision-maker discounts the value of the rewards of each option exponentially over time."

"These are courageous assumptions!"

"Yes, indeed," confirmed Eve. "First, options are rarely finite and known. You can choose from a myriad, a nearly unlimited number, of destinations, hotels, rentals, and Airbnbs. Second, outcomes or rewards are typically unknown. How could you know how satisfying your experience is going to be at a particular new hotel or destination if you've never been there? Third, probabilities – even if unknown – are rarely fixed. They may change all the time, and they may depend on choices made by other people (March, 1991). Say, many tourists also book their vacations at a specific destination, such as the hotel you were planning to explore. Now very busy, the hotel may not be able to keep up its quality of service."

"Yes, that makes sense," said Isabelle.

Eve continued: "And, finally, fourth, you probably cannot discount the expected value of the outcomes exponentially into the future (Cohen et al., 2007). And you are not alone. It is unlikely that any human could calculate the Gittins index when deciding. Human rationality is limited, or bounded as Nobel Prize-winner Herbert Simon put it (Simon, 1979). We do not always have all the information we need; our cognitive abilities are generally limited. Not everyone has an IQ of 140 or so. We usually have little time to reflect and study all possible options before deciding. Against this background, we tend to look for satisfying solutions rather than optimum ones. We are 'satisficers' (Simon, 1979). We can safely conclude that none of the theoretical assumptions necessary for the Gittins index to work hold in practice. There is no known general rule for exactly solving exploit-explore dilemmas, and there is no reason to believe we may ever have one (Cohen et al., 2007)."

"Yes, but we still make decisions?" asked Isabelle.

"While we cannot calculate the optimal exploit-explore balance exactly, we may be able to approximate a 'good-enough' or 'satisfactory' exploration-exploitation balance," said Eve. "Our brain seems to consider seven decision rules or rules of thumb – I call them heuristics – when doing so (Figure 3.3). Four of them are situational and three relate to the individual making the decision."

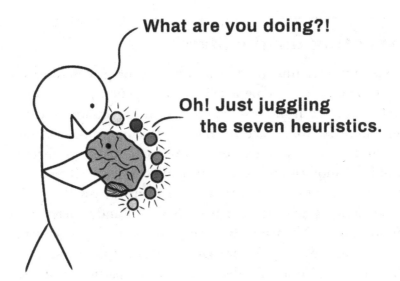

Figure 3.3   Seven heuristics.

"So, our brain uses seven decision rules to approximate a satisfactory decision? What are those heuristics?," asked Isabelle.

"Let's return to our simple dilemma," said Eve, "where to go on vacation with the family this year. Should you go to your favorite place in the Swiss mountains, as you always do, or should you explore new places, perhaps in Italy? The first factor that your brain will consider is the ambitiousness of your goals."

"Ambitiousness of goals?" asked Isabelle.

"Yes. Let's assume that your family is telling you that last year's vacation in the mountains was great, and that is all they want this year, too, you probably won't explore other destinations. But if your kids say that this year, they would like to have an exceptional vacation ('the grandparents are joining us, and you know how picky they are'), you are more likely to explore new destinations, perhaps in Italy, to be able to satisfy their wishes. The choice of a balance between exploit and explore depends on the ambitiousness of your goals or objectives. If exploitation activities alone are hitting, or exceeding, your goals, you are not likely to waste time exploring other possibilities. On the other hand, if the expected rewards from exploring fall short of your goals, you are likely to explore more (March, 1991)."

Shooting for the Stars?

Extensive literature on the importance of goal setting for performance achievement exists. Goals generate motivation and action, both in personal life and in organizations. Goals give meaning to our actions, help us develop plans to achieve them, and drive us to execute our plans. Goals are connected to higher motivation, self-esteem, and confidence. Over 1,000 studies involving over 40,000 participants across the globe have demonstrated that high goals significantly increase an individual's performance on nearly 90 different tasks, regardless of how these goals are set. Goals set by managers, for instance, can be as effective as self-set or participatively set goals (Latham and Locke, 2006).

But can goals be too ambitious and end up harming performance and exploration? Yes, they can. The relationship between goal ambitiousness and activation is not linear but looks more like Figure 3.4.

Research by Emily Balcetis, a social psychologist from New York University, suggests that we can detect how goals affect our level of planned effort or anticipation by measuring

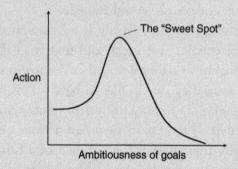

Figure 3.4 The relationship between ambitiousness of goals and actions towards achieving them.

our systolic blood pressure (SBP) (Balcetis and Dunning, 2010). Our SBP increases when our body is preparing to take action. If a goal is easy to achieve, the SBP increases a little. If a goal is moderately hard to achieve, that is, it seems feasible but challenging, the SBP increases significantly. However, if a goal is seen as impossible to achieve, we disengage and shut off completely. In the brain this pattern also shows up in the medial prefrontal cortex (MPFC). The MPFC helps us to envision how a goal may be achieved. But when a goal looks unrealistically ambitious, the MPFC hardly gets activated (Comaford, 2015).

Studies suggest that you may be able to raise the ambitiousness of your goals ("moving the sweet spot" to the right, see Figure 3.4) and increase your level of goal achievement if you do the following:

1. Visualize your goals. Studies have shown that visualizing goals, a popular technique among professional athletes, tricks our brain in making goals look closer and more realistic (Cole et al., 2013). It may enhance the likelihood of going for ambitious goals and achieving them.
2. Make your goals important to you. Goals can matter for many reasons. They may reflect a need, your values, or your personality, for instance. Either way, our brain makes our most important goals look closer, which increases the likelihood of goal achievement (Balcetis and Dunning, 2010).
3. Write your goals down. A study found that individuals who wrote down their goals increased goal achievement by 42%. The impact increased further when they shared their written objectives publicly, for instance, sending their written goals to a friend (Matthews, 2007).

"OK, got that. Ambitious goals. That is the first heuristic. What's the second one?" asked Isabelle.

"The second one is opportunities. If, while you are thinking about this year's vacation, you find a brochure in your mailbox about a new acclaimed, family-friendly boutique hotel in Capri, you are more likely to explore the Italian island off Naples than if you hadn't opened your mail. The choice of balance also depends on information about opportunities. The inclination to explore increases when information about new opportunities becomes available."

"Makes sense. Goals and opportunities. What's the third one?" asked Isabelle.

"The third one is time," answered Eve. "If you have time to gather information about great places and hotels in Italy, call up some colleagues who have recently traveled to Italy to ask for advice, and read some reviews on the internet, you may be more likely to explore a new destination in Italy than you were when you simply had to decide on the spot. People are more likely to explore when they have more time left to complete a task or meet their objectives (Cohen et al., 2007)."

"So, if we have time we can explore more and be more innovative, right?" asked Isabelle.

"Yes, that's right. Think about Google's '20% time' rule. The company encourages its engineers, in addition to their regular activities and work, to spend 20% of their time working on new stuff. Google is agnostic about what that 'new stuff' is, as long as it benefits the company in some way. It gives employees the time and space to explore, that is, to be more innovative and creative," Eve answered.

She continued: "The fourth heuristic is social context. If all your friends are switching to Italy as a vacation destination this year, and you were not planning to do so, you'll look into it when you learn what they are doing. 'Why are they all going to Italy this year? Am I missing something?,' you may ask yourself. You may or you may not decide to explore Italy, and, after all, you may not want to go where everyone else is going. But the fact that other people are going to Italy signals to you that you may want to think about it. Social context matters. We are more likely to explore the environment when we have information about others doing so or when we face competition for resources (Cohen et al., 2007)."

"OK, got it. Does this also mean that we are also more likely to focus on exploitation if we are expected to do so, say, from superiors – in my case, the board – or peers?" asked Isabelle.

"Yes, very much so."

"OK, we got four. There are three to go. What's the fifth one?"

"The fifth one is your personality and values," Eve answered. "If you are a curious and open-minded person, you are more likely to explore Italy than if you were conservative and risk-averse. Your inclination to taking risks matters. Risk-oriented people tend to explore more, as do curious and open-minded people (Keller and Weibler, 2015). The inclination to think, especially about the future, and learning-orientation may also matter (Kauppila and Tempelaar, 2016)."

"And the sixth one?"

"The sixth one is your skills," answered Eve. "If you learned Italian in school, you may also be more inclined to explore Italy; after all, you could leverage your skill to ask around, to find great places, and to order exquisite food for your family. Your skills, or rather your belief in your skills, what psychologists call self-efficacy beliefs, matter (Schunk and Pajares, 2002). We are more likely to choose options that build on skills that we believe we have."

"So, if I have confidence in my coaching skills, I may be more inclined to consider decisions that leverage coaching abilities. Would this be a good example?" wondered Isabelle.

"Yes, very much so," and Eve continued, "And, finally, the last and the seventh one is your mood."

"Mood?"

"Yes. Your mood matters. When you are tired and stressed, you are less likely to spend the evening exploring other destinations in Italy. You'll tend to stick what has worked so far. 'That will be good enough,' you say to yourself, and move on. If you are relaxed and energized, you may be more inclined to try out a new destination in Italy. Moods, or cognitive states, as I call them, influence your decisions. When you feel safe, relaxed, energized, and inspired you are more inclined to take risks and explore. On the other hand, when you feel stressed and under pressure, you may be more inclined to become pessimistic, absorb negative information, and 'play it safe' (Sharot, 2017)."

"No decisions if I have a bad day?" asked Isabelle.

"Well, sometimes you can't avoid making decisions. That said, for important decisions, say, you want to buy a house or hand in your resignation, the proverbial 'sleeping on it' may be a good thing. When tired or stressed, you may end up being too conservative, or 'over-exploiting' so to speak."

"Hmmm. . . lots of heuristics. Lots of content. Lots to bear in mind," said Isabelle, who was feeling slightly irritated, noticing she was having trouble keeping everything in her mind.

"Yes, here, look, this slide might help," said Eve, inviting Isabelle to have a look at a page she was holding in front of the camera (Figure 3.5).

"This is super-helpful! Thank you, Eve. By the way, do these heuristics also hold when approximating the right decisions in the context of a company?" asked Isabelle.

Situation
- Goals (e.g., objectives, ambition, etc.)
- Opportunities (e.g., availability of additional options, additional information, etc.)
- Time (time horizon)
- Social context

Exploit ◄─────────────────────◯─────────────────────► Explore

Individual inclinations
- Behavioral inclinations (e.g., openness to new opportunities, risk orientation, values etc.,)
- Skills, capabilities (e.g., empathy, attention control, etc.,)
- Cognitive states (e.g., feeling safe, being rested, etc.,)

Figure 3.5   The seven factors (heuristics) that influence the exploit-explore balance for the individual decision-maker.

"Yes, companies also face exploit and explore dilemmas, and like individuals, they combine exploit and explore activities in their strategies. Companies typically optimize their current business, executing yearly plans, improving their operations, and continuously driving for efficiency, while at the same time also exploring new opportunities, pursuing innovative ideas, launching new products and services, acquiring new businesses, and experimenting. The approach of simultaneously exploiting and exploring is called ambidexterity. It comes from Latin. In Latin, dexter means 'right,' or related to the right side. Since most people are more skillful with their right hand, dexter came to be used to describe being capable or skillful. In the seventeenth century, the English author Sir Thomas Browne combined the term dexter with ambi, which in Latin means 'both,' to create the expression ambidextrous: 'Some are. . . right-handed on both sides,' he wrote."[1]

"Yes, that reflects my experience in my former role in Denmark. The company did both and did well."

"I am not surprised," said Eve. "Various studies suggest that an organization's ability to explore and exploit simultaneously – that is ambidexterity – is essential in gaining a sustainable competitive advantage, in achieving both short-term performance and long-term survival, especially in a dynamic, fast-changing environment, and in taking advantage of disruptive new business models and new technologies (He and Wong, 2004; O'Reilly and Tushman, 2008; Raisch and Birkinshaw, 2008, Junni et al., 2013, Birkinshaw et al., 2016; Hill and Birkinshaw, 2014). In other words, combining exploitation-oriented and exploration-oriented initiatives improves an organization's short-term, that is, operational, and long-term, that is, strategic performance (Schulze et al., 2008)."

"But also, with companies there is a question about the approximately right balance, correct?" asked Isabelle.

"Yes. Some companies tend to focus too much on execution and spend too little resources on innovation. Some other companies do the opposite. The relationship between ambidexterity and company performance is U-shaped (inverted U, Tushman and

O'Reilly, 1996). Firms that put too much emphasis on exploitation, focusing excessively on optimization, efficiency, and short-term results, may miss innovation opportunities, and hence adapt poorly in uncertain and dynamic environments. They may experience declining revenues, growth rate decreases over time, and they see their valuation and multiples decrease. They may become take-over targets. On the other hand, companies that spend too many resources and time on innovation may see their profitability erode. They may run out of financial resources to fund innovative projects and growth."

"Makes intuitive sense. So, without going to extremes, how can companies find the right balance between exploitation and exploration? Do they use the same heuristics that we discussed before?" wondered Isabelle.

"Yes, they do," confirmed Eve. "Organizations seem to use the same seven heuristics, but in a slightly adjusted form. In my thesis, I call them the seven heuristics of exploit-explore optimization. Let me take you through them, one by one:

Heuristic I: The more ambitious the objectives, the more explorative the chosen option or strategy.

"To illustrate: when you give incremental targets to your team, the team members will optimize their existing strategy, maybe reducing discretionary expenses marginally. However, if you ask for a 30% improvement in performance as opposed to a 5% improvement, your team is more likely to 'think outside of the box,' and explore new ways to achieve the results. Research suggests that when objectives are not ambitious enough, organizational members try to salvage impaired, partially functioning routines – that is, exploitation-oriented activities – whereas when objectives are ambitious, they are forced to explore and to rethink and re-create routines. As with individuals, the relationships between the ambitiousness of goals and behavior in organizations is not linear (Brauer and Laamanen, 2014).

Heuristic II: The more opportunities, the more explorative the chosen option or strategy.

"To illustrate: you and your team may choose to expand your company abroad, if you and your team visit another country, and you learn about opportunities for your organization's products there. Increasing the amount of information and knowledge about opportunities increases the propensity to explore.

Heuristic III: The more time and resources available, the more explorative the chosen option or strategy.

"To illustrate: if your boss urges you to improve profitability so that the company can meet its quarterly earnings targets, you are more likely to focus on short-term measures than on newer, more innovative but also longer-term initiatives. However, if your boss asks you to improve profitability by the end of year three, you'll be more inclined to use the extra time to explore and experiment with new ideas and technologies.

Heuristic IV: Competitive actions can influence the exploit-explore balance in different ways.

"The social context for organizations is broad. It could include expectations from varied stakeholders, politicians, the government, suppliers, the public, etc. Importantly, it includes the actions and initiatives of your competitors. Competitive actions play two signaling roles. First, they signal what may be important trends. Say, for example, that you and your team notice that some of your company's competitors are experimenting with blockchain to improve a product. You and your team will be more inclined to do so as well. Second, competitors' actions may increase competitive intensity and signal that a given opportunity is now less attractive. Say a competitor launched an innovative new product. The competitor has entered a market successfully, is gaining significant share of demand, and is building entry barriers (e.g., distribution channels, brands, etc.). Under these conditions, you and your team may not be inclined to follow your competitor, or you would do so, but a with a differentiating approach.

Heuristic V: A chosen option or strategy is likely to be consistent with a work organization's culture and values.

"To illustrate: if a company values getting things done, with a focus on execution and making short-term-objectives, the chosen strategy is likely to reflect that and to be more exploit-oriented in nature.

Heuristic VI: A chosen option or strategy is likely to be consistent with a work organization's capabilities.

"To illustrate: if your organization is believed to be a competent acquirer and integrator of other firms, its strategy is likely to reflect that. Organizational capabilities (or, more precisely, beliefs about organizational capabilities) that match opportunities in the market increase the propensity to explore these opportunities.

Heuristic VII: A chosen option or strategy is likely to reflect the general mood in a work organization.

"To illustrate: if the management and employees are confident about the future and the opportunities ahead, they are more likely to engage in explorative, riskier strategies and options."

"This all resonates. Again, lots of content and insights," said Isabelle.

"Yes, you are right. I am glad you find it insightful. Here is a page that summarizes the seven heuristics in a model I developed, the Decision Navigator," said Eve as she clicked the "Share" button on the menu in the video conference (Figure 3.6). You start from the dilemma and then you look at possible options and finally you use the heuristics to select the right option."

Eve continued: "We can illustrate the importance of the seven heuristics looking at how they are reflected in the differences among companies' strategies. Let's look at two innovative firms in

1. Dilemma				
2. Options on the Exploit-Explore continuum	Exploit ←			→ Explore
	Option	Option	Option	Option
The seven heuristics	**3. Assumptions**	**3. Assumptions**	**3. Assumptions**	**3. Assumptions**
a) Objectives				
b) Opportunities				
c) Time				
d) Competitive actions and stakeholder expectations				
e) Our values and culture				
f) Our capabilities				
g) Our "mood" or prevalent collective cognitive states				

↓

4. Resolution

Figure 3.6 The four-step Decision Navigator.

totally different industries when it comes to maturity and uncertainty. Both ExxonMobil Corporation (an American multinational and one of the leading firms in the oil and gas industry, commonly shortened to Exxon) and Meta Platforms, Inc. (an American social media and virtual reality company, commonly shortened to Meta) regularly make it in the list of the top 50 most innovative firms globally published annually by Boston Consulting Group, a consultancy firm (Manly et al., 2023). Relatively speaking, the oil and gas industry is much older, more mature, and stable. Less uncertain. Social media and virtual reality are newer industries. They did not exist 30 years ago. It is a very dynamic space continuously reshaped by new technologies and new competitors. These industries are more uncertain. When we look at the differences in strategy and culture, Exxon emphasizes continuous improvements and optimization, that is, exploit, while Meta emphasizes continuous innovation, that is explore."

"So, Exxon would have a more exploit-oriented balance in its strategy?"

"Yes, let me illustrate this," said Eve. "Exxon states its objectives as achieving 'superior financial and operating results while adhering to high ethical standards.' It operates in a relatively mature (compared to Meta) industry with less opportunities for innovation. The company is public. The three largest shareholders, owning roughly 19% of the shares, are money managers. The focus is rather short-term. Exxon competes in the oil and gas market, which prioritizes incremental innovation. Exxon's strategic posture or exploit-explore balance emphasizes exploitation. The guiding principles of its strategy read as follows: 'Exxon Mobil Corporation is committed to being the world's premier petroleum and chemical manufacturing company. To that end, we must continuously achieve superior financial and operating results while adhering to high ethical standards.'[2] The guiding principles further state a series of commitments to shareholders ('We are committed to enhancing the long-term value of the investment dollars entrusted to us by our shareholders. By running the business profitably and

responsibly, we expect our shareholders to be rewarded with superior returns'), to customers ('We commit to being innovative and
responsive, while offering high-quality products and services at
competitive prices'), to employees ('We are committed to main-
taining a safe work environment enriched by diversity and characterized by open communication, trust, and fair treatment'), and to
society ('We commit to being a good corporate citizen in all the
places we operate worldwide. We will maintain high ethical standards, obey all applicable laws, rules, and regulations, and respect
local and national cultures. Above all other objectives, we are dedicated to running safe and environmentally responsible operations').
Exxon's guiding principles close with, 'We aspire to achieve our
goals by flawlessly executing our business plans. . . .'"

"Exploit-oriented indeed. They talk about executing plans,"
said Isabelle.

"Yes, indeed," continued Eve. "Compare this to Meta. Meta's
ambition is enormous, no less than: 'Giving people the power to
build community and bring the world closer together.'[3] The industry is very dynamic, and opportunities for innovation abound. Also,
the focus is more long-term. Mark Zuckerberg is Meta's largest
shareholder, owning 13.4% of its shares. However, Zuckerberg
controls 61.9% of all votes thanks to owning super-voting shares.
Meta competes in the broader tech industry, where innovation is
rather disruptive. Meta's strategic posture or exploit-explore balance emphasizes explore. Its principles read as follows: 'Give People
a Voice, Build Connection and Community, Serve Everyone, Keep
People Safe and Protect Privacy, Promote Economic Opportunity.'
I show this on the following slide," said Eve, who shared again her
screen (Figure 3.7).

"OK, lots of food for thought. Let me try to summarize,"
said Isabelle.

"Yes, please do," responded Eve, grabbing a pen to take notes.
She really liked Isabelle's ability to synthesize her work.

Isabelle continued: "So, decisions under uncertainty present
themselves as exploit-explore dilemmas. That is, should we keep

Heuristics	Exploit — ExonMobil	Explore — ∞ Meta
a) Objectives	Achieving "superior financial and operating results while adhering to high ethical standards".	"Giving people the power to build community and bring the world closer together".
b) Opportunities	Mature industry with limited opportunities for innovation.	The industry is very dynamic, and opportunities for innovation abound.
c) Time perspective	The three largest shareholders owning roughly 19% of the shares short term are money managers.	Mark Zuckerberg controls 61.9% of all votes thanks to long term owning super-voting shares.
d) Competitors' actions and stakeholder expectations	Exxon competes in the oil and gas market, where the focus lies on incremental innovation.	Meta competes in the broader Tech industry, where innovation is rather disruptive.
e) What consistent values and culture do we assume we have?	"Work flexibility, safety and security, recognizing human rights, integrity and diversity and inclusion"	"Move fast together; Build awesome things; Focus on long-term impact; Live in the future; Be open"
f) Our relevant capabilities	Likely to include continuous innovation skills, execution capabilities, etc.	Likely to include breakthrough innovation skills, technology capabilities, etc.
g) Our "mood" or prevalent collective cognitive state	Likely cautious ("Safety and security")	Likely optimistic ("Live in the future; Be open")

Figure 3.7 Comparing Exxon to Meta.

what we know and optimize it? This is called exploit. Or should we try something different, exploring something new? This is called explore. While exploit-explore dilemmas appear as choices between two options, they are in fact choices between an infinite number of options on the exploit-explore continuum. There is no known general rule for exactly solving exploit-explore dilemmas, but there are heuristics, decision-rules our brain uses when facing such dilemmas. There are seven: objectives, opportunities, time, social context, our personality, our skills, and our mood."

> There is no known general rule for solving dilemmas, but there are seven heuristics, decision-rules, that our brain uses when facing dilemmas.

"Yes, correct!" said Eve, making notes.

Isabelle continued: "Like individuals, companies combine exploit and explore initiatives in their strategies. The strategy of exploiting and exploring at the same time is called ambidexterity, which is essential to ensuring both short- and long-term results. Combining exploit and explore decisions help deal with uncertainty. Each decision to some extent optimizes the current state while allowing the exploration of opportunities for future development. It creates options for the future. The 'satisfactory' balance of exploit and explore activities for companies depends on the same seven heuristics. Like those for individuals, they are objectives, opportunities, time, competitive context, company's culture, the organization's capabilities, and the cognitive state of the organization's employees."

"Perfect! This summary is really helpful!" said Eve, thanking Isabelle.

Isabelle thanked Eve for her time and insights. Their video call was scheduled to last one hour, and they only now realized that they had spent 90 minutes talking. Immersed in the content, they had lost track of time. They ended the call agreeing to continue speaking in the coming weeks. Isabelle wanted to reflect on the conversation and get back to Eve with more questions.

But she also needed to reflect on her decision on Alessandro, but she felt now better equipped to approach it wisely.

Key Takeaways

- Decisions under uncertainty usually present themselves as "either-or" dilemmas, i.e., exploit-explore dilemmas: should I stay (exploit) or should I go (explore)?
- While exploit-explore dilemmas appear as choices between two options, they are in fact choices between an infinite number of options on the exploit-explore continuum.
- There is no mathematical formula for solving exploit-explore dilemmas, but there are seven heuristics that the brain uses to arrive at "satisfactory" decisions: goals, opportunities, time, social context, our personality, our skills, and our mood.
- Like individuals, companies combine exploit and explore initiatives in their strategies. The strategy of exploiting and exploring at the same time is called ambidexterity. The "satisfactory" level of ambidexterity is driven by the same seven heuristics that individuals use.

To frame and optimize your decisions you can use the following Decision Navigator that has four steps (Figure 3.8):

1. Identify the exploit-explore dilemma.
2. Develop multiple options on the exploit-explore continuum.
3. Identify underlying, relevant assumptions for each of the options using the seven decision-making heuristics.
4. Decide.

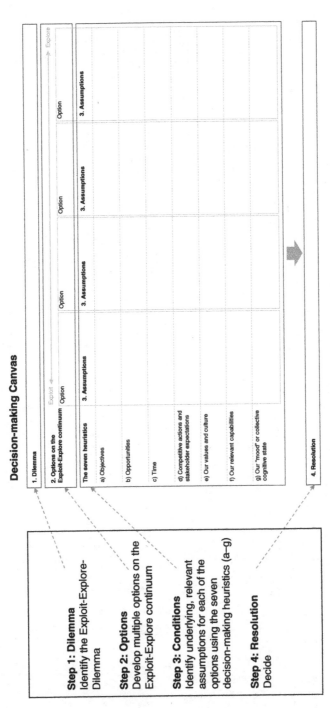

Figure 3.8 Summary of the four-step Decision Navigator.

Part Two

MAKING DECISIONS UNDER UNCERTAINTY

Chapter 4

Case 2: Making Strategic Decisions

**Claudio Feser, David Redaschi, and
Karolin Frankenberger**

In the evening after the conversation on heuristics with Eve, Isabelle was having a late dinner with Marco. It was late, as so often happened when coming back from the office in the evening, and the girls were already in bed.

But she was still energized by the discussion with Eve, and wanted to discuss the "Alessandro issue," as she called it, with her husband.

Marco listened attentively and asked: "Why don't you give Alessandro a chance? Could you tell him your expectations and give him an ultimatum? Say, you give him three months. If you don't see any improvement in his behavior, you let him go."

"An ultimatum? That's not me. I want to talk clearly to him and transparently share my assessment of him. But I don't like giving him an ultimatum. That sounds like a threat," countered Isabelle.

"Well, I didn't mean threatening. I simply meant that you may want to be clear with him about your expectations, and then you'll see if anything changes."

"Yes," Isabelle agreed, "maybe I should do that. But what if nothing changes in his behavior? I will have lost three months. What then?"

"Well, maybe you could use the time in between to talk to Jakob or other potential candidates and see if you can find a suitable alternative. And if Alessandro keeps being destructive and passive-aggressive toward you, you'll make a change," responded Marco, but then he continued, "by the way, you may have another option."

"What do you mean?" Isabelle asked.

"Well, you said that in the coming three months, you may need all hands on deck to address the profitability challenges that ATG is facing. And that Alessandro knows ATG's system inside-out. Why don't you focus him on IT only? Ask him to identify and capture cost improvements in IT, managing him closely and forcefully. In the meanwhile, you hire someone else – a Chief Digital Officer (CDO) – to do a digitization project. If that goes well and the new person integrates well, you may let Alessandro go at a later stage and expand the role of the new CDO to also include IT."

The more they spoke, the more options for addressing Isabelle's dilemma emerged. She noticed that, exactly as Eve had explained, when debating a dilemma in a team or simply with someone else, new options appear. What looked like a choice between two bad options was in fact a choice between many options. They converged on four potential options:

1. To continue to work with Alessandro and to manage him more forcefully.
2. To give transparent feedback and state clear expectations for the coming months, while exploring alternative opportunities, that is, Jakob and other candidates.
3. To focus Alessandro on IT and to hire a CDO.
4. To let Alessandro go.

Then they evaluated the four options using the framework that Eve had shared in their last discussion.

"Let's start with objectives," said Isabelle, "my objective is to have the GET to be able to work effectively as one team. That's true for all the options."

"OK," responded Marco, "let's turn to opportunities. When would it make sense to continue working with Alessandro?"

"Well, first, if Alessandro wants to continue, that is, he can get to terms that he hasn't been appointed as CEO and is willing to continue. Second, if there were no other Chief Information Officer (CIO) candidates available," responded Isabelle, "but that's probably not the case. I think it is safe to assume that there are CIO candidates available, including possibly Jakob. So, this kills Option 1."

"Makes sense to me. What about time? If you let Alessandro go, do you have time to look for another candidate?" asked Marco.

"No, I don't. We are in the middle of a crisis. I can't afford to operate for months without a CIO!" responded Isabelle.

"OK, that kills Option 4. What about competitors?" asked Marco.

"Not sure it is that relevant what our competitors are doing, so I would disregard this condition," responded Isabelle.

"Ok. Let's look at the next one: values and culture. Which options are mostly consistent with the values and culture of the organization?" asked Marco.

"Hmmm. . .ATG has a very people-oriented, caring culture. Fits better to Options 1 and 2, I think. Options 3 and 4 would probably require a more performance-oriented culture, which ATG clearly doesn't have," answered Isabelle.

"OK, we seem to converge toward Option 2, which, however, would require that you are able to coach and develop Alessandro, and Alessandro is willing to be coached," said Marco.

"Yes, you are right. But I believe I can coach him, if he accepts that," responded Isabelle.

"OK, final condition. Would the decision to keep and coach Alessandro while looking for other candidates be consistent with the state of mind of ATG's employees?" asked Marco.

"Hmm. . . good question," responded Isabelle and continued: "ATG isn't doing well, employees know that. In addition, the economy is slowing down, and ATG has a newly appointed CEO. I assume that a lot of our employees are anxious and wonder whether there will be cuts and lay-offs. Letting Alessandro go as my first big decision would probably magnify that anxiety. Keeping and coaching him would probably signal to our employees that we care about our people, and we help them, even in difficult situations. Yes, I think Option 2 is probably consistent with the prevalent state of mind of our people."

While she was speaking Marco wrote down her answers to produce an evaluation of the four options (Figure 4.1).

"OK, Option 2 it is," said Isabelle and she thanked Marco for brainstorming with her and being so supportive.

"Why don't you sleep on it and decide tomorrow?" said Marco. "It is late now, and I think you need some sleep."

She thanked and kissed him, before going to bed. Marco also had news, and he wanted to share it with his wife. A prestigious British publisher had offered him a multi-book contract for his *Charlemagne's Secrets* mystery series and was hinting at a movie deal. But since Isabelle was so absorbed by the decision on the "Alessandro issues," he decided to wait and tell her over breakfast the next day. She needed time to sleep now.

The next morning, he got the full onslaught of attention and celebratory congratulations his news warranted as Isabelle and the girls hugged him joyfully and toasted *Charlemagne's Secrets* with coffee and hot chocolate.

Driving to work a bit later, Isabelle reflected that Marco had known his news the night before but had given her the space to think only about ATG. She hoped she would remember to thank him.

She also reflected on her decision on Alessandro. Using the heuristics discussed with Eve, Option 2 emerged as the best of the four options that she and Marco had developed.

1. Dilemma	Continue working with Alessandro or let him go			

Exploit ← → Explore

2. Options on the Exploit-Explore continuum	Continue working with Alessandro	Give Alessandro feedback. Explore other candidates	Focus Alessandro on IT. Hire a new CDO	Let Alessandro go
The seven heuristics	**3. Assumptions**	**3. Assumptions**	**3. Assumptions**	**3. Assumptions**
a) Objectives		← Have a GET that is able to work effectively as one team →		
b) Opportunities	None. No other CIO is available	Other CIOs are available	Other CIOs are available	Other CIOs are available
c) Time	No time	No time	No time	Time available
d) Competitive actions and stakeholder expectations		← Probably not relevant here →		
e) Our values and culture	Caring-oriented values	Caring-oriented values	Performance-oriented values	Performance-oriented values
f) Our capabilities	Isabelle is a good coach	Isabelle is good at coaching	Isabelle is good at managing inter-personal tensions	Isabelle is good at recruiting
g) Our "mood" or prevalent collective cognitive states	Employees are anxious	Employees are anxious	Employees are not anxious	Employees are not anxious

4. Resolution	Give Alessandro feedback. Explore other candidates

Figure 4.1 Four-step Decision Navigator with solution for Case 1.

Option 2 would ensure that she could build a GET that worked efficiently as a team. She would immediately be able to tackle IT performance issues, while guaranteeing that she would have a back-up if Alessandro did not behave as expected. Importantly, Option 2 was in line with her own – and the company's – values, and with her skills. She had proven at The Travel Group that she was able to coach individuals very effectively. Also, Option 2 allowed her to signal to the organization that she was willing to give people a chance. The mood in the organization wasn't good. Replacing the former, growth-oriented CEO just as the economy was going into a recession didn't seem like a good omen. Many feared that headcount reduction would soon follow. Isabelle didn't want to fuel those fears, although she didn't yet know how to address ATG's collapsing profitability.

Option 2 assumed, however, that Alessandro was willing to commit to ATG and engage with the GET.

It is an assumption that Isabelle decided to test when she arrived at the office. She asked Alessandro for a one-on-one meeting.

The conversation with Alessandro – which was tense and emotional at times – was very helpful. By her design, he spoke more than she did.

She learned of his deep disappointment at not being appointed CEO. And, more importantly, she learned about the limitations that her predecessor always placed on Alessandro: "to mind his own business." Alessandro was an entrepreneurial personality with many ideas about how to use technology and how to digitize the business. He was full of new technology-enabled business ideas. But people often misunderstood his ideas and suggestions and saw them as criticisms of his colleagues, perhaps because of his harsh communication style. Also, the previous CEO hadn't been interested in creating a collaborative working mode in the GET. Instead, he led hierarchically, like "Louis XIV, the Sun King," as he was sometimes called. The former CEO had repeatedly asked Alessandro to focus only on his own area and, in time, that's all he did.

But Isabelle was different from the old CEO. She welcomed new, diverse ideas that could help her and the GET move ATG forward. She encouraged conflicting views, if they were handled in a constructive and productive way within the team. On that basis, she encouraged Alessandro to speak up more and do more for the team and ATG as a whole.

After talking with Isabelle, Alessandro felt liberated and encouraged for the first time in years. He appreciated that Isabelle was direct and proactive in addressing the tensions between them. In the week following their conversation, he began to behave noticeably differently. To the surprise of most of the team – but not Isabelle – his changed approach was on display a week later at the next GET meeting. The agenda was to debate how to deal with the current situation, the market slow-down, and ATG's collapsing profitability.

In preparation for the meeting, Kosta did some fact-gathering and tried to substantiate some of the elements of the prior week's GET discussion.

He shared information about ATG's competitors (see Appendix 6). He also completed his strategic review and presented an analysis of relevant market trends plus a SWOT analysis for ATG (see Appendices 7 and 8).

In the constructive conversation that followed, many different competing options emerged. The GET converged on four.

Option 1 was to launch an aggressive cost-reduction and cash-flow optimization program, as Hugo, the CFO, had proposed. It comprised four elements: (1) shutting down 25% of the branches, that is, those with the lowest contribution margins; (2) discontinuing the B2B business. While it deemed B2B strategically attractive, it seemed that ATG couldn't make the B2B business work; (3) a 25% linear cost reduction in all functions (i.e., Finance, HR, IT); and (4) selling selected non-core assets (three hotels that ATG still owned) to secure enough funding for the following 24 months.

Hugo strongly favored this solution. Isabelle was also in favor of it. The option would have led to a quick improvement of profitability. Both had a PE background, and they feared that unless they took drastic actions, ATG could become a take-over target. Alessandro also supported this option, even though it would have meant reducing the IT staff by a quarter. Frank, Conny, and Alison strongly opposed this option. Their concerns ranged from shutting down recently opened agencies (Frank and Conny) to potentially very negative union reactions (Conny), to losing critical employees (Conny), and, with them, critical skills and capabilities that might have been necessary for future growth (Alison).

Like Option 1, Option 2 also included an aggressive cost-cutting program. The difference was that Option 2 was more forward-looking; it called for re-investing some of the money saved in building a digital attacker, a "TravelTech." The digital attacker, which would be marketed under a separate brand, would emulate Booken.com, but focus on niche segments, such as customers with "complex needs" and those who wanted more personalization than they could receive from mass market companies like Booken. com. Personalization and digital offerings were important trends that emerged from Kosta's analyses.

The support for Option 2 was polarized into two camps. On one side, Alessandro, who probably saw a role for himself in the new "TravelTech" venture, was adamantly in favor of it. Isabelle and Hugo, who were keen to quickly restore profitability, also supported it. On the other side, Frank, Alison, and Conny were unyieldingly against Option 2, for the very same reasons that they opposed Option 1.

Option 3 was like Option 1, but it was less aggressive on the cost side. It called for shutting down 15% of ATG's agencies. Further, it included a 10% cost reduction in all functions and areas by digitizing all processes, that is, both front- and back-office processes. Digitization of the front-office processes was an important element of this option, which also had the aim of increasing ATG agents' ability to develop digitally personalized offerings for customers. It also aimed at improving service (adding 24/7 accessibility online) and customer retention. Building experience-based service offerings and providing them digitally was an emerging trend, and ATG seemed well positioned for it. However, because Option 3 cost reductions would come mostly through digitization, savings would have accrued only after two to three years. Under Option 3, ATG would continue to invest in the B2B business, but only in Switzerland where its brand was strongest.

The support for Option 3 was lukewarm, at best. Frank was the strongest proponent of this option, alongside Alison. Alessandro also liked the option and the focus on digitization. Kosta wasn't comfortable about leaving the B2B investment in Switzerland as the company's only remaining growth initiative. Alison was supportive too. Isabelle and Hugo were concerned about the time it would take to restore profitability. Hugo, however, signaled that he might have supported Option 3 if ATG stopped its B2B investment altogether.

Option 4 was to take a long-term view and to manage through the crisis; after all, ATG was competing in an attractive industry with many new growth opportunities. Option 4 included selling a few selected non-core assets (the three hotels) to ensure enough funding for the next 36 months, shutting down only chronically unprofitable agencies, which Frank guessed were no more than 5% of the agencies, and digitizing internal processes to create simple order-to-cash procedures and further reduce costs. Further, it included continuing to build the B2B business, and investing in new emerging business models, in particular, gaming tourism and VR-enabled tourism.

Kosta was adamant about Option 4. "We may not be able to catch up with online marketplaces like Booken.com, but we can become a leader in emerging technology-enabled business models." Alessandro, Frank, Conny, and Alison were also supportive. Interestingly, the signals coming from the board of directors seemed to support this option, too. Hugo was obviously and ferociously against it. He feared that the B2B business and the new technology-enabled business models might become significant drags on results and eat up all the savings stemming from shutting down agencies and digitizing order-to-cash processes. Worse, it could lead to bankruptcy. Isabelle didn't support Option 4 either. Her background in PE included a difficult experience that wasn't easy to forget.

Kosta produced a slide, summarizing the four options (Figure 4.2).

The GET needed to decide which option to propose to the Board of Directors, which was expecting their proposal.

What bothered Isabelle is that she was now left alone to decide which proposal to make to the board. All four options seemed reasonable and coherent, to her, yet they were all different.

She wondered, why couldn't she get everyone aligned behind one of them? All the GET members (and Kosta) seemed to care for ATG, not their own area of responsibility. They had a constructive attitude and used the same information. Yet their views differed significantly. Why was that?

Questions for Reflection

Based on what you know about the situation now, what should the GET do?

Which option should the GET select?

- Option 1?
- Option 2?
- Option 3?
- Option 4?
- Or develop further options?

You may want to write down your answer before continuing.

Options	Considerations	"Champion"

Option 1: Launch an aggressive cost-reduction and cash-flow optimization program
• Shut down 25% of the branches, that is, those with the lowest margins
• Discontinue the B2B business
• A 25% linear cost reduction in all functions (i.e., Finance, HR, IT)
• Sale of selected non-core assets (three hotels that ATG still owned)
	• Quick improvement of profitability
	• Risks
	  – Lack of future growth
	  – Negative union reactions
	  – Loss of talent
		Hugo

Option 2: Reduce costs and re-invest in TravelTech • Reduce costs as aggressively as in option 1 • Re-invest in building a digital attacker, a "TravelTech" focusing on niche segments under a separate brand	• Quick improvement of profitability • Capturing the TravelTech trend • Risks similar to option 1	Alessandro

Option 3: Reduce costs moderately and digitize
• Shut down 15% of the branches
• 10% cost reduction in front-functions
• Digitization of all main front and back-office processes
• Invest in B2B but only in Switzerland
	• "Modernization"
	• Risks
	  – Lack of future growth (no new trends, closing of new branches)
	  – Slow reduction of costs
		Frank

Option 4: Take a long-term view and manage through the crisis
• Sale of few selected non-core assets (the three hotels)
• Shut down of chronically unprofitable agencies (5%)
• Digitize internal processes
• Continue to build the B2B business
• Invest in new emerging business models
	• Becoming a leader in emerging technology enabled models
	• Risks:
	  – Bankruptcy
	  – To become a take-over target
		Konstantinos

Figure 4.2 Summary of the four strategic options considered by the GET.

Chapter 5

Identifying Assumptions and Testing Them

Claudio Feser, Daniella Laureiro-Martinez, and Stefano Brusoni

The greatest minds are capable of the greatest vices as well as the greatest virtues; those who go forward but very slowly can get further, if they always follow the right road, than those who are in too much of a hurry and stray off it.
—René Descartes, *Discourse on the Method* (2018)

"Thank you for making time again, Eve, at such short notice. I appreciate your flexibility," said Isabelle as she started the video call with Eve.

"No worries," answered Eve. "What's up?"

"First of all, I wanted to share with you that our conversations have proved to be very helpful. Debating dilemmas helped me see more and better options. And the seven heuristics proved to be very helpful for making the decision on the issue we discussed last time."

"I am glad to hear that!" said Eve.

"Well, but I feel I am stuck with another decision now. As you had suggested, I ensured that we have a well-performing team, a team in which all members contribute, respect, and trust each other, and feel safe. As a result, I feel that we get lots of different and good options. Yet, when it comes to decisions, and even when we have access to the identical facts, we seem to interpret the situation differently, and are unable to come to an agreement."

"Is your question, how can all your top team members look at the same information and interpret it so differently?"

"Yes, exactly!"

"Hmmm, let me show you a chart," said Eve as she shared a page on the video call that had only a large letter T written on it (Figure 5.1). "The letter T has two segments, two lines. A horizontal and a vertical one. Which segment is longer, or are the two segments of equal length?"

Figure 5.1 The T experiment.

"Well, I think that the vertical line is longer," said Isabelle, slightly irritated by the question. She wasn't in the mood for playing guessing games.

"Really? In fact, they are exactly of equal length. However, if you show this chart to different people, and ask them the same question, you may receive different answers."

"Why are you telling me this?" asked Isabelle impatiently.

"Let me explain. What I am showing you is the essence of an experiment done by neuroscientists in the 1980s. They showed the letter T to a group of research participants. Both segments of the letter were of equal length. When asked whether one of the two segments was longer than the other or whether they were of the same length, the participants gave – as you would expect – three different answers. What was somewhat unexpected and eye-opening was that the answers depended on the personal background of the participants. Participants, who lived or who had grown up in a flat environment, for instance, in the Netherlands, tended to see the horizontal segment as longer. Participants, who lived or had grown up in a mountainous region, such as Switzerland, for instance, overwhelmingly believed that the vertical segment was longer. They were biased to think in terms of up and down. Only few participants responded that the two segments were equal in length (Hayward and Varela, 1992)."

"Are you saying that personal background of an individual influences how he or she processes and interprets information?"

"Yes, that's exactly right! Our background, our history, our past experiences shape how we experience reality. Our past experiences shape out perceptions and our interpretation of facts, as if we were wearing glasses that shape how we see things," confirmed Eve.

"Hmmm. . . , got it," said Isabelle reflecting on her own insecurities about some of the suggested strategic options for ATG, because she might be seeing the overall situation through the frame of her previous experiences of acquisitions and having PE firms represented on the board.

Everyone has a unique genetic make-up and a unique set of experiences that influence and color how they process information.

Eve continued: "What's really important to know is that we
cannot take these glasses off. In fact, we are not even aware that we
are looking at reality through them. In other words, the process of
interpreting and coloring information is largely unconscious."

"Unconscious?"

"Yes," responded Isabelle and asked, "Have you heard about the
concept of unconscious biases?"

"Yes, I read about it. I picked up a few books on biases at the
airport last year. Interesting topic," said Isabelle.

Eve continued: "The literature on cognitive biases is volu-
minous (Tversky and Kahneman, 1974; Kahneman and Tversky, 2000; Kahneman, 2002; Gilovich et al., 2002; Thaler and
Sunstein, 2008; Kahneman, 2012; Schirrmeister, Göhring, and
Warnke, 2020) and I am not going to go into it. I just want to
mention one point: many cognitive biases are largely based on
experiences that have created unconscious associations as cause-
and-effect relationships. If you have experienced in your career
one or more unfriendly take-overs that ended badly – say, you or
individuals close to you lost their jobs – you are likely to frame a
new take-over bid as potentially negative, instead of maybe looking at both opportunities and threats. Your brain is going to say
'Uuh, bad. Take-over means pain,' and you are likely to draw negative implications."

"I understand," said Isabelle nodding.

Eve continued: "Cognitive biases are often described as being
something negative, leading us to making make poor decisions.
But that is not correct. Building on the glasses-analogy, cognitive
biases are like glasses that allow us to recognize patterns, interpret
the situation, and act quickly when we have to make a decision.
Saying that biases are negative would be like saying that experience

is useless. On the contrary, cognitive biases help us make efficient and fast decisions in most situations we encounter daily.

"But sometimes cognitive biases can be misleading, that is, when we see patterns when in fact there aren't. That's the case when we encounter novel situations, that is, new unfamiliar dilemmas. In addition, even for known dilemmas, they may also limit our thinking, reduce our option space, and lead us on to wrong beaten paths. Since in your team you are combining different experiences, you may have very different cognitive biases, or assumptions at work. That may explain why your team members see more options and don't get the same view of the situation."

Why the Brain Forms Biases and Why They Are Useful (Most of the Time)

To understand the concept of biases we need to take a detour and explore the brain. The detour will help us grasp the cognitive and biological foundations of the exploit-explore optimization process. Neuroscience can help us understand how these glasses develop, and why we are not conscious of wearing them. These glasses are well-established and persistent thinking patterns that influence how we routinely process information, and that shape our behavioral routines, that is, habits.

Our detour starts with an introduction to our brain. The brain is the core of our central nervous system. It manages and regulates the actions and reactions of our body and is the center of our thinking and our feelings. It weighs about 1.5 kg, that is, it represents about 2% of our body weight. However, and that gives you a sense of how much is going on in our brain, it eats up 20% of the body's glucose, that is, total energy (Raichle and Gusnard, 2002). Its structure is similar to

(continued)

(continued)

the structure of brains of other vertebrates, but relative to the brain of a typical mammal with a comparable body size, it is three times larger. Relatively to body size or weight, humans have the largest cerebral cortex of all vertebrates.

Let's look at a cross-section of the human brain (Figure 5.2). The brain is composed of different areas, which perform different tasks. This becomes evident when neuroscientists use imaging technologies to shed light on the intensity of the activity in different areas of the brain when individuals are carrying out physical or cognitive activities, or when the brain is experimentally or accidentally impaired (Feser, 2011).

Let's start with the inner part. That's the part of your brain that is toward the back and the bottom of the brain. Here we find the brainstem. The brainstem processes sensory functions, such as vision, hearing, smell, and balance, and it manages basic functions of the body, including body temperature, heartbeat, blood pressure, and breathing. In addition, it regulates instinctive reflexes such as coughing or sneezing. The brainstem is quite fundamental. It keeps the body in balance, so to speak. A severe lesion of the brainstem usually leads to death.

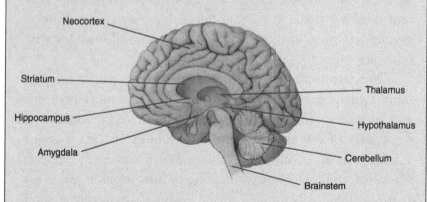

Figure 5.2   The human brain.
Source: Adapted from Feser (2011).

Another part which is quite important for balance is the cerebellum, which is next to the brainstem. The cerebellum manages the body's balance and movements. It makes our body movements fluid, coordinated, and effective. When the cerebellum is injured, the body movements become clumsy and unsteady, which is called ataxia. If we move further upward and forward (dorsally and anterior), we arrive at the thalamus and the hypothalamus. The thalamus is like a relay station. It relays sensory information to the other areas of the brain, and then back to the body. The hypothalamus is responsible for homeostasis, that is, when the all systems are in balance so that the body can function properly.

Homeostasis happens through processes that are for the most part unconscious, like most activities performed by the parts of the brain situated in the back (posterior) and bottom part of our brain – the brainstem, the cerebellum, the thalamus, and the hypothalamus. We do not consciously think that we should cough or blink. Our brain takes care of that, and most of the time we don't even notice. Many believe that these parts of the brain developed first in the evolution of our species. Interestingly, if we compare the human brain with that of other vertebrates – fish, amphibians, reptiles, birds, or mammals – we will find striking similarities in the back and lower part of the different brains.

Let's now move toward the front (anterior) and upward (dorsally) in the tour of the brain. As we do so, the activities of the brain become gradually more deliberate, more complex, and importantly, more conscious. The first area that we encounter is the limbic system, which includes the amygdala and the hippocampus. The amygdala is the brain's emotion-processing center. It is the part of the brain that instinctively reacts to situations – whether threatening, dangerous,

(continued)

(continued)

or joyous – and that generates emotions associated to them. Because emotions play an important role in the formation of memories, the amygdala works closely together with the hippocampus, the brain's memory center. Besides storing information and facts, the hippocampus, plays a central role in forming long-term memories. It is interesting to note that our limbic system works largely instinctively, and that it does not change much or mature over the course of a lifetime. When it is stimulated – say, you feel attacked – it makes us instinctively react like 2-year-olds, even when we are adults (Bolte Taylor, 2008). Luckily, while our emotional reactions do not mature, our ability to control our behavior does.

However, even when we are adults, in the very moment when something unexpected happens, the amygdala generates a strong emotional reaction. But we have learnt not to let those emotions steer us.

There is one more part associated with the limbic system that matters here: the striatum. It "sits" above the hippocampus and plays an important role in planning and executing movements. It is believed to play an important role in the memorization of habitual behaviors, that is, in the formation of habits, capabilities, or skills. Further, the striatum appears to react strongly to rewards and punishments (Rock and Schwartz, 2006; Linden, 2008) and – working closely with higher parts of the brain – to be involved in a variety of more complex, and conscious cognitive processes. Because we share the structure of this part of the brain – generally described as the limbic system – with other animals, especially with mammals, this part of the brain is sometimes called, in colloquial language, the mammalian brain. Dog owners will say to you that they think their beloved dogs can sense their emotions. That may in fact be right.

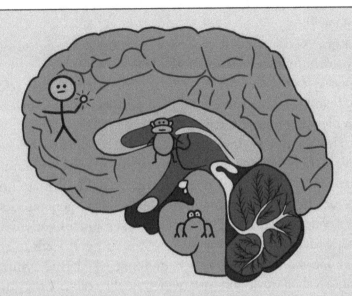

Figure 5.3   Three brain layers work together.

And now, finally, let's come to the cerebral cortex, believed to be, in evolutionary terms, the newest, most recently developed part of the brain. It has a left and a right part. The two parts are called hemispheres. The thinking activities in the neocortex are largely conscious, and the neocortex is involved in thinking processes that require attention control, awareness, and reflection (Feser, 2011). When we reflect about our own thoughts, that is when we think about thinking, it is the neocortex that is at work, so to speak (Figure 5.3).

You may now ask yourself: how does all this relate to decision-making?

We know that two regions of the brain are particularly active in the process of decision-making, regulating exploration and exploitation activities (Laureiro-Martinez et al., 2010; Laureiro-Martinez et al., 2015). The first is the mammalian brain, which encompasses the limbic system and the

(continued)

(continued)

striatum. As discussed, it processes emotions, evaluates rewards, and stores memories and habits. The thinking process in the limbic system is mostly automatic, unconscious, and effortless. It tends to be active when we perform exploit-oriented activities (Laureiro-Martinez, 2014).

The second is the neocortex, which tends to be more active when we focus on explorative activities (Laureiro-Martinez et al., 2015). The neocortex holds the attention control circuits of the brain, needed to plan, generate ideas, and develop strategies. The neocortex is conscious and deliberate, which requires effort. Using it is tiring. It leads to cognitive fatigue. Try, for instance, dividing 417 by 23 (without using a calculator), and you will quickly realize how much effort it takes.

Sustained thinking efforts of the neocortex are exhausting. Traditional explanations of this phenomenon have focused on the impact of brain activities on energy consumption. They assumed that the thinking process of the cortex was responsible for the glucose consumption of the brain. However, newer research suggests that cognitive fatigue results from an accumulation of glutamate in the neocortex (Wiehler et al., 2022). Glutamate is an excitatory neurotransmitter that plays a role in learning and memory-formation. In other words, extended thinking processes in the neocortex lead to chemical changes in the brain that express themselves as cognitive fatigue. We are learning more about this every day!

So, when exploiting, the "mammal system" is leading. The thinking processes are effortless and largely unconscious. When exploring, the neocortex takes the lead. That, however, leads to cognitive fatigue.

But it is the interaction between the two systems which interests us. That's where the music plays, so to speak.

When we have to make a decision between two or more options, that is, when we have to address a dilemma, the "mammal system" and the neocortex work together to resolve it.

Let's see how the neocortex and the mammalian brain interact, say, when our brain confronts a challenge, and going back to our vacation example, where to go on vacation, knowing that your never-satisfied parents-in-law will join you and your family.

Initially, a dilemma activates the "mammal system." During that first step, the limbic system generates an emotional reaction that says, "Hey, pay attention! This is important!" Such signals include emotions like joy, love, sadness, anger, and fear (Linden, 2008). Then, after the initial activation of the limbic system, comes the second step, at which the brain starts to reflect on how to address the situation and develop options or strategies to overcome the challenges. At this stage, the neocortex is activated in the process of thinking of options, that is, exploring ways to resolve the dilemma. The process somewhat resembles the way biological organisms create variation, with the neocortex generating ideas for alternative courses of action while planning and testing possible strategies. This is a process of reflective thinking, which particularly activates the frontal part of the cortex, also called the PFC or prefrontal cortex (Bechara, 2005).

This process used by the prefrontal cortex requires attention and concentration, and it leads to cognitive fatigue. But the prefrontal cortex can hold only a limited amount of information, and cope with only a limited amount of cognitive load. Therefore, in a third step, our brain selects the courses of action that have worked in the past and discards those that did not work, as it focuses on scaling the former.

(continued)

(continued)

Useful information, that is, exploration activities that worked successfully, are memorized, stored, and pushed down into our "C drive," that is, the automatic limbic system. Emotions play an important role in the recording of this information. For example, you may remember in great detail, sometimes after many decades, a particular day or event when something of high and positive or negative emotional intensity occurred. Such events could include something personal, like winning a prize or being told that a close relative has died, or an intense public event, such as the terrorist attacks of 9/11. But you may not remember anything that happened in the days before or after that event. What I am saying is: events and experiences connected with strong emotions result in more consolidated memories. The striatum is also involved in this process. It is believed to steer habitual activities and procedures that we carry out without energy or effort, or, as we might say, "without much thought" (Rock and Schwartz, 2006; Linden, 2008).

Let us take an example. You and your partner live together in a small village far away from the nearest city, and you have no public transportation options after working hours. Most of your friends already have a driver's license. You have no driver's license. Your partner, who also does not have a driver license, is frustrated that your friends are going out after work and driving to the city, while you can't. You are frustrated too. Your brain takes note. That's step 1. You decide to get your driver's license, and you start taking driving lessons. In your first lesson, performing all necessary activities in the sequence required to get started – buckling up, checking your surroundings, pressing the gear pedal, starting the engine, and so forth, let alone driving – will require a great deal of attention and concentration, and will produce a lot of pleasure when done well! This is step 2. But then, after you pass the exam and do this sequence a thousand times, driving becomes routine, which is step 3. All driving activities seem to happen correctly, as if by magic, without much thinking. Now you can drive to a far-away place without much thought. This is because driving is now stored in your automatic system."

This three-step process is the very process, the "circuitry," by which new routines are formed. Habits, skills, or competencies are all forms of exploitation routines. They can be carried out without much cognitive effort. They are the results of the brain's effort to save energy. "You thought about them long and hard, and you tested them, so why put so much additional energy in thinking more about these strategies?" says your brain. So, you don't, and the routines become largely unconscious. In other words, today's exploitation strategies are yesterday's exploration strategies. They have been stored in the limbic system so that the neocortex can focus cognitive energy on new dilemmas. And so, we fly on autopilot, so to speak. This partly explains why we tend to stick to habits and why we have an aversion to change.

This three-step process, the "circuitry" that helps free up cognitive energy to focus on novel issues, is also the very process by which we form experience-based cognitive biases. We are exposed to millions of bits of information at any given time. We cannot process, evaluate, integrate, and use all this information for decision-making because people's mental capacities are limited (Newell and Simon, 1972). Therefore, we form cognitive biases as strategies to reduce complexity. Cognitive biases – sometimes also referred to as prejudices, stereotypes, or simply biases – are efficient because they are cognitive simplification mechanisms or mental shortcuts.

(continued)

> The brain constantly develops – through experience – new such shortcuts throughout our lifetime.
>
> However, while allowing for efficient and fast decision-making in familiar situations, cognitive biases can lead to distortions (the glasses) and poor decisions in novel, unfamiliar situations.

"Yes, but since they are largely unconscious, how can I surface them in order to overcome the default mechanism to exploit and to use potentially harmful unconscious assumptions?" asked Isabelle.

"In my habilitation thesis, I developed a stepwise approach to overcome your brain's tendency to use experience-based biases. You can use the approach to prepare decisions under uncertainty," answered Eve. She continued:

"Step 1 is to start from the problem and *to identify the exploit-explore dilemma*. Should I stay or should I go?

Step 2 is to *widen the option space on the exploit-explore continuum*. Recent advances in neuroscience relating to exploit-explore optimization suggest that thinking in options of different level of uncertainty (relative uncertainty) counterbalances the brain tendency to exploit, that is to build on experience and to use biases. It appears that in situation of relative uncertainty, the choice of options is regulated by an "uncertainty bonus," a value associated with exploring novel options or uncertain options if there is the possibility of gaining knowledge that can be exploited in the future (Gershman and Tzovaras, 2018; Tomov et al., 2020; Cockburn et al., 2021)."

> Thinking in options counterbalances the brain tendency to exploit, that is, to build on experience and to use biases.

"This sounds a bit theoretical. What does this mean?" asked Isabelle, who seemed a bit lost.

"In a nutshell, thinking in options fosters rational thinking and exploration," responded Eve. "The research suggests that thinking of options that have different levels of uncertainty, that is, different balances on the exploit-explore continuum, leverages the uncertainty bonus and counteracts the brain's natural tendency to exploit. Cognitive biases are less potent when we think in options. We become more rational."

"So, developing many options makes us more rational, and less victim of experienced-based biases?"

"Yes, exactly," answered Eve. "Widening the option space is a well-known approach to de-biasing decisions under uncertainty (Heath and Heath, 2013). The new facet in my proposed approach is to widen the option space along various levels of uncertainty or, in other words, along the exploit-explore continuum."

The comment made Isabelle think. She noted that that was exactly what she and Marco did, when they discussed whether ATG should let Alessandro go or not. They had developed four options along the exploit-explore continuum.

"Importantly, and to build on the earlier discussion on teams, teams are particularly effective in widening the option space," said Eve, sharing another slide on the screen (Figure 5.4).

"As you can see here" she continued, "the secret of teams is that they tend to look at a broader solution space and to develop more options. Further, thinking of options along the exploit-explore continuum also allows us to identify in a targeted way the assumptions underlying each of the options, that is, to identify assumptions for the seven heuristics that influence the optimization of exploit-explore balances."

"What do you mean?" asked Isabelle.

"Well, when a team member proposes an option, you can ask him or her, 'Why do you believe the option will work?' That will lead to the third step."

"Third step?"

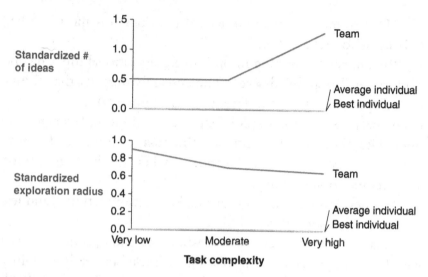

Figure 5.4 The secret of groups: more ideas, broader solution space.
Source: Adapted from Almaatouq et al. (2021).

"Yes, step 3 is to *identify unconscious assumptions for each of the options along the seven exploit-explore heuristics.* So, you would ask a team member who had proposed an option, 'Why do you believe that that option will work? What do you assume are the objectives? What do you assume are opportunities? What is your hypothesis, how much time do we have? What's your hypothesis on what competitors will do? Why do you assume that the option fits us in terms of culture, competencies, and cognitive states?' It is important to note that you do not have to identify all seven heuristics for each option. Some options are driven by objectives, opportunities, and competencies, and then you focus on these three. Some by objectives, opportunities, and values, so that's where you focus your attention. Some options follow other heuristics. The seven heuristics can serve as a checklist to help you identify and categorize the assumptions that you are making or that a team member is making."

"What do you mean? Can you give an example?" asked Isabelle.

"Sure. Say you are an energy producer and are to decide whether to invest in an oilfield, or alternatively in a wind park. Say that member A of your team, Jack, proposes Option 1. Jack's option, investing in an oilfield, might be driven by his assumptions that the objective is to maximize profits, that there is a concrete opportunity to invest in, and that the company has the competence to develop the oilfield. Say another member, member B or Anna, believes that the company should invest in a wind park. Her conclusion may be driven by her assumptions that the company must make a reasonable profit, that there is the opportunity to invest in a wind park, and that it is important (values) that the company invests in sustainable, renewable energy," responded Eve.

"Got it," said Isabelle.

Eve continued:"No matter which assumptions drive your options; it is important to write them down. Writing hypotheses, or assumptions if you prefer, along the seven explore-exploit heuristics on paper helps make them explicit. It also helps to de-personalize them."

"De-personalize assumptions?"

> No matter which assumptions drive your options; it is important to write them down. It helps to de-personalize them.

"Yes, when working in a team, we may sometimes feel the urge to argue and defend our option, as if losing an argument is a personal defeat. However, basing our conclusions on arguments – hypotheses or assumptions – and writing them down, separates them from the person who is using them. They become testable and, if wrong, they change the conclusion, but they do not affect the person. It becomes, 'the assumption was false,' rather than, 'I was wrong.'"

"Makes sense. So, all we need is to write down the assumptions or reasons for the option and we can use the seven heuristics of optimization of the exploit-explore balance as a check-list to identify our assumptions and to structure our thinking?" asked Isabelle.

"Correct, most of the time writing down the rationale for an option is already sufficient to uncover unconscious assumptions," answered Eve, "but sometimes that is not sufficient. Sometimes the assumptions written down don't fully justify an option. That's because there may still be some assumptions that haven't been made explicit. Two more approaches can help make all unconscious assumptions explicit. The first approach is critical reasoning, that is, determining whether an argument is valid or not. If the argument is valid, the proposed option does indeed follow from the assumptions stated. Then, no more hidden assumptions are involved. But if the argument is not valid, check carefully to understand what additional assumptions should be added to the argument that would make it valid. Some assumptions may still be hidden if the stated assumptions only partly justify the proposed options. Or, in case of non-sequitur reasoning, if there is no logical connection between arguments, that is, assumptions, and conclusion, that is, the option (Toulmin, 2003)."

"OK, once the assumptions are in plain sight, we can ask ourselves if the conclusion is logical, as we assume that the person proposing an option is thinking rationally, right?"

"Yes, correct," answered Eve. "There is another approach and that is persistently ask why: 'Why? Yes, but why? Yes, but why.' Repeatedly asking why a conclusion would hold, may help unearth additional or missing assumptions."

"OK, I assume the next step is to test assumptions, right?"

"Yes, that's right. Step 4 is to *test assumptions*," answered Eve. "Once assumptions are in plain sight, they can be tested. You can gather evidence and facts to determine whether an assumption is false or not. That takes time. Not all assumptions require testing, however. Some assumptions are reasonable, that is, they are well understood and widely accepted, such as, 'a large market provides more potential than a small market,' for instance. Some assumptions are immaterial, that is, even when false, they do not materially change the conclusion. You can simply disregard them. You also can prioritize assumptions for testing. Those that have the largest, and the most material impact on the conclusion are the ones you might want to test."

"Can you give an example?" asked Isabelle.

"Yes, sure. Assume that you want to launch a new product to address changing customers' needs. Your hypothesis is that the product that you have developed will be effective in addressing clients' needs. Investments in production – a new manufacturing plant, new machinery, hiring of staff in production – and a marketing campaign are so significant, that you are likely to bet the company on this one decision to launch the product. In such a case, you will want to test your hypothesis extensively. You may run market tests, surveys, do a regional pilot and so forth."

"Hmmm. . . sounds like a lot of work," noted Isabelle.

"Yes, testing requires work," responded Eve. "But testing can be done efficiently. Some testing methods require more effort than others. For instance, creating a prototype or a minimum viable product (MVP), running usability tests, or conducting large-scale, representative quantitative surveys, take more time and resources. However, some testing requires less work. The use of analogies or analogous offerings, that is, similar mechanics, by another industry, or another country, the use of publicly available data such as country statistics, company reports, and so forth do not require a lot of work. Nor does leveraging experiments others have done, think of academic studies, market research reports, for instance, nor does conducting qualitative market research, such as interviewing a handful of subject experts."

Isabelle thought about her first one-on-one conversation with Alessandro. She realized that when reaching out to him to understand the reasons for his passive-aggressive behavior, she was in fact testing an implicit assumption. She was unconsciously testing the hypothesis whether Alessandro was in fact willing to commit to ATG and engage with the GET.

"I think I understand," she said. "Sometimes a simple discussion is sufficient to test a hypothesis, for instance, about another individual's motivations."

"Yes, that's exactly right. Sometimes the information to test an assumption is easily accessible. But for us to decide how to test assumptions, we first must become aware of them. It is all about making assumptions explicit. Once they are, you can design an effective and efficient testing strategy, so to speak," confirmed Eve.

While Eve was talking, Isabelle was taking notes. At least, that's what Eve thought. In reality, Isabelle was drawing a slide which she promptly shared on the video call (Figure 5.5).

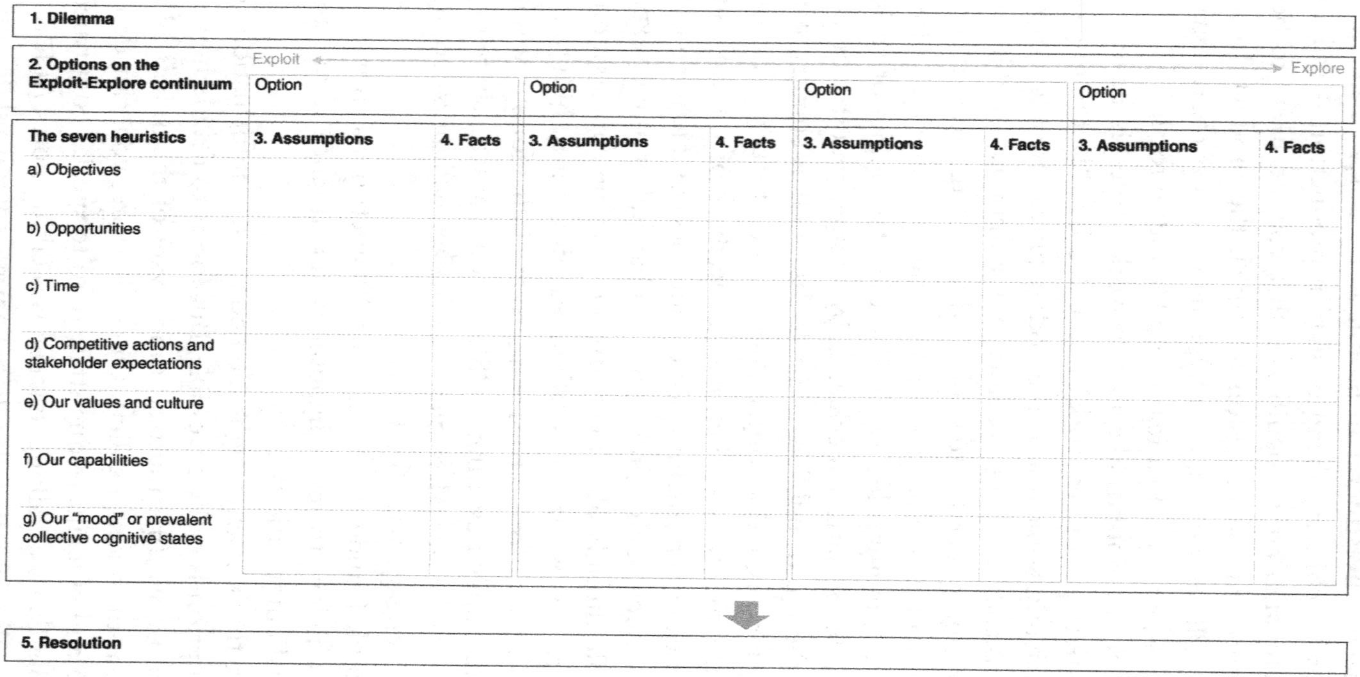

1. Dilemma

2. Options on the Exploit-Explore continuum

Exploit ————→ ————→ Explore

The seven heuristics	Option		Option		Option		Option	
	3. Assumptions	4. Facts	3. Assumptions	4. Facts	3. Assumptions	4. Facts	3. Assumptions	4. Facts
a) Objectives								
b) Opportunities								
c) Time								
d) Competitive actions and stakeholder expectations								
e) Our values and culture								
f) Our capabilities								
g) Our "mood" or prevalent collective cognitive states								

5. Resolution

Figure 5.5 The 5-step Decision Navigator.

"I tried to summarize the discussion and, building on the framework that you had shared last time, I added a column. The new column is to validate the assumptions with facts," she said.

"Wow! Cool. That's super helpful. Could be used as a template when making decisions under uncertainty!" said Eve enthusiastically as ever. "Let's try an example to apply it!"

"Yes, let me try that too," said Isabelle. "Say, you would like to expand your company abroad. Where should you go? There are theoretically an unlimited number of explorative moves you could make, and uncertainty is total. But let's say you develop two exploration options instead. The first is to expand into a specific adjacent country. Some relevant elements of uncertainty are known; for example, the potential new market's culture and legislation are probably like those in your home country, and your current business model may work well in this new setting. The second option is to expand into a specific far-away country, maybe a larger one that offers more potential. The latter option comes with more uncertainty attached. You are less familiar with the culture and business practices in that distant country, and it is unclear whether your business model might work there. You then ask yourself, 'What would I need to believe to be true for my business model to work if I take the second option?' and then you can develop hypotheses to test. Maybe you could do market research that surveys potential customers about their needs, maybe you could arrange interviews with local authorities, or perhaps you could launch a small pilot project, making an initial foray into the new country to try to gain the information you require and raise your confidence to take the second, potentially more lucrative, option."

"Fantastic, well done. The student is surpassing the teacher here!" said Eve with a big smile.

"The Sorcerer's Apprentice," said Isabelle jokingly. She recalled a Disney movie that she used to watch together with the girls when they were 5 and 3 years old or so. The movie was about the story of a wizard who had a young apprentice (Mickey Mouse). The apprentice was bright and very eager to learn to be a wizard.

However, he was a little too eager and started practicing some of his mentor's tricks before knowing how to control them, leading to the flooding of the wizard's cavern.

"That's funny," said Eve. They both laughed.

"Going back to the framework, I have one more question," said Isabelle. "When applying it, I asked myself, doesn't relative uncertainty differ by person? What I may perceive as uncertain, may not bother someone else, right?"

"Yes, that's correct. It is important to remember whenever you consider uncertainty that individuals' different experiences and knowledge mean that a factor which may represent high relative uncertainty for one person may not mean uncertainty for someone else. Perhaps you have already worked in the far-away country and gained experience there. If that was the case, you may experience less relative uncertainty between the two options," responded Eve.

"Sounds intuitive, but also quite mechanical. And it takes diligence and effort to use."

"Making decision under uncertainty well is demanding. There is no simple way to produce high-quality decisions. While you might think that it takes effort and time, just think of how long it takes to revert a wrong decision. Also, if you practice making decisions using the model, doing so becomes an automatic process, second nature, so to speak. It can become an important skill when making decisions under uncertainty and managing exploration-exploitation trade-offs effectively. I also believe that if this skill is widely developed in an organization, it may create a learning environment and a culture where exploration is seen as an experiment or a series of experiments, and where failing initiatives are not stigmatized and personalized, but rather seen as steps toward new knowledge, insights, and adaptation," said Eve.

"I agree, making great decisions takes time and effort," noted Isabelle.

"Yes, you are right. But you don't have to make every decision this way. The approach is probably not efficient for use in most decisions you make in a day. But when you encounter novel situations and the decision really matters, say, when the survival of a company is a stake, when you are betting the company on a large investment, when your employees' careers and families are at stake, it is probably worth taking the time and making the effort," noted Eve.

"Yes, I agree. Thanks for sharing it, Eve," said Isabelle. "Let me summarize: our brain constantly develops, through experience, largely unconscious cognitive biases. Making decisions causes cognitive load. Biases reduce cognitive load in that they simplify the decision-making process. They are short-cuts. While helpful and efficient in most situations, cognitive biases can harm decision-making performance, especially when we encounter new, unfamiliar situations. In particular, cognitive biases may reduce our option space. Our experience may make us explore fewer options. It may also lead us to choose sub-optimal ones. Widening the option space on the exploit-explore continuum creates innovative solutions, and identifying the relevant assumptions that must hold for each option to be valid helps reduce the potential harmful effect of cognitive biases in novel situations. It helps unearth unconscious assumptions or hypotheses, which can then be validated or falsified with evidence, that is, facts. This process should be used for decisions that really matter though, as it takes time and effort."

> While helpful and efficient in most situations, cognitive biases can harm decision-making performance, especially when we encounter new, unfamiliar situations.

"A great summary once again. Super helpful! Thank you, Isabelle," noted Eve.

"I need to reflect on this conversation. Also, I want to try the approach you outlined in the GET. Maybe it will help us get out of the impasse we are in. Thank you for now!" said Isabelle ending the video call.

Key Takeaways

- Under uncertainty decisions are biased. The way you interpret information, the assumptions you make about the situation, and hence the options you consider are biased, that is, they are colored by your own experience and patterns of thinking.
- Biases reduce your option space, and make you choose sub-optimal options.
- Widening the option space, identifying the assumptions that must hold for each option to be valid, helps you to develop innovative solutions and to reduce the effect of biases.
- You can use the seven heuristics of exploit-explore balance optimization as a check-list to identify and categorize the relevant assumption that drive each option. Once done, you can test your assumptions.

Our Decision Navigator now has five steps (Figure 5.6):

1. Identify the exploit-explore dilemma.
2. Develop multiple options on the exploit-explore continuum.
3. Identify underlying, relevant assumptions for each of the options using the seven decision-making heuristics.
4. Use facts to test the relevant assumptions.
5. Decide.

The process of widening the option space, unearthing unconscious assumptions, and testing them takes time and effort. Don't rush important decisions.

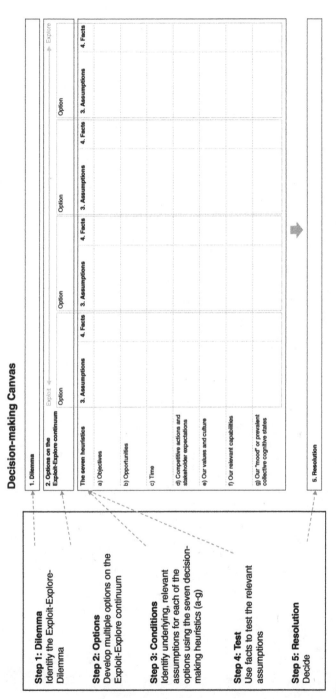

Figure 5.6 Summary of the five-step Decision Navigator.

Chapter 6

Case 3: Making Decisions About Company Growth

**Claudio Feser, David Redaschi,
and Karolin Frankenberger**

T
he GET needed to decide how to address ATG's current challenges. The board of directors was expecting a proposal from them. But the GET weren't ready to go to the board. They decided to invest more effort and time to debate the options, and to apply the model for decision-making that Isabelle had shared with them.

As a first step, Isabelle asked the most vocal ones (the "champions") to argue for the option that they were most in favor of, that is, Hugo for Option 1, Alessandro for Option 2, Frank and Conny for Option 3 and Kosta for Option 4.

She started with Hugo.

"Hugo, why are you in favor of Option 1?" she asked, "what is your objective?"

"I want to reduce the costs quickly."

"Why?" she asked.

"Well, because I assume that if we don't reduce costs, ATG risks going bankrupt, having funding issues, and possibly becoming a take-over-target," he responded.

Isabelle noted the assumption on the sheet she had developed with Eve. "OK, I understand. What about opportunities? Why do you believe that we can cut costs rapidly?" she continued.

"My assumption is that we can close a significant number of underperforming agencies rapidly. Also, I don't believe that we can turn around the B2B business rapidly and that we should shut it down. And I assume that we have enough overcapacity in many functions and that we can take a 25% linear cut without major disruptions," Hugo answered.

"What about time?" Isabelle asked.

"I think we should act fast," responded Hugo.

"Why?" asked Isabelle.

"Well, first, because we are running a loss, and this can't go on much longer. Besides profitability, we risk having funding issues. Also, I assume that there are competitors already looking at us. I assume that we are at risk of being a take-over target."

"OK, I understand, what about competition?" she asked.

"Not sure," responded Hugo, "I assume our traditional competitors will also be hit by the slow-down and try to reduce costs."

"What about values and culture?" Isabelle asked.

"Well, I think if we do this well, involving the unions, communicating transparently and helping people impacted by the cost reductions, I assume that we can implement Option 1 in line with our people-centric and caring culture," he responded.

"OK, what about our competencies? Do you assume that we have the capabilities to implement Option 1?" she asked.

"I think we can implement Option 1 effectively."

"Why do you believe that?" asked Isabelle.

"We have never done a major cost reduction program, but I believe that if we work well as a team, we can pull this off," responded Hugo.

"What about the mood and morale of our employees?" she asked.

"I think that many of our people are anxious. They also see that the economy is cooling and expect us to react. But it can be done, to my mind," responded Hugo.

"Why do you believe that?" asked Isabelle again intending to identify Hugo's assumptions.

"Because I assume that we can implement Option 1 in a manner consistent with our value and culture."

After having identified Hugo's assumptions supporting Option 1, Isabelle then did the same for the rest, asking the proponents of Options 2, 3, and 4 to argue for their options. Isabelle persistently asked why the proponents of each of the options favored it, noting the identified assumptions on the evaluation sheet.

What emerged was a list of assumptions on which each option was based (Figure 6.1).

Writing the assumptions on paper proved to be very helpful. Now, the question no longer was "who is right?" but rather "which assumption is correct?" This not only made the discussion less tense and even more constructive, but it also helped uncover the source of the GET members' real differences in conclusions. Now, the GET members could go back to the data that was available and test their assumptions.

"Let's use facts to check the assumptions for Option 1," suggested Isabelle.

"Option 1 assumed that we must act immediately to prevent a bankruptcy or a funding problem. That said, if I look at the financial data and the latest financial projections, we are well capitalized, and our cash flow is positive. So, the facts don't support the assumptions that we run a risk here or that we need to act immediately," said Frank.

1. Dilemma — In a slowing market, focus on reducing costs (exploit) or continue to invest in growth (explore)?

2. Options on the Exploit-Explore continuum (Exploit → → Explore)

The seven heuristics	Aggressive cost-reduction and cash-flow optimization program		Cost-reduction and re-investment into TravelTech		Moderate cost-reduction and digitization		Taking a long-term view and managing through the crisis	
	3. Assumptions	4. Facts	3. Assumptions	4. Facts	3. Assumptions	4. Facts	3. Assumptions	4. Facts
a) Objectives	Improve short-term profitability (funding, unsolicited take-over)		Improve short-term profitability (funding, unsolicited take-over)		Focusing on both profitability and growth creates most value		Focusing only on growth maximizes value	
b) Opportunities	Potential for significant cost red. Potential (agencies, B2B, functions)		Potential for significant cost red. Potential but also for digitization		Potential for selected cost reduction not impacting growth		Many growth opportunities Closing agencies reduces profit growth	
c) Time	Limited time as competitors are preparing a bid		Limited time as competitors are preparing a bid		Time and resources are available		Time and resources are available	
d) Competitive actions and stakeholder expectations	Focusing on reducing costs		Both focusing on reducing costs and investing into growth		Both focusing on reducing costs and investing into growth		Investing in the future	
e) Our values and culture	If executed well, Option 1 is in line with ATG's culture		If executed well, Option 2 is in line with ATG's culture		If executed well, Option 3 is in line with ATG's culture		Creativity, innovation, entrepreneurship	
f) Our capabilities	Cost management and team collaboration		Cost management Scaling innovation "TravelTech" capabilities		Cost management Scaling innovation		Scaling innovation, accelerating growth	
g) Our "mood" or prevalent collective cognitive states	Employees are anxious but if executed well, Option 1 is accepted		Employees are anxious but if executed well, Option 2 is accepted		Employees are anxious but if executed well, Option 3 is accepted		Employees are optimistic and see the opportunities	

5. Resolution

Figure 6.1 Five-step Decision Navigator with solution for Case 2.

"Yes, that's correct," said Alison, "but what about the potential take-over risk?"

No GET member had an answer, but a few telephone calls with two subject experts, investment bankers who specialized in take-over defenses, provided a new perspective: if ATG had a credible value-creation plan, one that combined cost reduction measures with growth initiatives, the risk of an unsolicited take-over was minimal.

"What about opportunities? What facts support the assumption that we can close 25% of the agencies?" asked Isabelle.

"Well, I included in the financial projections shared last week an analysis on the profitability of each agency," said Hugo. He continued: "The analysis groups agencies into decile according to their contribution margins. The data validates the assumption."

"Yes, that's right," responded Frank, "but it also validates another assumption, one for Option 3. The analysis also shows the average age of the agencies in each decile, as well as the percentage of agencies that had opened in the past few years. It suggests that ATG wouldn't lose profit growth momentum by shutting down not 15%, but probably even 20% of the agencies. The agencies' data by deciles are averages. But the data validates the assumption for Option 3 that we can close a significant number of agencies without losing growth momentum."

The discussion unfolded with the GET members working through the data available. Where data was not available, but an assumption felt reasonable, it was noted accordingly, as it was when no data was available at all. What emerged is shown in Figure 6.2.

It emerged that Option 3 was probably the best of the four options.

It did address short-term profitability issues, at least partially. Even though the savings would not kick in immediately, having a credible plan protected ATG from a competitor's potential take-over attempt.

It also captured short-term improvement opportunities. The measures would include reducing the number of agencies by 20% and closing the B2B business completely, which was neither – as

T (True), F (False), R (Reasonable), ? (Open, unclear)

1. Dilemma	In a slowing market, focus on reducing costs (exploit) or continue to invest in growth (explore)?							
2. Options on the Exploit-Explore continuum	Exploit → → → Explore							
	Aggressive cost-reduction and cash-flow optimization program		Cost-reduction and re-investment into TravelTech		Moderate cost-reduction and digitization		Taking a long-term view and managing through the crisis	
The seven heuristics	**3. Assumptions**	**4. Facts**	**3. Assumptions**	**4. Facts**	**3. Assumptions**	**4. Facts**	**3. Assumptions**	**4. Facts**
a) Objectives	Improve short-term profitability (funding, unsolicited take-over)	F	Improve short-term profitability (funding, unsolicited take-over)	F	Focusing on both profitability and growth creates most value	T	Focusing only on growth maximizes value	T
b) Opportunities	Potential for significant cost red. Potential (agencies, B2B, functions)	T	Potential for significant cost red. Potential but also for digitization	T / T	Potential for selected cost reduction not impacting growth	T	Many gr. opportunities / Closing ag. reduces profit growth	T / F
c) Time	Limited time as competitors are preparing a bid	F	Limited time as competitors are preparing a bid	F	Time and resources are available	T	Time and resources are available	T
d) Competitive actions and stakeholder expectations	Focusing on reducing costs	?	Both focusing on reducing costs and investing into growth	?	Both focusing on reducing costs and investing into growth	?	Investing into the future	?
e) Our values and culture	If executed well, Option 1 is in line with ATG's culture	R	If executed well, Option 2 is in line with ATG's culture	R	If executed well, Option 3 is in line with ATG's culture	R	Creativity, innovation, entrepreneurship	R
f) Our capabilities	Cost management and team collaboration	T	Cost management / Scaling innovation / "TravelTech" capabilities	T / ? / ?	Cost management / Scaling innovation	T / ?	Scaling innovation, accelerating growth	?
g) Our "mood" or prevalent collective cognitive states	Employees are anxious but if executed well, Option 1 is accepted	R	Employees are anxious but if executed well, Option 2 is accepted	R	Employees are anxious but if executed well, Option 3 is accepted	R	Employees are optimistic and see the opportunities	F

5. Resolution	Moderate costreduction and digitization

Figure 6.2 Five-step Decision Navigator with solution for Case 2 (including testing).

Konstantinos had claimed – the only growth opportunity available to ATG, nor a particularly attractive one, as recent experience had shown. It also included a digitization initiative of front- and back-office activities to reduce costs.

ATG was well capitalized and had enough time and resources not only to focus on reducing costs, but also to continue investing in building a stronger corporation in the future. Konstantinos' analysis had highlighted a few growth opportunities that played to ATG's strengths and could provide venues for future growth, this included the areas of advice-intense, experience-based and personalized tourism. The attempt to digitize the front-office, reduce the administrative activities of agency staff members, and provide more time for customer service would also enable selling new experience-based products and services.

While it was not clear what ATG's competitors were doing, it was clear to the GET that Option 3, if executed well, was consistent with ATG's values, culture, and competencies (although after the B2B adventure, some members still questioned the organization's ability to scale innovation effectively).

The GET also felt that ATG's employees would support this option, if executed well, because it provided an inspiring path for future growth. The GET started to converge on Option 3, but Konstantinos was still not on board.

Isabelle asked Kosta why.

Kosta said that he feared that with Option 3, ATG would be missing out on some of the trends that were shaping the travel industry. The question that emerged is whether ATG could – given relatively limited funding – find and execute selected smaller investments in future growth areas.

Kosta promised to do some more fact-finding to answer this question, and Isabelle adjourned the meeting.

Three days later, she reconvened the GET.

In the interim, Kosta had identified three potential acquisition targets – start-ups in VR-tourism – that ATG could acquire to build competencies that might be relevant to it in the future. He presented the VR-tourism opportunity by explaining, "People want to have unique and unforgettable experiences. However, I believe there is a market for experiences where you don't have to suffer the agony of traveling, standing in line at the check-in counter, waiting for delayed planes, searching for lost luggage, or staying in a hotel with a poor internet connection. This is where the power of virtual reality comes into play. Customers could go on vacation without leaving the comfort of their homes. People could experience day-long simulations and games for all sorts of things via virtual reality. For example, virtual reality could enable travel to 'impossible' destinations. Have you ever dreamed of flying to the moon? Or, flying like a bird inside a volcano?"

While his presentation was convincing, he was the youngest person present, and his idea sounded strange and a bit far-fetched. But Isabelle and the GET felt it was still worth looking into, at least as a means for building competencies that might become relevant in the future.

They unanimously decided to propose Option 3 to the board of directors. The board fully endorsed the strategy.

★ ★ ★

In the following 18 months, the implementation of the strategy progressed well. Closing agencies is always a difficult process, especially when it requires letting go of long-standing, loyal employees. But the GET handled the communication well. The unions also praised the GET for the support ATG provided to departing employees. Thanks to a generous redundancy package, and funding for retraining and outplacement, most departing employees had time and the capabilities to find other attractive job opportunities.

Digitization also progressed well, especially in the back-office area. Front-office digitization was lagging, but not by much. The strategy to transform ATG's offerings to include more experience-based services and packages was also progressing, albeit more slowly than expected. Still, a few agencies were making big inroads with experience-based offerings, a fact that demonstrated the validity and the profit growth potential of the new concept.

After two years under Isabelle's leadership, ATG was in great shape. It was innovative, and it had mastered the use of technology to optimize its front- and back-office processes, and to enable its experiential travel strategy.

The numbers were good too. ATG was now a smaller company, but one that was growing, although not by much. The profit-growth of younger agencies had started to kick in, and ROE was back to pre-crisis levels, even though the European travel industry was still fighting against a weak economy and stagnant demand.

Isabelle received a lot of praise and recognition, both from the board and from analysts covering ATG's stock, who, after initial skepticism, were now more positive about the work being accomplished by Isabelle and her team.

Success brought more confidence in the GET, across the organization, but also among the board members, who nudged the GET to look beyond the stagnating European travel market. Increasing affluence in Asia, Latin America, and Africa was transforming those regions into big growth markets for tour operators in general and for ATG, in particular. The board believed in the scalability of the experience model. The digital platform was easily scalable, as were its capabilities, if ATG could acquire young organizations or quickly scale local frontline organizations outside of Europe.

Even though she had a lot on her plate, Isabelle was also keen to expand internationally. The year before, she and Marco had spent two weeks in Asia with their girls. As they explored the region, she grasped the huge potential of bringing the concept of experiential travel to Asia. The market for experience-travel was clearly underdeveloped, and she believed that customers' needs were not being met.

As the GET planned for expansion, two perspectives or options emerged.

One option involved Matthew Clark, an energetic, dedicated Bostonian who had been with ATG for many years. He was the head of its tiny business in the United States, which he had built from nothing into a player in the small but profitable adventure travel niche. He felt that the best use of the funds available for growth would be to expand the US business. While America wasn't an emerging growth market, ATG already had a strong position in its adventure niche from which it could expand rapidly, if given the resources. The US is a large market, and ATG's position was insignificant, so it clearly had room for growth. In addition, the market was more familiar, culturally, and language-wise, than other foreign markets. Further, it was subject to the same trends that affected the European travel market.

Reporting to Frank de Vries, head of foreign sales, Matthew already operated four ATG agencies in large US cities, Boston, New York, Chicago, and Los Angeles, providing the company with many years of experience as a foundation for expansion. And, his US agencies were already capable of selling experience-oriented offerings, at least in their niche.

The second option centered around Thomas Huan, a Swiss-Chinese dual citizen, the son of a Chinese physicist (his mother taught at ETH) and a Swiss private banker. He grew up in Zurich and – after his parents' divorce – in Hong Kong. He built his career with Lee Travels, one of Asia's leading tour operators at the time. He stood out at Lee for his excellent skills in strategy, scaling up new businesses, and executing business plans. For these reasons, Frank had been trying to poach him for ATG for some time, and he eventually succeeded. ATG had no presence whatsoever in Asia, but Frank, Isabelle, and Thomas, as an "insider and connoisseur" of the Asian region, saw a lot of potential in this market for ATG's experience-based business model. The market was humungous and attractively underdeveloped.

Discussions at GET meetings – and later at the board of directors' meeting – revolved around North America, with the focus being the United States, and Asia, with the focus being China. The board of directors strongly felt that ATG should expand into only one region, either North America or Asia.

Although ATG's valuation had improved, the board did not approve a capital increase, so funds for investment were limited. However, the main reasons for the decision to limit expansion to only one region were the complexity of expanding and the associated commitment of resources. One of the biggest resources was the time commitment required from the GET, particularly Frank, who was still preoccupied with executing the new strategy in Europe, even as he supervised both Thomas and Matthew.

Focusing on just one region for expansion led to another problem for Frank, Isabelle, and the GET: the choice between Matthew and Thomas. As GET discussions dragged on for several months, the arguments between Matthew and Thomas became increasingly heated and eventually personal.

As in the past, Isabelle asked Kosta and Hugo to work together to produce an analysis of the relevant financial data for both options (Appendix 9).

But Isabelle wasn't concerned only about the strategic and financial aspects of this choice. She was also concerned about the personal touch underlying this decision: picking between Thomas and Matthew. Both were great personalities, successful, principled, committed. Isabelle feared losing one of them or – if the conflict between them continued to escalate – even both.

She didn't want to lose any management talent in these challenging times, but she didn't like any of the options the GET was presenting to her. She was facing yet another dilemma.

Questions for Reflection

What would you decide as Isabelle or as a member of the GET? What should ATG do?:

- Expand in North America or in Asia?
- Appoint Thomas or Matthew to lead the new business?
- Do something else?

You may want to write down your answer before continuing.

Chapter 7

Developing Better Options

Claudio Feser, Daniella Laureiro-Martinez, and Stefano Brusoni

I know nothing except the fact of my ignorance.
                    —Socrates, cited in *Lives of the Philosophers*
                                        by Diogenes Laertius

O ver time, Isabelle's video calls with Eve had become a bit less frequent. But she enjoyed her conversations with Eve and was looking forward to seeing her. They had only met once in person, but strangely, she felt connected to her. Eve seemed to care for her and be willing to share her knowledge to help, and she always acted selflessly, never asking anything in return. Isabelle felt a sense of trust, a feeling that so far, she had only experienced with Oscar, her childhood friend, and with Marco and the girls. Consciously or not, she had come to see Eve as her "nerdy, little sister," the little sister she never had.

This time, Isabelle was eager to share with her little sister some insights she had gained when applying the four-steps model. Isabelle opened the conversation: "I think your four-steps model is awesome and super helpful. But it is not complete."

"Incomplete? What do you mean?" asked Eve, slightly worried that she might have missed something in her research.

"Yes," answered Isabelle. "Let me tell you what happened in the GET when we applied it. First, we applied it for our discussion on strategy. It really helped to get everyone aligned on a strategy, both the GET and the board. The process of identifying and testing assumptions worked well, and, as you had told me, it de-personified the discussion of options and made the team work together very effectively."

"That's great. I am glad it was helpful," said Eve.

> The process of identifying and testing assumptions de-personifies the discussion of options and makes teams work together effectively.

"Yes, but when we applied it a second time," Isabelle continued, "on the discussion on where to expand internationally, we got stuck, and we had to improve the model."

"How?" asked Eve, curious to understand what she might have missed.

Isabelle continued: "In discussing the dilemma and developing more options with the GET, we developed three options. The first two were obvious:

Option 1: Expand the US business with Matthew.

Option 2: Build the Asia business with Thomas.

In both options, we would, however, have lost one talented individual. It would not have met our objectives and therefore we developed one more option:

Option 3: Build the business in Asia – which looked more attractive than the US market – with Matthew and Thomas as co-leads."

This time it was Isabelle sharing a slide: "Our three options and their evaluation along the seven heuristics are graphically depicted in the figure I am sharing (Figure 7.1)."

"Well done. This looks great. I feel proud to see that you are using the outcome of my research," noted Eve.

"Thank you," said Isabelle, and continued: "Based on our analysis, Option 3 appeared to be the best of the three options. There were clear risks involved. Importantly, the risk of an expansion in the less familiar market and with a value proposition, which was largely untested in Asia. But the option looked superior to the other two options."

"OK, but what happened next?" asked Eve, who was wondering where the problem was.

Isabelle continued: "After a debate in the GET, we jointly decided to expand into Asia, and therefore also to appoint Thomas and Matthew as Asia co-heads. Thus, it fulfilled the board's requirement and goal of expanding only in one region, and it allowed us to retain both Matthew and Thomas. The decision also made strategic sense. The market was huge, and the intensity of competition in ATG's niche was small. And Thomas and Matthew could find enough qualified personnel in Asia to build ATG's new business. The figures that Hugo, the CFO, had prepared clearly reflected the attractiveness of the Asia option. The necessary investments were high, but the capital and time were available: I and the GET believed that this choice would put us ahead of the competition. In addition, the strategy suited ATG's culture. The company already had the skills to be successful in its niche in Asia, and after the successful turnaround at the beginning of my tenure, and the recent successes of the experience- and consulting-based approach to travel services, our people had renewed confidence in the organization. The decision in the GET was unanimous. Following the meeting of the GET, I asked to meet with Carlo, the board chair, the following day. I wanted to propose the chosen option – Asia and Thomas/Matthew – to him, and after winning his approval, to the entire board of directors."

1. Dilemma	Expanding in the US or building in Asia? With Matthew or Thomas?							

2. Options on the Exploit-Explore continuum Exploit → Explore

The seven heuristics	Expanding in the US with Matthew		Building Asia with Thomas		Building Asia with both Matthew and Thomas as co-leads		Option	
	3. Assumptions	4. Facts	3. Assumptions	4. Facts	3. Assumptions	4. Facts	3. Assumptions	4. Facts
a) Objectives	Expand in one market Retain M and T	T / F	Expand in one market Retain M and T	T / F	Expand in one market Retain M and T	T / T / T		
b) Opportunities	US is an attractive growth opportunity	T	Asia is an even more attractive growth opportunity than US	T	Asia is an even more attractive growth opportunity than US	T / T		
c) Time	Limited funds and mgmt. capacity available	T	Limited funds and mgmt. capacity available	T	Limited funds and mgmt. capacity available	T		
d) Competitive actions and stakeholder expectations	Competitors are expanding internationally	?	Competitors are expanding internationally	?	Competitors are expanding internationally	?		
e) Our values and culture	Less risk-oriented (market is familiar, value proposition tested)	R	More risk-oriented (market is unfamiliar, value prop. untested)	R	More risk-oriented (market is unfamiliar, value prop. untested)	R		
f) Our capabilities	Matthew is known, and capable	T	Thomas is capable, but integration is unclear	T	Both Matthew and Thomas are capable	T		
g) Our "mood" or prevalent collective cognitive states	We are pessimistic as to whether we can keep both	T	We are pessimistic as to whether we can keep both	T	We are optimistic as to whether we can keep both	F		

5. Resolution	

Figure 7.1 Five-step Decision Navigator with solution for Case 3.

"OK, sounds like the correct decision. But where was the problem?" asked Eve impatiently.

Isabelle continued: "That night I couldn't sleep."

"You couldn't sleep?"

"No, I couldn't," answered Isabelle. "Marco woke up at about 2 a.m. and noticed that I was tossing around and that I was obviously worried. He asked me, 'What's on your mind. . .the Asia decision?' I confirmed it was, apologizing for having woken him up. I said: 'Going with Asia with Thomas and Matthew as co-heads is a logical decision, but is it the right one? I'm excited about expanding into Asia, but Thomas is new to ATG. Is it wise to entrust him with our entire growth strategy? Matthew would also be there, but I don't know of many successful examples of co-head models. What if they fight and Matthew leaves? We are back to Option 2.' Also, I was worried about whether ATG's competency in personalization would be a success factor in Asia. The culture there may have been very different from in the West. I was uncomfortable with the assumption that ATG's competency was scalable in Asia."

"Hmmm. . . interesting. So how did you proceed?"

Isabelle continued: "When I got out of bed in the morning, I still had a queasy feeling. I decided to convene the GET again. I told my GET colleagues that I was having second thoughts, and I wanted to bring this back to the GET for a second look. At core, I was concerned that we hadn't fully checked our assumption that our business model was really going to work in Asia. Also, Thomas had a great reputation, but could he be as successful at ATG as he had been in the past? And would he work well with Matthew? Would Matthew make it work? I wasn't sure anymore if Option 3 was our best option."

"OK. What happened then?"

Isabelle continued: "A discussion ensued, and it ended with Hugo asking, 'Is the board of directors' requirement to expand only into one region a given, rigid fact — or can we challenge the board and ask it to reconsider?' Hugo went on: 'I can speak only for my function. I trust my team to be able to serve two new regions with financial services. And if the board is willing to let us expand into two regions, then maybe we could come up with another, better option, such as expanding into North America with 80–90% of the resources – and with Matthew, a tested, known ATG leader – and make a small push into Asia with the rest. It would give us time to test two assumptions. First, whether our business model can be successful in Asia. Secondly, whether Thomas can be integrated into ATG and succeed.'"

"Interesting. You kind of changed a boundary condition, so to speak."

"Yes, exactly," said Isabelle. "The GET – after a short discussion – supported the proposed new option and gave me the task of talking to Carlo and the board. Until now, I had always followed the chairman's instructions, so going to see him and challenging his guidance didn't come naturally to me. I anticipated a tough discussion. To my surprise, it wasn't all that hard: Carlo understood the dilemma and agreed with the board to drop the requirement to expand only in one region, but he didn't concur before he made sure – and had sufficient facts – that every single GET member – especially the support functions of Hugo, Alessandro, and Alison – could actually and effectively support two more regions."

"Thus, a new, better option emerged," noted Eve.

"Yes, exactly," said Isabelle. "In addition, the chairman had confirmation that I had succeeded in pulling the executive team together."

"Congratulations, Isabelle," said Eve, who started to piece together the discussion. "So, what you are saying to me is that when none of the available options is satisfactory, you can create new ones. To do so, you need to identify which of the seven heuristics of optimization of the exploit-explore balance are significantly limiting the option space and investigate whether you can change them. This is like in an optimization algorithm. It optimizes within the defined boundary conditions. If you lift

> When none of the available options is satisfactory, you should try to create new ones.

selected boundary conditions, the algorithm has more space to optimize, right?"

"Yes, exactly. That's exactly what we did!" answered Isabelle. "We chose the best available option, scrolled through the tested assumptions, and asked ourselves, what options would emerge if we decided to lift this assumption. We thought that two interconnected heuristics were particularly limiting:

1. The board's guidance to expand only into either North America or Asia.
2. Limited management resources.

"Then we asked ourselves, what if ATG lifted them? Say, the board agreed to expand into both markets, and management could make provisions – such as hiring additional capacity or using external resources – to be able to support not one but two international expansions? With those boundaries lifted, at least one new reasonable option emerged."

"One new option?" asked Eve.

Isabelle continued: "Yes, namely Option 4: with the larger part of the available funding, expand the North American business under Matthew's leadership. Then fund a limited build-up in Asia under Thomas's leadership as an experiment to validate ATG's value proposition in Asia and to weigh Thomas' ability to integrate into ATG. We then evaluated this new option and chose it (Figure 7.2). That's how we solved it!" concluded Isabelle.

"Wow, that's great! Thank you for sharing," said Eve, who was visibly excited about how Isabelle had taken and improved her four-step model. "Since we switched roles today, and you have

| 1. Dilemma | Expanding in the US or building in Asia? With Matthew or Thomas? | | | | | | | |

2. Options on the Exploit-Explore continuum (Exploit → Explore)

The seven heuristics	Expanding in the US with Matthew		Building Asia with Thomas		Building Asia with both Matthew and Thomas as co-leads		US with 80% of resources and Asia with 20% of resources	
	3. Assumptions	4. Facts	3. Assumptions	4. Facts	3. Assumptions	4. Facts	3. Assumptions	4. Facts
a) Objectives	Expand in one market Retain M and T	T / F	Expand in one market Retain M and T	T / F	Expand in one market Retain M and T	T / T	Expansion in 2 markets Retain M and T	T / T
b) Opportunities	US is an attractive growth opportunity	T	Asia is an even more attractive growth opportunity than US	T	Asia is an even more attractive growth opportunity than US	T	Both Asia and US are attractive	T
c) Time	Limited funds and mgmt. capacity available	T	Limited funds and mgmt. capacity available	T	Limited funds and mgmt. capacity available	T	Limited funds, but management capacity available	T
d) Competitive actions and stakeholder expectations	Competitors are expanding internationally	?	Competitors are expanding internationally	?	Competitors are expanding internationally	?	Competitors are expanding internationally	?
e) Our values and culture	Less risk-oriented (market is familiar, value proposition tested)	R	More risk-oriented (market is unfamiliar, value prop. untested)	R	More risk-oriented (market is unfamiliar, value prop. untested)	R	Allows testing of both the business model and Thomas integration	R
f) Our capabilities	Matthew is known, and capable	T	Thomas is capable, but integration is unclear	T	Both Matthew and Thomas are capable	T	Both Matthew and Thomas are capable	T
g) Our "mood" or prevalent collective cognitive states	We are pessimistic as to whether we can keep both	T	We are pessimistic as to whether we can keep both	T	We are optimistic as to whether we can keep both	F	We are optimistic that we can make the option work	T

5. Optimization	Option 3 is unstable. Change boundary condition only 1 market and check management capacity available
6. Resolution	Option 4

Figure 7.2 Six-step Decision Navigator with solution for Case 3.

been explaining to me how to improve the model, let me try to summarize the discussion. In essence, you have expanded the decision-making model for dynamic and uncertain situations. The model now has six steps:

Step 1: *Dilemma* – Identify the exploit-explore dilemma.
Step 2: *Options* – Widen the option space along the exploit-explore continuum. Develop several options, ideally at least three or four.
Step 3: *Conditions* – Identify assumptions for each of the options along the seven exploit-explore heuristics, asking yourself, 'What assumptions need to hold for this option to be valid?' Uncover hidden assumptions by writing them down, applying critical reasoning, and persistently looking for the rationale, that is, asking why, why, why.
Step 4: *Tests* – Test the relevant assumptions. Testing takes time and energy, but you don't need to test reasonable and non-material assumptions. Conduct testing efficiently, focusing on the most material assumptions and the least expensive tests.
Step 5: *Optimization* – Change boundary conditions to expand the option space. When you cannot find any satisfactory options, seek to change limiting assumptions along the seven heuristics to develop more satisfactory alternatives.
Step 6: *Resolution* – Decide."

"That's a great summary, Eve. Well done!" said Isabelle, proud to have contributed to Eve's thesis. "One more thing. You need a name or an acronym for your model, so that your readers can memorize it easily. As I was listening to you, I noted down one letter for each of the six steps: D for Dilemma, O for Options, C for Conditions, T for Tests, O for Optimization of Options, and R for Resolution. You could call your model the DOCTOR model of decision-making in dynamic and uncertain situations!"

"I like the acronym. It captures the scientific nature of the approach," noted Eve.

"Scientific?" asked Isabelle.

"Yes, the approach of developing options, identifying hypotheses or assumptions if you prefer, and testing them is in fact a scientific approach. Research has shown that such an approach leads to significantly better decisions," said Eve.

"Significantly better decisions?" asked Isabelle.

"Yes. Let me explain," responded Eve. She continued: "Recently a group of researchers led by Arnaldo Camuffo and Alfonso Gambardella at Bocconi University in Milan ran an experiment with over a hundred Italian founders of start-ups in various fields (Camuffo et al., 2020). The start-ups were in an early stage of development, that is, they either had only a business idea, or they had already started working on a product or service. None of them had revenues at the start of the experiment. The founders participated in a program in entrepreneurship, in which they were taught four subjects. First, how to develop a business model canvas for their business ideas, that is, they had to design a model of a firm that would deliver their business ideas. Second, how to interview potential customers to understand the market and the customers' needs, and to collect feedback about their business idea. Third, to develop a minimum viable product, an MVP. An MVP is a basic version of their offering with just enough features for customers to experience it. And, finally, fourth, to develop a prototype to deliver the idea. The participants of the program were – without being told – randomly assigned to two groups, a 'scientific thinking group' and a control group. The training of all participating founders was identical, except that the members of the scientific thinking group were trained to think about their business model as theories, and about interviews, the MVPs, and the prototypes as experiments to rigorously measure and test their theories, and as means to update and further refine their theories.

"Then in the year following the program, they measured the results for the two groups.

"First, they measured the progress along three points. One, they counted exits. Exits are a normal course of action for many start-ups as their business ideas get validated in practice and as time passes. Two, they counted the number of start-ups that had launched their products or services and that were generating revenues. Three, they counted all others, that is, start-ups that were still working on their plans.

"Second, they counted pivots. Pivots were defined as major changes of the business idea. A change could be a change of the core value proposition of the product or service, or a change of target customer segments.

"Third, they measured the flow of revenues of the firms that were started.

"Figure 7.3 shows the results they measured."

"The rate of exits, launches (revenues), and 'still working on it' were similar across the two groups. The scientific thinking group had fewer 'still working on it' start-ups, but the differences were not large.

"However, the rate of pivots in the scientific thinking group was significantly higher than in the control group (49% to 21%). As with superforecasters, who tend to update their predictions more frequently than others, it seems that founders thinking about their business ideas and business models as hypotheses and testing them

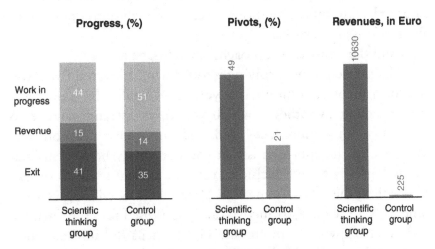

Figure 7.3   The impact of scientific thinking on entrepreneurial decision-making.

rigorously, made more revisions and updates. And as with super-forecasters, it led to better results: the average revenues for the year of the start-ups that had launched their products or services in the scientific thinking group amounted to more than EUR 10,600, while the average revenues for the year in the revenues control group amounted to less than EUR 250.

"If we assume that higher revenues can be taken as a proxy of improved decision quality, one could say that scientific thinking increased the average quality of decisions in this experiment manyfold, by nearly 4000%."

"Wow! That's impressive!" noted Isabelle.

Eve continued: "What's unique about the model is that it combines and leverages the best of two alternative scientific research and problem-solving approaches, the inductive and the deductive one."

"What do you mean?" asked Isabelle.

"Well, you can solve a problem bottom-up," responded Eve and continued: "This is called inductive problem solving. In essence, you start from facts or observations, you see a pattern, and you develop a theory, a solution. It is easy and fast, and that's how we solve problems daily. In science, it is used in exploratory research, as it is creative and as it leads to new discoveries. The caveat is that it tends to lead to biased solutions, since the conclusions drawn from observations are personal."

"And the deductive approach?" asked Isabelle.

"Deductive problem solving is top-down," answered Eve, "You develop a theory, a solution, that you believe will solve a problem. It is based on hypotheses, which you then test and validate to come up with a valid, fact-based, and unbiased conclusion. The advantage of the approach is that you come to valid conclusions, that is, logically sound decisions. You can explain them to others, who will come to the same logical conclusions when given the same facts. In science, deductive thinking is used for confirmatory studies. That's what Camuffo and Gambardella did in their study at Bocconi. The drawbacks are that it seldom leads to new insights, and that it takes time. I have summarized the main advantages and

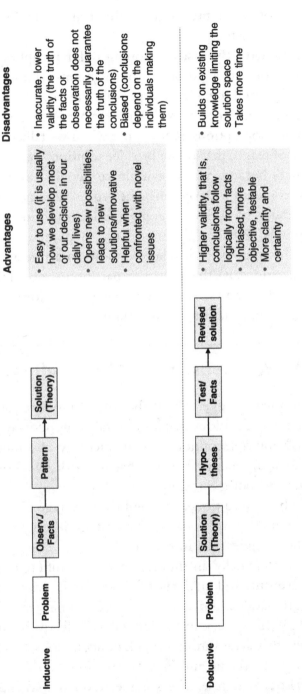

Figure 7.4 The decision-making model combines the best of inductive and deductive reasoning.

disadvantages of the approaches on this page," said Eve sharing Figure 7.4 on the screen.

Eve continued: "By first developing different options, that is, different solutions to a problem, the decision-making model is using inductive thinking. That is especially the case when working in teams, as you can access very different experiences and thinking patterns to develop options. Remember when we talked about the secret sauce of teams, that is, the broader solution space that teams explore. That's because we have multiple people using inductive thinking to come up with options. The process leverages biases and thinking patterns of different people and leads to more and often creative options. But then the model uses hypotheses and testing to validate the options. It de-biases options to arrive at valid and fact-based decisions. It's the deductive part of the model that helps to overcome the brain's natural tendency to exploit and to use cognitive biases in situations of uncertainty."

Should You Trust Your Gut Feelings?

Sometimes we are asked about the role of intuition, after all, there are many decisions that are not taken by actively deliberating on multiple options and deductively choosing one. Instead, there are many decisions that are made by taking into consideration "our gut feelings."

But what is intuition, and should we leverage it?

Intuition is not as straightforward as it might sound. Researchers argue that instead of being an homogeneous concept, it is actually an umbrella term for different cognitive mechanisms and an array of models exist when talking about automatic-intuitive processes (Glöckner and Witteman, 2010). Intuition can be defined as "affectively charged judgments that arise through rapid, nonconscious, and holistic associations" (Dane and Pratt, 2007). One of the defining characteristics that researchers agree upon is that intuition does not involve active deliberation, but is rather an automatic process, one that often occurs outside our conscious awareness (Kopalle et al., 2023). Intuitive processes operate outside our conscious control, they arise fast, they recognize features or patterns, and they are emotionally driven. Research has shown that when decision-makers are in a positive mood, they tend to use more intuition than deliberative approaches (Weiss and Cropanzano, 1996).

Many executives use an intuitive approach to decision-making, particularly in unstable environments (Kopalle et al., 2023). It is important to recognize that intuition is helpful because it allows us to quickly grasp patterns in complex, ambiguous situations, to reduce the cognitive burden of extensive analysis, and to accelerate the process of decision-making. In other words, intuition is efficient.

But how effective is it? How good are decisions based on intuition? The study of the effectiveness of intuition is an evolving debate, and more empirical research is needed to understand when intuition works, and when it doesn't.

That said, researchers agree that intuition ideally works in concert with formal, fact-based analysis (Calabretta et al., 2017; Kolbe et al., 2020; Kopalle, et al., 2023). In other words, when decisions really matter, intuition should be augmented with a deliberate, deductive approach of testing assumptions.

"I got it," said Isabelle, "In fact, the model combines the best of these two worlds. It combines the advantages of two usually alternative and competing problem-solving approaches: it creates innovative and at the same time unbiased decisions."

"That's exactly right!" noted Eve.

"Yes, but isn't the approach a bit 'scientific'? I am a businesswoman, not a scientist. None of ATG's associates is a scientist," said Isabelle wondering whether the approach could be used effectively by her team and ATG in practice.

"Thinking scientifically is not a profession. Sure, researchers are paid to think and work like scientists. But thinking scientifically is a mindset and a skill, not a profession. It is about questioning what we know, it is about being open-minded, and it is about updating our views when new facts emerge. The decision-making-model is a method of decision-making, and methods can be learned and practiced, and can turn into skills," responded Eve, addressing Isabelle's concerns.

"You are probably right. I want to try to make this the way we take important decisions at ATG, not only in the GET but throughout the organization," responded Isabelle.

"I want to thank you for this discussion and how you helped me to further the model," said Eve, and continued: "I like the DOCTOR acronym, but I prefer calling the model differently. I was thinking about calling it The Decision Navigator."

"The Decision Navigator?"

"Yes. As you may have noted in the past months, each decision you make depends on decisions you have made in the past, and again shapes the decision you will make in the future. In dynamic and uncertain situations, decisions unfold as journeys, not as single, discrete, and independent events. Decision journeys are how we navigate dynamic situations."

"I understand. I like the name The Decision Navigator," said Isabelle.

The Importance of Confident Humility

Using the proposed decision-making model effectively requires having a scientific mindset.

Psychologist Adam Grant coined the term "Confident Humility" to describe it. The term describes a mindset of feeling confident about yourself, about your abilities, but not about your tools, your theories, or your beliefs (Grant, 2021). It describes a mindset in which you doubt your own knowledge and theories, you stay curious, and you enjoy discovering something new.

The prolific inventor Thomas Edison ran thousands of failed experiments before being able to produce the light bulb. When interviewed about the failed experiments, Edison was quoted as saying, "I have not failed. I've just found 10,000 ways that won't work." Thomas Edison had confident humility. He had confidence in his own abilities, but he didn't trust his science. He repeatedly tested his assumptions with experiments.

Confident humility may protect you from the Dunning-Kruger effect (Kruger and Dunning, 1999).

First described in 1999 by the psychologists David Dunning and Justin Kruger, the Dunning-Kruger effect describes a bias of individuals with low competence or knowledge to overestimate their own competence and knowledge (the peak of Mount Stupid in Figure 7.5).

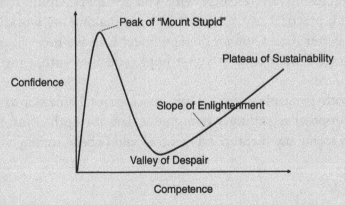

Figure 7.5   The Dunning-Kruger effect.

Among many others, senior executives might be at risk of falling for the Dunning-Kruger effect. Senior executives who focus on general management tasks might at times not be deep experts in areas of competence relevant for the company they lead, for example, in the technologies used, in the minutiae of the production processes, or in knowledge areas relevant to the front line. If their companies are nevertheless successful, the Dunning-Kruger effect may lead them to overestimate their own competence. Another insight of the work of the two psychologists is that those suffering from the Dunning-Kruger effect, don't realize it. This contributes to explaining why sometimes individuals not only lack the competence, but also the ability to recognize that they are doing so, and hence resist opposing views and challenge.

We all have fallen for the Dunning-Kruger effect at times in the past. Remember the last time you were on Mount Stupid, take a mental picture of yourself standing on the peak, and look at it regularly. It will remind you to stay humble.

"Discussing my research with you is super-helpful. It makes my work practical and accessible. You are making my work better. Much better than a sorcerer's apprentice! Can we meet in person next time? I want to give you a hug!" said Eve with a big smile on her face.

"With great pleasure! I'll ask my assistant Franziska to make some proposal regarding a convenient date for both of us. I look forward seeing my mentor and mentee," said Isabelle, smiling as well.

Key Takeaways

- Sometimes — even after widening the options space — none of the available options is satisfactory.
- Once all your assumptions are explicit, you not only can test them, but you can also question and sometimes change them to arrive at better options and hence better decisions.
- Always ask yourself, "what options would emerge if this specific assumption were no longer to hold?"

Our Decision-Making Canvas — the Decision Navigator (Figure 7.6; https://timgroup.ethz.ch/Decision_Navigator .html) — has now developed further to include six steps:

1. Identify the exploit-explore dilemma.
2. Develop multiple options on the exploit-explore continuum.
3. Identify underlying, relevant assumptions for each of the options using the seven decision-making heuristics.
4. Use facts to test the relevant assumptions.
5. If no satisfactory options exist, change the boundary conditions (assumptions) to develop new ones.
6. Decide.

The Decision Navigator leverages the advantage of combining inductive and deductive problem-solving approaches. It is explorative and leads to innovative solutions, and it validates options and leads to unbiased, fact-based decisions.

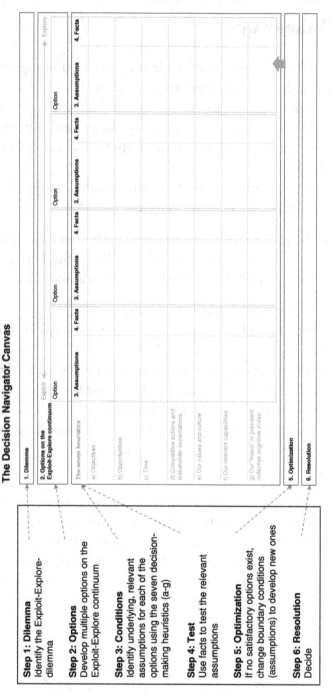

The Decision Navigator Canvas

1. Dilemma

2. Options on the Exploit-Explore continuum

Exploit ←————————→ Explore

	Option		Option		Option	
	3. Assumptions	4. Facts	3. Assumptions	4. Facts	3. Assumptions	4. Facts
The seven heuristics						
a) Objectives						
b) Opportunities						
c) Time						
d) Competitive actions and stakeholder expectations						
e) Our values and culture						
f) Our relevant capabilities						
g) Our "mood" or prevalent collective cognitive states						

5. Optimization

6. Resolution

Step 1: Dilemma
Identify the Exploit-Explore-dilemma

Step 2: Options
Develop multiple options on the Exploit-Explore continuum

Step 3: Conditions
Identify underlying, relevant assumptions for each of the options using the seven decision-making heuristics (a-g)

Step 4: Test
Use facts to test the relevant assumptions

Step 5: Optimization
If no satisfactory options exist, change boundary conditions (assumptions) to develop new ones

Step 6: Resolution
Decide

Figure 7.6 Summary of the 6-step Decision Navigator.

Part Three

MANAGING
THE TENSIONS CREATED
BY DECISIONS UNDER
UNCERTAINTY

Chapter 8

Case 4: Implementing Decisions

Claudio Feser, David Redaschi, and Karolin Frankenberger

oughly six months later, it started to become increasingly clear that the transformation of ATG's sales approach had stalled. The problem wasn't in the US or Asia, where momentum and initial customer feedback were strong, but in its core business in Europe.

With ATG's new experiential travel strategy, Isabelle and the GET not only wanted to lead the industry in taking advantage of the trends of experience-oriented and personalized travel, but they also aimed to make ATG one of the most innovative, high-growth, and profitable companies in the European travel industry. With the digitization of front-office processes, the GET also targeted massively increasing customer satisfaction (measured in net promoter scores (NPS)) and customer loyalty (measured in reduction of churn).

The implementation of the new strategy required agencies' staff members to build new capabilities to deliver experience-based services and packages. These new capabilities included being able to integrate more complex offerings (combining excursions, guides, special events, etc.) into complete, comprehensive experiential travel offerings. It required agency employees to become better listeners, so they could gain an improved understanding of customers' needs. It also required them to become more creative in packaging different offerings, and more entrepreneurial to spot further opportunities to develop experienced-based packages. But the attempt to build these new capabilities simply did not get off the ground.

Worse, a recent employee survey suggested only limited workforce buy-in for the new strategy (see Appendix 10).

While the development and implementation of the front-line digital platform progressed well under Alessandro's leadership, it appeared that frontline staff members only marginally supported the transformation. In addition, the GET saw little "entrepreneurial energy" emanating from ATG's staff. Agency travel advisors seemed to be concerned only with meeting their targets by selling traditional products, and they had little desire or energy for "the new thing." The change that Isabelle and the GET were striving for was simply not happening, despite the hands-on efforts of Conny in domestic sales and Frank in foreign sales. Alison had stepped up HR's training efforts to be sure ATG salespeople were up to date and understood their new pitch and new products, but little had helped.

Faced with being stuck, the GET decided to put a lot more energy into change management. It established and staffed a Project Management Office (PMO), and it prioritized its change initiatives. Each initiative had a charter that summarized its goals, actions with deliverables, responsibilities, and milestones. Despite all these measures, the transformation faltered.

Isabelle invited Kosta, whom she had promoted to Head of Strategy & Innovation, to come to a GET meeting to help address this problem. He asked if the new experience-based business model had been properly integrated into existing organizational and management structures, or whether implementing the new strategy required reestablishing a separate, parallel business unit specializing in experiential travel with its own agencies and resources.

Conny, who carefully approached change quite slowly, feared imposing too much disruption on her department. She also advocated building a separate experiential-travel organization, adding, "I don't know of any organization that successfully leverages existing business while tapping into new potential. It just doesn't work."

Hugo strongly disagreed with Kosta and Conny. "As CFO, I have to forcefully point out that building a separate business unit for experience-based travel offerings is expensive," he stated. "We should not repeat the mistake we made with the B2B attempt. A separation does not allow us to exploit synergies – it just introduces complexity and costs. In addition, we would need to reduce our objectives for the penetration of the new products and services – as we would only leverage the dedicated business unit to sell the new product and services, and not the entire agency network. We might need to revise the budget."

Isabelle reacted promptly, "I certainly don't want that. I don't want to go back to the board and ask for a budget adjustment."

Yet, Conny would not give up her idea of separating the old ATG from the "new ATG," that is, the offering of experiential travel with its different value proposition and more advisory-heavy staff role. She saw separation as crucial to protecting her traditional sales and marketing efforts, making Isabelle wonder if the "new ATG" needed, at least, separate promotional work. "If we can't make it a separate business, could we at least select agencies to specialize in the new offering?" she proposed. "We would need to convince fewer people and train fewer people, and we would be faster to market. In addition, we could create some competition between the 'new-ATG' agencies and the traditional ones."

Alison pushed back from an HR perspective. "I disagree! We would create an A-team and a B-team. It would probably divide our employees and fuel envy and jealousy because working on a new, cool, prestigious business model is seen as a reward, as being the favored part of ATG," she cautioned. "I assume that separating these functions would massively demotivate the largest part of our workforce, as at first, we'd focus only a handful of agencies as specialists on the new value proposition."

"And it wouldn't solve the budget issue," added Hugo.

Isabelle noticed with approval that Alison had stepped forward and was stating her assumptions explicitly. She took pleasure in that. But only briefly. Her thoughts went back to the issue at hand: the stalled transformation.

While Isabelle also wasn't sure whether or not to separate experiential travel from traditional mass vacation travel in ATG's internal operations, her biggest concern was the organization's lack of energy and commitment. She felt that with a separate business unit or with specialized agencies, the "new ATG" could get traction quickly, but she was concerned about losing the majority of ATG's employees on the way. In fact, she felt she had already lost them. It was clear that most of ATG's people in the core European market hadn't bought into the transformation.

"I understand your arguments, Alison, but, as a head of HR, what would you suggest?" she asked.

Alison paused and then said: "My hypothesis is that we need to increase the portion of each agency's incentives devoted to new products and services, talk more about the successes of the branches that are already marketing the 'new ATG' effectively, and invest more in training. We know how to do that. And maybe we should take another go at engaging our employees more. We haven't held a town hall for over a year now, and we could convene our workforce around the 'new' ATG."

That sounded reasonable, but also not fully convincing.

Personally, Isabelle was excited about the new value proposition. She believed that it could be instrumental in achieving her ambitious goals of building a European travel company that led the way in growth, customer satisfaction, and profitability. She was also excited about the customer-orientation and creative skills the new value proposition required from ATG staff. It required them to spend more time listening and understanding client needs. They would have to learn to "put themselves in the shoes of the customers," and to combine more offerings creatively to create more complex, integrated travel experiences. Such packaging also required agents to become more open-minded and entrepreneurial about new offerings and possible combinations.

These are great skills and mindsets, Isabelle thought. But I don't understand — and neither does the rest of the GET, whether they are for a separate experiential travel set-up or not — why our staff doesn't share our enthusiasm. After all, working for a very successful company that is growing, has happy customers, and is profitable is very satisfying.

Isabelle didn't know what else to do.

She met with a specialized consulting firm which recommended that she should "create a crisis," that is, make it clear to the organization that the company was in crisis and risked losing touch with its market. The consultants advised using "symbolic" actions (such as firing some agency leaders who opposed the new strategy and didn't cooperate with it), to make members of the organization understand the urgency of the change. Isabelle disliked such actions. They were not compatible with her values.

Frank, the head of foreign sales, was very happy that Matthew and Thomas were doing well in their separate jurisdictions, and he believed no further measures were necessary on the new experiential travel project. "Change is always slow," he said, "We should simply give ATG's staff more time. I assume that the situation will look different in twelve months. Most of our staff will have learned to deal with the new products and will start selling them. Maybe we should go back to the board and ask for a budget adjustment."

But Isabelle had the impression that resistance to the planned changes was growing slowly but surely within the organization.

The GET's discussion yielded four potential options going forward:

1. Slow the pace of transformation to address increasing change resistance.
2. Set up a dedicated unit – a "speedboat" Kosta called it, to market the new experience-based product- and service-line separately from the main organization.
3. Select 30% of ATG's agencies to market the new experience-based product- and service-line.
4. Make stronger use of incentives, "advertise and celebrate successes," invest more in training, and re-engage the organization.

Questions for Reflection

Which option do you think should be adopted as ATG's approach to implement its new strategy in Europe?

- Option 1?
- Option 2?
- Option 3?
- Option 4?
- Other options?

You may want to write down your answer before continuing.

Chapter 9

Managing Change

Ana Procopio Schön, Claudio Feser, Daniella Laureiro-Martinez, and Stefano Brusoni

Πάντα ῥεῖ. There is nothing permanent except change.

—Heraclitus

Isabelle and Eve connected more and more sporadically. Isabelle didn't have much time. Even though Isabelle loved and missed the conversations with her "little sister" Eve, the CEO job was absorbing every minute of her time. She worked 60–70 hours per week, Mondays to Fridays and sometimes weekends.

Eve missed the conversations too. She admired Isabelle for her decisiveness, strong character, and action-orientation. She looked up to her and wished she had more of all those traits herself. But she was also busy and in the final stages of submitting her postdoctoral thesis and preparing the defense of it.

When they finally connected again, they did so as usual per video conference. They had planned to meet in person, but Franziska, Isabelle's assistant, called on short notice asking to do a video call instead. "Mrs. Dubois is very sorry, but she will be out of the country and asked me to schedule a video call instead," she said.

When they connected, Isabelle apologized for any inconvenience the change in plans might have caused to Eve.

"No worries. I understand," said Eve.

Then, they talked briefly about their private situations. Eve had got engaged and had fixed a date for her wedding. Raul, her fiancé, was an academic she had met at a conference on cognitive biases in Madrid a year earlier. "Congratulations! This is great news," said Isabelle enthusiastically, "I hope we, my husband and I, get invited to your wedding!"

"All your family is, Isabelle. The girls are invited as well," said Eve with a big smile.

Then, the discussion moved on to ATG. Isabelle shared the situation at ATG and her frustration about the fact that the transformation was stalling, and she was wondering why there was so much resistance in relation to the new value proposition in the organization. She wondered whether she and the GET had missed something when making the decisions regarding ATG's strategy.

"What you and the GET are experiencing is not uncommon, Isabelle, and often the result of making decisions under uncertainty," Eve noted.

"What do you mean?" asked Isabelle surprised.

Eve continued: "Well, making decisions under uncertainty that optimize the explore-exploit balance often generates a combination of execution-oriented, short-term initiatives, for instance, closing poorly performing travel agencies, and innovation-oriented, longer-term initiatives, for instance, refocusing on customized, personalized travel. All initiatives are pursued simultaneously and, more often than not, compete for funds and management attention. Such competition creates organizational tensions."

"Tensions?"

"Yes, in my thesis I call them tensions," said Eve. "They are the product of running two very different businesses simultaneously in an organization. For instance, such tensions exist in a matrix organization between line functions, which are short-term oriented and focused on making quarterly sales targets, i.e., exploit, versus corporate functions, whose focus might be on more long-term developments, such as building capabilities, i.e., explore. In functional organizations, such tensions could emerge between production and sales units (exploit) versus R&D (explore). Or, for instance, differing goals could spark tension between an agency-based distribution channel (exploit) and a separate direct-to-consumer business unit selling new products (explore). Companies often face conflict between a mature technology, say, an internal combustion engine (exploit) and a new technology, like an electric engine (explore)."

> Tensions are the product of running two very different businesses simultaneously in an organization.

"I understand," noted Isabelle. "Such tensions are now affecting ATG, where employees need to 'sell the new,' that is, selling the new value proposition, while continuing to perform the 'old' paradigm, that is, continuing to market the old value proposition."

Eve continued: "Yes, as the decision-making efforts of ATG's GET demonstrate, exploitation and exploration strategies have very different profiles and characteristics (Tushman and O'Reilly, 1996). And, in most organizations, as with ATG, they have different advocates among organizational leaders. The strategic intent of exploitation-oriented activities and businesses is mostly cost- and profit-oriented; critical tasks include operational efficiency and continuous innovation; the competencies are also rather operational; the organizational structure is formal and minutely defined; margins and productivity are core KPIs; the culture is oriented toward customers, efficiency, and quality; the organization is risk-averse; and the leadership style is top-down (Tushman and O'Reilly, 1996). In exploration-oriented activities and businesses, the strategic intent turns toward innovation and growth; critical tasks include exercising adaptability, creating new products, and practicing breakthrough innovation; the competencies are rather entrepreneurial; the organization structure is rather loose and adaptable; the culture fosters willingness to take risks; the organization prizes flexibility, speed, and the curiosity to experiment; and the leadership style tends to be visionary (Tushman and O'Reilly, 1996)."

"Why do the tensions come out now?" Isabelle asked.

Eve continued: "Internal tensions typically increase when organizations launch transformation programs – that is, they launch new exploration initiatives – while continuing to execute their exploitation-oriented strategies. Most organizations fail to manage these tensions effectively, and their transformation programs falter. According to some accounts, between 60% and 70% of corporate change initiatives fail (Beer and Nohria, 2000; Ewenstein et al., 2015). Whenever academics have looked at these statistics over the last 40–50 years, they noticed a failure rate of 60–70%. Despite better knowledge about change management and the psychology of change, that number is remarkably constant over time (Ashkenas, 2013)."

"Sounds familiar. . . How does one address this?"

"To succeed, ambidextrous organizations, that is, firms that pursue both exploit-oriented and explore-oriented initiatives and businesses, can pursue three approaches to manage tensions: (1) keeping exploration and exploitation activities separate; (2) concentrating tensions into high-performing top teams; and (3) changing – or at least influencing – how people behave in firms. These strategies are not mutually exclusive," said Eve.

"Keeping exploit-oriented and explore-oriented businesses separate?"

"Separation is the first approach that helps organizations effectively manage ambidexterity," answered Eve. "Generally, when it comes to exploration and exploitation, people are not particularly good at multi-tasking. People are not good at pursuing exploration and exploitation simultaneously (Sana et al., 2013; Janssen et al., 2015; Laureiro-Martinez et al., 2015). People generally do one or the other. Also, as discussed, a few months ago, under pressure, people tend to revert to their default mode, that is, exploitation, since it reduces cognitive load. When this happens, the organization stops exploring, or at least exploration suffers. But organizations can direct their staff members to specialize on one mode only, that is, on either exploitation or exploration."

"How?"

"There are three separation approaches. One, structural ambidexterity, that is, one uses organizational structures to get people to specialize in either exploration or exploitation. Two, contextual ambidexterity, that is, separating exploitation and exploration activities in time. Three, temporal ambidexterity, that is, changing the organization over time to adapt to the changing strategy," answered Eve.

"Structural ambidexterity?"

"Yes, with structural ambidexterity organizations use organizational structures to separate exploration from exploitation (O'Reilly and Tushman, 2004). With structural ambidexterity, some of an organization's employees specialize in exploitation activities, while others focus on exploration. Examples of such specialization abound. One simple and classical example is the functional organization. In a functional organization, some departments, for example, the sales department, focus on short-term, incremental objectives, that is, exploitation, while some other departments, for instance, R&D, are assigned to develop innovative solutions that will impact the business in the coming years, that is, exploration. Another example would be an organization that creates an independent unit to launch and grow a new product. That is, while the traditional organization focuses on continuous, incremental improvements, an independent business unit or subsidiary could, for instance, focus on launching a new direct channel. Skunk works offer another example of structural ambidexterity. Skunk works are completely autonomous units that leaders separate out from the rest of a company in order to give them the freedom to innovate, and the flexibility to capture new opportunities as they arise. For example, Gilead, a pharmaceutical company, keeps Kite Pharma, a leader in the new and fast-growing area of gene therapy, as an independent business unit. In a press release, Gilead's CEO said that giving Kite autonomy would promote entrepreneurial energy, agility, and innovation. He said: 'Cell therapy oncology is an ultra-competitive area.' He added that Kite 'will wake up and go to sleep every day thinking about how to be the leaders in oncology cell therapy' (Barba, 2019). And Apple's Macintosh personal computer, the Mac for short, was created by 'a small autonomous team with a pirate flag flying from the mast of a separate building' (Beinhocker 2006)," said Eve.

"Got it. We are actually thinking about that at ATG. What is contextual ambidexterity?" asked Isabelle.

"With contextual ambidexterity, organizations keep flexible work environments so that people can switch between exploitation and exploration activities (Gibson and Birkinshaw, 2004)," answered Eve. "In such organizations, employees 'specialize' for a time. For example, some staff members might focus on exploration for a time before switching to exploitation. An example of a time-limited exploration activity is the strategic planning process. It is a process in which executives step back from the day-to-day work and reflect on their organization's challenges and their industry's trends. In the process, they select new activities, which are subsequently executed, that is, exploited. Another example of contextual ambidexterity is the lean production method. When applying the lean method, organizations use kanban sessions. During a kanban session, a production team works to identify challenges, and addresses them by exploring alternative and better approaches. For instance, they might make and test new components before going back to the production line to exploit their fresh ideas. Agile teams composed of individuals from different functions and who work together for 10–12 weeks are another example."

"OK, got it. What's the last one, temporal ambidexterity?"

Eve answered: "With temporal ambidexterity, organizations adapt their structures over time, and as a response to changing requirements to the organization (Tushman and O'Reilly, 1996). For instance, when a start-up that has been operating with contextual ambidexterity approaches matures and changes, that is, formalizes its structure by specializing its people more. When a start-up grows and matures, it typically goes from being informal and explorative to becoming more stable, structured, and execution-oriented."

"And when does one use separation? We are having this discussion currently in the organization and are wondering whether to specialize a few agencies on selling our new value proposition."

"Structural separation is typically the most straightforward approach to manage organizational tensions. But it works only when there is a low level of integration between exploitation and exploration activities."

"Low level of integration?" asked Isabelle.

"Yes," answered Eve and continued: "For example, when exploitation and exploration activities share few synergies or require very different capabilities, or if the business models are very different, that is, they may have different brands or very different distribution channels."

> Structural separation is typically the most straightforward approach to manage organizational tensions.

"OK, get it, then you can still specialize in time, can't you?" asked Isabelle.

"Yes, that's right. However, contextual and temporal ambidexterity require better, more skilled leadership. They require leaders who can switch employees' attention from exploit to explore activities continuously over time."

"OK, got it. What about the second approach to managing tensions: concentrating top tensions into high-performing top teams?"

"Yes, that's the second approach," answered Eve. "Sometimes you can't fully separate exploit and explore activities in different businesses. You may still need to operate different business units, but connected ones, as they may leverage a common expertise or a common operations platform, or that may depend on one another. In this case, one approach is to concentrate the tensions to the very top of the organization's hierarchy: to the top team. If different members of a top team are responsible for different parts of the strategy – say, two line managers for hitting the quarterly sales targets (exploit) and a central product management function for launching a new product (explore) – tensions will show up in the top team. The line managers may complain that product management is trying to launch an unsellable product, or that selling the new product requires too much time, time that the sales organization doesn't have as it tries to hit its quarterly targets. At the same time, the product management function may complain about the lack of support or interest by the sales organizations, or for the fact that the sales organization may be actively 'sabotaging' the launch of the newly developed product. However, if the three representatives trust each other and want to help one another succeed, they may find ways to achieve both the line's and the central function's objectives. They may agree to some minor changes of the new product, to a phased launch, to a change of priorities of the line organization, and so forth."

"Got it," said Isabelle.

Eve continued: "Research suggest that top teams matter a lot for ambidexterity (Carmeli, 2008; Carmeli and Halevi, 2009; Lubatkin et al., 2006; Tarba et al., 2020). Top teams are capable of behavioral complexity. That allows them to deal with a dynamic, uncertain environment as well as the complexities and contradictions that characterize ambidextrous organizations."

"Behavioral complexity?" asked Isabelle.

"Yes, teams that have a high degree of so-called behavioral complexity tend to manage organizations effectively in dynamic and changing environments (Carmeli and Halevi, 2009). Behavioral complexity means that teams integrate a wide range of experiences and leadership styles. You can use the term diversity if you prefer," answered Eve.

"Oh, I see."

Eve continued, "Diversity dominated discussions about top team and board appointments in recent years, and many firms have diverse top teams now, at least on paper. But the benefits of diversity can only be captured if the top team members value diverse perspectives and opinions. That is, diversity is more than having diverse people on a top team. It is a matter of mindset. Therefore, diversity alone is not sufficient. Team dynamics matter just as much. Another term to describe effective team dynamics is the expression 'behavioral integration.' Hambrick (1998), a management professor at the Pennsylvania State University, describes it as 'the degree to which the group engages in mutual and collective interaction.' The higher the degree, the more effective the team dynamics. Teams with effective team dynamics tend to lead more effectively in dynamic environments (Carmeli and Halevi, 2009)."

> Diversity is a matter of mindset. The benefits of diversity are only captured when team members value diverse perspectives and opinions.

"I understand," said Isabelle. "That's probably why it mattered so much to Carlo, our chairman, that I learned to mesh with the existing GET team. It was a daunting challenge at first, especially with Alessandro, but in time I achieved a level of integration and teamwork in which the members function together with respect, and they cooperate even when they disagree on matters of policy. I feel that each GET executive supports the company's decisions even if the outcome is contrary to their initial wishes."

"That sounds great. Well done!" said Eve. "Probably each member contributes in different ways to the team decisions."

"Yes, that's right!" answered Isabelle. "For instance, Kosta's youthful, forward-looking optimism about strategy and Hugo's pragmatic, even pessimistic focus on cost could hardly be more different, but their mutual concern for shaping the best future for ATG makes them allies."

"But don't underestimate your role as a leader, Isabelle," noted Eve. "As a leader of the GET you are instrumental to effective team dynamics. You can achieve effective team dynamics by setting mutual goals, by ensuring that the GET members meet and discuss frequently (Carmeli and Halevi, 2009), by giving them equal opportunities to contribute and be heard (Woolley et al., 2010), by encouraging them to collaborate with one another (Zaccaro et al., 1991), by allowing decisions to be made jointly (Hambrick, 1994), and by making the team members feel safe, that is, by ensuring that they can speak up safely if they disagree (Edmondson, 1999; Duhigg, 2016). Being an effective leader of a top team requires attention and real work, as you do, Isabelle."

"Thanks for noticing. It's indeed real work to get them to collaborate so well."

Eve continued, "Yes, but it is usually worth it. Top teams that score high on team diversity and team dynamics develop something called collective intelligence, a form of intelligence that exceeds the sum of the individual intelligence of all the individual team members. Collective intelligence beats individual intelligence and skills (Woolley et al. 2010)."

Isabelle commented, "I am happy that I was able to build this collective intelligence. It really helps us. When we look at challenges, we see more options to address them. And we can make more nuanced decisions. This, despite the fact that I inherited the team. Unlike many other team leaders, I did not have the opportunity to select my team members. I had to accept the diversity I inherited."

"Yes, that's right," added Eve. "But maybe that was a blessing in disguise. If you only had selected individuals that you liked, you might have run the risk of reducing diversity. Building on the diversity that you inherited luckily worked, and your day-to-day leadership at ATG has led to the emergence of effective team dynamics, of collective intelligence or 'teamness' (Hambrick, 1998)."

"OK, understand. We spoke about specialization or different forms of separation of activities as a means to manage organizational tensions. We also spoke about the importance of top teams to manage tensions. But you also mentioned a third approach: changing how people behave in organizations. Can you tell me more?" asked Isabelle.

"Sure," said Eve, and continued: "Sometimes separating and using top teams to manage tensions isn't enough. Sometimes exploitation and exploration activities need to be integrated in the day-to-day job of most, if not all, employees in an organization. In the case of ATG, as I understand it, your employees in the agencies need to sell effectively the existing products, while, at the same time, start to sell the new products and services. To do so, ATG's employees need to become better listeners, more skilled at aggregating products and services, and more entrepreneurial, in order to promote and effectively sell their new experience-oriented value proposition. This requires employees to change their behaviors. They must learn to be more proactive and less reactive in identifying potential customer needs."

"Yes, that's right."

Eve continued, "But behavioral change is hard, not only in strategy transformations and in organizations, but in daily life. This issue comes up in every area of life. For instance, think of weight control. Many people want to lose weight. Many want to look and feel in good shape, hence many have plans to exercise and follow a healthier diet. But few follow through and they find excuses for not executing their plans. After a few days they tell themselves, 'This week doesn't work. I have so many invitations and business lunches. I'll try to start next week.'"

"Yes, that sounds familiar. . ."

Eve continued, "Changing behavior is hard even when it is about life or death. For instance, medication nonadherence is a big issue in medicine. An estimated 40–50% of patients with chronic diseases such as diabetes or elevated blood pressure (hypertension) do not adhere to the medication regimen prescribed by their doctors (Kleinsinger, 2018). The condition of these patients remains uncontrolled, despite significant risks. Worse, medication nonadherence affects even many patients who have had coronary bypass surgery. Even though the patients are aware of the risks of suffering a stroke or another cardiac incident, many do not follow through with their prescribed medication regimen (Feser, 2011)."

"Wow! I wasn't aware of this. Yes, you are right. Change is hard. But why?"

Eve continued, "Reducing 'cognitive load' is one explanation for the human resistance to change, as we discussed a few months ago. But there is one more explanation. Change requires attention and focus. Though the neocortex handles exploration activities, the limbic system can sometimes hijack the explore-exploit process. Change tends to generate feelings of fear, stress, and anxiety (Laureiro-Martinez et al., 2015; Brusoni et al., 2020). The amygdala is essential to this process since it moderates the brain's emotional reactions. It triggers the release of different neurotransmitters, which in turn activate the hippocampus, where memory is stored. Stressful situations, such as imminent danger, can very rapidly activate the amygdala and some portions of the insula (bypassing other areas of the brain) and replace reflective thinking. When we are in situations of stress or perceived danger, our instincts seem to take over – as, in fact, they do."

"What has this to do with businesses or ATG?" asked Isabelle.

Eve continued, "Many of the routines in an organization – how people behave and interact, how they work, how they make decisions – are exploitation strategies, that is, habits, skills, or simply 'the way we do things around here.' Changing those exploitation strategies takes a lot of attention and effort. Under pressure and stress, we may feel uncomfortable, become afraid, resist change, and revert to 'standard,' safe, and proven behaviors, that is, to a state of exploitation."

"Well, you are making it sound a bit dramatic," commented Isabelle.

> Many of the routines in an organization – how people behave and interact, how they work, how they make decisions – are exploitation strategies, that is, habits, skills, or simply "the way we do things around here."

"I don't think so," answered Eve. "Managers sometimes underestimate the anxiety and fear employees can experience when they face a negative change in their working context, such as news about bankruptcies in their industry, or some close friend or relative losing a job due to a recession, or a shift in their working situation amid plans for organizational restructuring. Change can create discomfort and fear. This diminishes the brain's ability to focus, to explore, and to find new options to adapt to the new situation."

"OK, but how do we get employees to overcome their fears and change their behavior when new explorative initiatives require them to adapt?" asked Isabelle.

"Do you remember our discussion about heuristics, about circumstances when individuals tend to tilt their exploit-explore balance toward exploration? Can we use them to answer your question?" asked Eve.

"Hmmm. Let me try to do that," said Isabelle, and continued: "Applying the seven factors for optimizing individuals' exploit-explore balance to this question suggests that employees can change under the following conditions:

1. Objectives – They have ambitious goals they can't reach by exploitation only.
2. Opportunities – They see the opportunities and benefits that changing behavior might create or incentives it might earn.
3. Time and resources – They have time and other resources to experiment with new behaviors.
4. Others' actions – Their social context supports flexibility when they see other people change their behavior.

5. Values and culture – The changes they are required to make align with their values, the corporate culture, and their own personal standards.
6. Capabilities – They are able to make these changes.
7. State of mind – They feel safe and rested."

"That's exactly right, Isabelle. Well done! These seven factors align well with recent research (Lawson and Price, 2003; Basford and Schaninger, 2016; Feser et al., 2018) that suggests that behavioral change programs tend to succeed under four conditions: (1) the organization promotes the change with goals and rewards; (2) leaders become role models of the desired behavior; (3) the company communicates the desired change in an inspiring, clearly understandable way; and (4) organizations train employees and help them develop any necessary new abilities," said Eve.

"Can you say more?" asked Isabelle.

"Sure," responded Eve. "Let's look at these four conditions for success, one by one.

"First, using goals and rewards. Studies suggest that transformation programs tend to succeed when the organization reinforces expected changes with targets and incentives. In a sample of roughly 600 transformations, the percentage of transformations described as very or extremely successful increased 4.3 times more in organizations that reinforced the expected changes with targets and incentives than in organizations that did not (Feser et al., 2018).

"Targets and incentives play an important role in making people focus appropriately, either on exploitation or exploration. However, that doesn't necessarily mean that you need to pay employees to explore new behaviors, as some may think.

"Exploitation and exploration activities appear to require different types of incentives. For example, you may effectively promote exploration-related activities with financial incentives, according to researchers who have thoroughly reviewed the theoretical basis for the role of financial incentives as strong motivators. Several studies show that financial incentives are effective in creating a culture of performance (Stajkovic and Luthans, 1997; Peterson and Luthans, 2006). Financial incentives are effective when employees believe that there is a causal link between their individual actions and the outcome that the company is intending. Also, they are effective when that outcome can be easily measured. For example, financial incentives, such as offering bonuses to insurance agents, effectively encourage improved sales activities.

"However, three reasons explain why financial incentives may not be very effective in promoting exploration-related behaviors. First, such incentives tend to lead people to focus on the activities and outcomes you're paying for, while they may not give much attention to their other activities, despite their importance to the organization. For example, when financial incentives promote employees to achieve annual budget targets, they tend to engage in short-term goal-oriented behavior at the expense of pursuing longer-term work investments. Second, financial incentives can reduce the desirable social behavior that is important for exploration, such as cross-unit collaboration (Fehr and Falk, 2002). Third, monetary incentives can change people's understanding of what constitutes desirable social behavior and, thereby, crowd out intrinsic motivations (Gneezy et al., 2011).

"On the other hand, primarily non-financial incentives that build on intrinsic motivation – such as social recognition, performance feedback, and assignments to work on attractive tasks – may promote exploration-related behaviors (Peterson and Luthans, 2006; Fehr and Falk, 2002)."

"I understand. What's the second condition for behavioral change in organizations?"

Eve answered, "That leaders become role models for change. In a study, when leaders demonstrated the desired changes, transformation programs tended to succeed. This kind of role modeling increased results by 4.1 times.

"Role modeling plays an important part in showing members of the organization what matters and how to live ambidexterity in practice (Gist, 1987). Role modeling may include leaders' behaviors, changes in leadership, and recounting and celebrating the 'right successes.'"

"Got it. What's the third condition for behavioral change in organizations?"

Eve answered, "Simply, clear and inspiring communication. For instance, in the studies that I mentioned before, transformation programs tended to succeed when leaders communicated about them in an inspiring, clearly understandable way. Communicating successfully increased the success rate by 3.8 times. Inspiring leaders appeal to their colleagues' values and ideals in ways that stir their emotions (Yukl et al., 2008; Feser, 2016).

"An organization's mission statement often expresses its values and ideals, such as a health care provider that wants to help patients live longer, healthier lives or an insurance firm that wishes to help clients live safely. Inspiring leadership is likely to be more powerful when leaders bring their messages alive with emotional examples, stories, and metaphors. The alternative of using formal vision or strategy statements with lists of generic phrases and facts is not effective. While our brain has difficulty memorizing such lists, it handles emotional stories and metaphors much better.

"In fact, most of people's thinking, experience, and knowledge is organized as stories (Turner, 1996). Hollywood and Bollywood tell us stories. The Bible itself is a story. It is no coincidence that some of history's most inspiring leaders have been great storytellers, such as John F. Kennedy, who regularly used metaphors and positive visions to inspire people (Feser, 2011). Using stories to illustrate values and ideals arouses positive emotions that counterbalance the feelings of stress, anxiety, and fear connected to change and exploration."

"Interesting. What's the fourth and final condition for behavioral change in organizations?" asked Isabelle.

Eve answered, "Training and developing the necessary abilities. Transformation programs had better results when organizations invested in training and building the new, required capabilities. The success rate increased by 2.8 times."

"OK. Lots to keep in mind! Let me summarize," said Isabelle. "Making decisions under uncertainty generates strategies that combine execution-oriented with exploration-oriented initiatives. These initiatives often compete with one another and create organizational tensions. There are three approaches to managing these tensions in work organization: (1) separation; (2) high-performing top teams; and (3) fostering behavioral change. But when do I use which approach?"

Eve answered, "Each of these works best in certain conditions and has certain requirements. We have touched on some aspects of this already. To summarize, three factors seem to be particularly important. First, the level of integration between exploit and explore activities. If the level of integration is minimal, then structural separation is the most straightforward approach. If there are synergies or shared expertise to be leveraged, temporal separation and top teams probably work best. And when the integration is very high, that is, a large number of employees need to simultaneously perform exploit and explore activities, behavioral change programs are the way to go. Second, time available. Structural separation is straightforward and fast. Building performing top teams takes time, and behavioral change programs even more so. And finally, third, leadership repertoire."

"Leadership repertoire?"

"Yes, if you lead an organization which uses structural ambidexterity to separate exploit and explore activities into different business units, you as a leader need to be able to take different perspectives and adjust your leadership style depending on which unit in your organization you are dealing with. For example, you may lead discussions with the head of the sales department different than you may lead them with the head of the R&D department. Leading an organization that leverages structural ambidexterity requires good self-leadership, so to speak. However, if you leverage top teams, you also need to be good at leading others, understanding individual differences, motivating different individuals, and so forth. And, finally, if you go for behavioral change approaches,

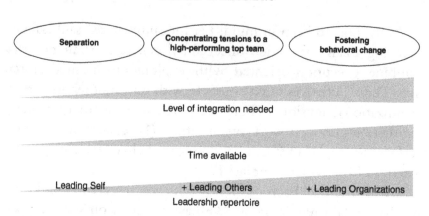

Figure 9.1 Approaches to managing organizational tension.

you need to be good at leading an entire organization, developing an inspiring vision, developing a strategy, designing performance management systems, designing incentive systems, communicating authentically, and so forth. I summarize this on the following chart, the higher the level of integration, the more time available, and the larger the leadership repertoire, the more one can use more demanding forms of managing organizational tensions (Figure 9.1)."

"Can you combine them. That is, could I work on the top team and organize ambidexterity structurally?" asked Isabelle.

"Yes, of course. The three approaches are not mutually exclusive and can be combined," answered Eve.

> Making decisions under uncertainty generates strategies that combine execution-oriented with exploration-oriented initiatives that often compete with one another and create organizational tensions. There are three approaches to managing these tensions: separation, top teams, and fostering behavioral change.

"You have given me a lot of food for thought, and some ideas on how I may approach the transformation of ATG. Thank you for this! Next time I really would love to meet in person. Time is always so tight that I never follow up on this intention, but maybe I could apply some of the approaches we discussed today. . . an incentive of a nice lunch perhaps!" said Isabelle.

"I would love that. If you don't mind me saying this, you seem to be working very hard, maybe too hard. Your work-life balance might also impact your decision-making. There is a section of my thesis devoted to this topic."

"Learning about that is a second incentive for me to meet soon over lunch. I'll follow up on it this time. I really look forward seeing you soon," said Isabelle, smiling.

Key Takeaways

- Making decisions under uncertainty generates strategies that combine initiatives that often compete with one another and create organizational tensions.
- Tensions are a source of innovation and progress but must be managed.
- To do so: (1) use organizational structure and processes to separate initiatives; (2) build diverse, high-performing top teams; and (3) increase your organization's and employees' ability to operate effectively with such tensions. There are four mechanisms to improve organization's ability to manage change: promotion of change with goals and rewards; role modelling; inspiring and clear communication; training and development of employees.

Part Four

BECOMING SUPER DECIDERS

Chapter 10

Case 5: Making Work-Life Balance Decisions

**Claudio Feser, David Redaschi,
and Karolin Frankenberger**

Isabelle wondered why ATG's transformation was stalling and what she could do about it. She was concerned that ATG was losing both momentum and its competitive edge in the niche of experience-oriented, personalized travel.

She looked at the four options using the Decision Navigator and building on the insights of the last discussion with Eve (Figure 10.1).

Her fourth option for accelerating change was the most convincing, but, even so, she was concerned that it wouldn't work. So far, change management hadn't been ATG's forte. She wasn't very optimistic about whether the company could mobilize its employees to promote and sell its new products and services. Also, using incentives and the like seemed risky. What if they didn't work?

Isabelle asked Carlo, the board chairman, to sit down with her, and she shared her concerns with him. She confessed that she

1. Dilemma	Should we slow down the pace of transformation or change the approach?							
2. Options on the Exploit-Explore continuum	Exploit ◄							Explore ►
	Slow down the pace of transformation		Set-up a dedicated unit separately from the main organization.		Select 30% of ATG's agencies to market the new products and services		Strengthen change management	
The seven heuristics	**3. Assumptions**	**4. Facts**	**3. Assumptions**	**4. Facts**	**3. Assumptions**	**4. Facts**	**3. Assumptions**	**4. Facts**
a) Objectives	Reengage the employees Reduced sales obj. for new ATG	T F	Fast implementation of the new ATG Reduced objectives	F F	Fast implementation of the new ATG Reduced objectives	F F	Reengage the employees Keep current objectives	T T
b) Opportunities	Regain the engagement of employees	T	Establish the new ATG in the market ahead of competitors	R	Establish the new ATG in the market ahead of competitors	R	Regain the engagement of the employees Establish the new ATG	T T
c) Time	Can wait for another 12 months	F	Need to move fast	T	Need to move fast	T	Need to move fast and at scale	T
d) Competitive actions and stakeholder expectations		?		?		?		?
e) Our values and culture	Caring, patient	R	Fast-execution, speed	F	Fast-execution, speed	R	Caring, ambitious	R
f) Our capabilities	Limited	T	ATG can manage ambidexterity structurally	R	ATG can manage ambidexterity structurally	R	ATG can manage complex change program	F
g) Our "mood" or prevalent collective cognitive states	Pessimistic that we can engage and mobilize the organization	T	Optimistic that we can mobilize part of the organization	R	Optimistic that we can mobilize part of the organization	R	Optimistic that we can mobilize the entire organization	F
5. Optimization	None							
6. Resolution	Option 4							

Figure 10.1 Six-step Decision Navigator for Case 4.

wondered why ATG's employees didn't seem to share her enthusiasm for becoming a leading tour operator in Europe, in terms
of growth, customer loyalty, and profitability. The goal seemed so
clear and meaningful to her.

"Should we launch the new service offerings as a separate business unit, just to get us moving?" she asked, "Or should I perhaps,
as a consultant specialized in change management has suggested,
try to mobilize the organization by creating a crisis?"

"Neither option sounds great," he answered. "Separation could
work if the objective was speed and if, for whatever reason, the
new value proposition was very different, even under a different
brand. But your objective is to transform ATG from providing
mass travel solutions to providing individualized travel experience
at scale – not just in some pockets. And creating a crisis works only
once or, perhaps, twice in a stretch. But we're in a very dynamic
environment, and if you continuously create crises when you want
to make changes, it will cultivate only cynicism and resistance."

"But what shall I do then?" Isabelle responded. "We have a
great concept that can make us a leader in our market and increase
profitability. This transformation invites employees to work on
more interesting tasks and learn new skills. Why don't they see it?"

Carlo listened to her carefully. "This is getting pretty frustrating
for you, isn't it?" he said empathetically.

"Well, I wouldn't admit it to anyone but you – or maybe
Marco – but, yes, it is. I work really hard and communicate the
vision non-stop. I host town halls and CEO breakfasts with smaller
groups. I published two interviews about our vision on the corporate intranet. But the organization doesn't seem to get it."

Usually serene and unflappable, Isabelle was aware that she
wasn't doing much of a job hiding her frustration and disappointment. "It's frustrating," she added. "Don't our employees want to
work for a leading European tour operator?"

Carlo paused and looked at her, "No, I don't think they
want that."

"What do you mean?" Isabelle was visibly surprised. She couldn't understand Carlo's reaction.

Carlo continued, calmer and wiser than ever.

"Well," he said thoughtfully. "That's what you and, maybe, the GET want to have happen. You are ambitious. You want ATG to become a leading tour operator in Europe. But why do you think our employees come to work every morning? Why do they work for ATG? What do you think makes them proud? What stories do they tell their children when they come home at night and talk about their work over dinner?"

Isabelle understood, "They're not talking about market share and profitability, are they?"

"Correct. Our people chose this industry because they love serving customers, providing them with unique travel experiences, opening new horizons, bringing cultures closer, and making people happy," Carlo continued, "They feel connected to the purpose of ATG, not the KPIs of the GET."

She thought about the last conversation with Eve and now what Eve had in mind when she spoke about inspiring leadership.

"You've laid out the transformation as a matter of strategy, KPIs, PMO, and initiatives. That's the hard side of transformation," Carlo continued, "It's correct, but it's not enough. Sit down with Alison and talk about the human side, too. Think about purpose, think about motivation, think about what employees care about. Think about their emotions."

Isabelle thanked Carlo and, as she left his office, texted Alison and made plans to go to lunch. Settled in a quiet corner of her favorite café, Isabelle explained, "I talked to Carlo, and I'm going about trying to get employees to buy into this transformation all the wrong ways – all head and no heart."

"We have the ability, with communication slides and outreach, to add the emotional component to explain to our people why we need this change," Alison reassured her. "But you know, I don't think that's what we need. This isn't about changing slides and the messaging. With all due respect, but this is about you and the GET."

"Me and the GET? What do you mean?" asked Isabelle, surprised at Alison's comment.

"If we just change the messaging, but not our own mindset, the communication will not be authentic. If we just care for sales and profits or our own interest, people will figure that out. They are not stupid. Just changing the messaging without reflecting on why you and we as a GET really want to do the transformation, will simply foster cynicism and even more resistance."

This conversation, also, was something of a revelation to Isabelle. Taken aback, it dawned on her that she had to change herself. Her confidence in her own all-business point of view softened as Carlo and Alison helped her see that if she wanted to touch her employees' hearts, she and the GET had first to connect to their common purpose or mission.

As the waiter delivered perfect crepes, Isabel asked, "Alison, will you help me facilitate a workshop with the GET? I want us to reflect why we are coming to work every morning, what we are talking about to our families in the evening when we tell them about our day in the office. I want us to find our common purpose."

"Of course," Alison said, "but after I give them the facts and findings, you'll be the best proponent to facilitate that discussion and lead ahead, because this shift reflects your awakening."

"Yes, I can do that. Thank you," said Isabelle, and as they were leaving the café, she turned to Alison, saying: "I really appreciated our conversation today. You were open and honest with me. I know that I can come across as self-confident at times and speaking up requires courage. But you really helped me. I thank you so much for that."

"Telling you what I thought was worth the risk, Isabelle," said Alison. "You are worth it!"

In the following weeks Isabelle and Alison worked together with the GET to create a common mission for ATG. They also revised ATG's approach to engaging the members of the organization in its new strategy.

Step by step, the GET made sure the change initiative came to fruition. The GET changed corporate communication about the transformation by including more personal stories and tapping into their own emotional satisfaction of guiding clients on new journeys. They involved front-line employees and led by example. The new approach spread through the sales force with help from Frank and Conny, while Alison's professionals adjusted ATG's training and incentives. Isabelle did face some initial tough questioning from Hugo, who felt that all these additional steps in the change initiative were too expensive, but he came around when positive outcomes began to appear. Isabelle was particularly pleased at how creatively Alessandro brought operations and IT into alignment with a more customized sales strategy.

Within a few weeks, employee resistance died down, and the ATG's European agencies began to reap success stories. Within six months the momentum had completely turned, and Isabelle felt that ATG was now "firing on all six cylinders," as Marco put it.

Alison was quick to run a survey that showed high employee engagement. ATG's people were proud to work at the company. Its new culture – entrepreneurial, customer-centric, caring, and respectful – was unique in the industry. Customers were satisfied, revenues were growing, and ATG was producing very strong results. Also, the expansion plans seemed to be working, both in the United States and in Asia. The concept of experience-oriented, personalized travel fitted both Asian and American customers perfectly.

ATG was about to become again the flagship company in its industry it once had been.

New Problems

However, due to a recession and the associated consolidation process in the travel industry, ATG soon faced another challenge. Its successful transformation and international expansion caught the attention of journalists, but it also prompted a different kind of attention. Suddenly, a much larger competitor made an unsolicited take-over bid. The move was also a surprise because ATG was now well valued.

It caught Isabelle and the GET on the wrong foot. She immediately contacted Carlo, her board chairman. As a former banker, he knew exactly what a take-over bid meant and how to handle it.

After Carlo and Isabelle touched base with their major shareholders and briefly discussed the matter with them, they immediately called in Hugo, the CFO, also an old hand at mergers and acquisitions (M&A). Carlo approached JC Logan Bank for support during the take-over defense battle. Late in the day, Isabelle and Carlo held a series of meetings with board members and the GET to discuss possible options for dealing with the hostile bid.

Amid the air of crisis, Isabelle received a message from her husband. It was already around 10 p.m. He texted, "It's a shame you couldn't make it to our anniversary dinner, but don't worry. I couldn't eat the *canard à l'orange* by myself (check the fridge)."

She hadn't even realized it was so late. How could she have forgotten? Isabelle was tired, frustrated, and annoyed with herself.

But the night got worse. When Isabelle came home around 11 p.m., Marco, as always understanding and caring about her and the children, though still aggrieved, told her that their 18-year-old daughter Marie was terribly upset and had decided not to talk to Isabelle anymore.

"I'll check on her before I go to sleep," he said, "but I should go upstairs now. I have an early Zoom with my publisher. Get something to eat and come on up. You look beat."

For several years, Marie, an earnest teenager who was passionate about her beliefs, had been actively campaigning for climate protection. She was upset not only because Isabelle spent so little time with her family and was often tense and irritable when she was around, but also precisely because her mother ran a big travel business. Marie saw tourism, especially aviation, as just another source of CO_2 emissions, and she had long since expected her mother to do something about it.

Isabelle was frustrated. She had to win this take-over defense battle. Her job was to save ATG's independence. She didn't want to lose her job as CEO. But, in the last few months, she admitted bleakly at the end of an already difficult day, she was losing her connection with her family.

She began to wonder if she could salvage her relationship with Marie before she started ETH's environmental science program in September. And how was Annelies doing as a younger teen caught up in a competitive sport? She seemed happy about her obsession with tennis, and was apparently glad to practice almost every day with her school team, but what was she thinking? Did she want to compete in the canton? Nationally? And how long would Marco's patience hold out?

Isabelle sat at the dining table trying to think. Tired and too disheartened to warm up leftover anniversary duckling, she poured a little milk into a bowl of muesli. She wanted to talk to her family, but everyone was already asleep.

Questions for Reflection

What would you do if you were in Isabelle's shoes?

- Resign and focus on family?
- Reduce your workload through delegation and ask for help, and spend time fixing family issues?
- Focus solely on work and address family issues later – or would that mean never?
- Something else?

You may want to write down your answer before continuing.

Chapter 11

Becoming Better at Making Decisions

**Claudio Feser, Daniella Laureiro-Martinez,
and Stefano Brusoni**

Everyone thinks of changing the world, but no one thinks
of changing himself.

—*Leo Tolstoy*

Isabelle and Eve met for breakfast at *Milchbar*, a trendy café in Zurich, the following morning. Breakfast was the only activity Isabelle was able to accommodate in her busy schedule. They had agreed to meet for a breakfast a few weeks earlier and Isabelle didn't want to cancel it this time, even though she was in the middle of a major crisis. Given the confidential nature of the situation at ATG, she didn't plan to discuss ATG this time. She just wanted to finally meet Eve in person again and give her a hug.

Isabelle arrived a few minutes late. She had had problems falling asleep the night before and had overslept. It wasn't the first time in the past months, and lack of sleep wasn't the only matter plaguing her. She often felt restless, had difficulty concentrating, was irritable, often felt worthless, and had lost interest in her hobbies.

Eve stood up to greet her, as always with a big smile on her face.

"Long time since we flew to London together. I really wanted to hug you and say thank you for all these wonderful and really helpful conversations we had in the past year," said Isabelle taking Eve.

"It is so nice to see you in person," said Eve, "but you look tired. Is everything OK?" She had noticed Isabelle yawning when she entered the café.

"How did you spot that?"

"You were yawning coming in, and, no offense, but you do look tired."

"Rough time, currently. I have been working really hard for a long time now. I enjoy the role that I am playing at ATG, and I am proud of my and the GET's achievements so far, even though we continue to face big challenges. But success comes at a price. I think it is just the way it is. There is no free lunch. I'll probably have to accept that to be a successful company leader, I must sacrifice a lot, especially in my private life," said Isabelle, yawning again.

"You make the work-life balance seem a zero-sum game: one can be either successful at work or at home."

"Isn't it?" asked Isabelle.

"I am not in your position, and I cannot judge your specific situation. As an academic I study decision-making processes at an individual and at a collective level. You will agree that making high-quality decisions consistently is important for success, in business and in life in general. Research suggests that living a balanced life has an impact on the quality of decision-making. Maybe it doesn't always need to be a zero-sum game," responded Eve.

Another of their insightful conversations had just started.

One line of Eve's work had been to identify the characteristics of individuals who repeatedly make high-quality decisions. Her objective had been to identify not only the individual characteristics of the great decision-makers, whom she called "Super

Deciders," but also whether those characteristics could be trained and improved over time.

First, she had to identify Super Deciders. To do so, in her lab at university, she assessed hundreds of executives using the multi-armed bandit (MAB) test.

She explained the test, "The MAB test is a robust model for assessing individual performance in making exploit-explore decisions. The MAB test − which looks like a game using multiple slot machines − asks people to make sequential resource allocation decisions as they choose among several competing alternatives.

"The MAB test captures the fundamental features of real-life situations where uncertainty is high, multiple alternatives change over time, and the environment changes continuously, so it is hard to tell what's going on. In the test, the rapidly evolving environment is represented by each slot machine's payoff, which not only changes continuously, but does so with some noise, so the trends are never crystal clear. Therefore, decision-makers should exploit the best paying option, but only for as long as its payoff is high, and once that payoff diminishes, exploration might lead to higher payoffs. To find the right slot machine, people must test alternative machines. However, in a noisy environment, it might be important to test the alternative machines multiple times to obtain a more accurate estimate of their value and the diminishing or rising trends that each specific slot machine is following (Laureiro-Martinez, 2022).

"For example, imagine that your company needs to select the best supplier from four options (A, B, C and D). You decide to test their quality to find out which one is best. After an initial exploration, you decide to go for the 'D' supplier."

Eve showed Isabelle a graph indicating arrow 1 to the D line (Figure 11.1).

Eve continued: "This is like winning on one of the multi-arm bandits. After a while, however, you notice that the quality of your results starts to decrease (like winning less on the bandit). Should you switch to a new supplier, or stay with your current one

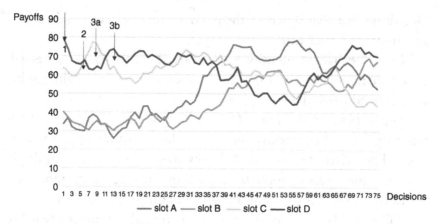

Figure 11.1   The MAB test.

(see arrow 2)? Let's say you explore the other three potential suppliers, and you find that 'C' gives you better quality. But after a while, 'C' gets worse, too, and you face the exploration–exploitation dilemma again.

"Timing is everything. If you explore at point 3a, you will not find a better alternative to 'C.' But if you explore at point 3b, 'D' will offer better quality. The longer you work with a supplier – or play a bandit – the easier it is to discern trends. But if you are betting on a loser, don't stick with it too long; instead, switch to another alternative as soon as possible (Laureiro-Martinez, 2022)."

"OK, so the MAB test shows the decision-making performance of an individual when making explore-exploit trade-offs, that is, when making decision under uncertainty, right?" asked Isabelle.

"Yes, that's right," answered Eve. "The MAB test captures the fundamental conflict between allocating resources with strategies that yield a high current reward (exploit) and making decisions that sacrifice a current reward to gain the possibility of a higher future reward (explore). Because decisions come with rewards – losses and gains – MAB tests are probably close to the experiences that decision-makers have when they face dilemmas in organizations."

"OK, I understand. The test allows you to rank decision-makers by their MAB test scores. The higher the individual score, the better the decision-maker. What did you do next?" asked Isabelle.

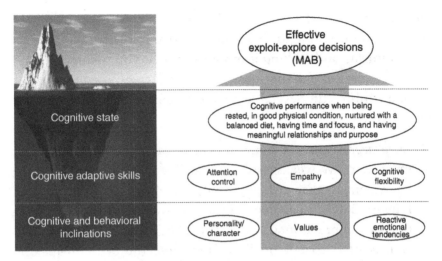

Figure 11.2 Seven factors that help explain exploit-explore decision performance of individuals.

"I reviewed studies and literature to identify individual factors that affect the MAB score, that is, individual characteristics that contribute to solving exploration-exploitation dilemmas effectively. This figure summarizes the main findings," answered Eve showing Isabelle Figure 11.2, and then she continued: "We can summarize and group the main findings in the literature into seven factors in three areas: cognitive state, cognitive-adaptive skills, and cognitive-behavioral inclinations (Brusoni et al., 2023)."

"Interesting figure. Why is there a picture of an iceberg on the left?"

"Austrian psychoanalyst Sigmund Freud used the iceberg picture to illustrate that most of what drives our behaviors – which are visible above the waterline – is submersed and not visible. The seven factors are not immediately visible, but important because they significantly influence decision-making behaviors."

"OK, got it. What are the first group of factors, the cognitive states?" asked Isabelle.

Eve answered: "The first group of factors influencing decision-making performance under uncertainty – or making effective exploit-explore decisions – concerns cognitive states. If you feel safe, relaxed, energized, or inspired, you are more inclined to explore. In contrast, when you feel tired, depressed, stressed, or under pressure, you tend to absorb negative information, generating pessimism, and making it more likely that you will favor 'playing it safe' over exploration (Sharot, 2017)."

She continued: "Several factors may negatively affect cognitive performance.

1. *Sleep deprivation*: Six hours of sleep per night for a period of more than two weeks results in a decline in mental performance equivalent to that of being awake for 48 hours (Durmer and Dinges, 2005). Sleep deprivation is known to disrupt the function of the pre-frontal cortex (PFC) (Chee and Chuah, 2008) and, as such, to potentially compromise the decision-making process. Importantly, the emotionally orientated contributions may become dominant in making decisions, leading – depending on personal inclinations – to overly risky (Killgore, 2015) or overly conservative decisions.

2. *Poor physical condition*: On average, fit individuals score 36% higher on standardized tests than those who rarely exercise (Tomporowski et al., 2008). Physical movement and exercise positively affect cognitive performance and play an important role in counteracting the degenerative effects of aging on the brain. In addition, Exercise promotes well-being (Mandolesi et al., 2018).

3. *An unbalanced diet*: Poor nutrition can lead to stress and fatigue and negatively affect the ability to think and work. Also, nutrition can induce behavioral changes when it comes to decisions. For instance, high-carb/protein diets may offer a non-pharmacological approach for effectively modulating the serotonin function, that – among others – regulates decision behaviors (Liu et al., 2021).

4. *Persistent high cognitive load and limited time for reflection*: People who meditate have increased amounts of gray matter in the hippocampus, and that reduces their levels of cortisol and stress (Congleton et al., 2015). Allowing space for deliberate

diffuse thinking also has important benefits, such as enhanced creativity (Kounios et al., 2008) and better learning (Parker-Pope, 2014).

5. *Lack of purpose and connection with others*: Research on the role of purpose suggests that helping others promotes physiological changes in the brain related to happiness (Post, 2014). Helping others can also help create a sense of belonging, friendship, and connection with a wider community (Brown et al., 2012; Pilkington et al., 2012)."

"OK, that makes sense. Not surprising, but I wasn't aware of the large effect that these factors have on cognitive performance and hence on decision-making," said Isabelle.

"Yes, they do," said Eve. Looking straight at Isabelle, she then asked: "Can I ask you something personal? How are you doing on these dimensions?"

"Hmmm. . . not well," answered Isabelle, "I haven't been sleeping well in the past months, I eat microwaved stuff in the evening, if I eat at all, and I have no time to work out. But the thing that is worse, is that I feel I have lost my connection to my daughters."

"To your daughters?"

"Yes, and to Marco, my husband. He is always supportive, but we haven't spent any quality time together for months now. I wonder how he feels."

Isabelle paused.

She then continued: "But that's the life of a CEO. I don't feel it is impacting my decisions at ATG, but I think that my GET colleagues and the chairman are helping a lot when we make decisions."

"Yes, you are probably lucky to have such support at work," responded Eve, "Still, you got to pay attention to this. You can't simply say, that's the life of a CEO. If this goes on for too long, you may experience signs of a depression and burnout."

"I think I may already be experiencing them."

She paused again.

Eve waited for a minute or two and then broke the silence: "I have good news for you. The effect of good sleep, healthy nutrition, working out, meditation, and improved relationships is not only large, but also immediate," said Eve. "You can regulate cognitive states relatively quickly. Any combination of a regular routine of seven to eight hours of uninterrupted sleep every night, taking several short breaks during the day to unplug and recharge, performing two to three hours of vigorous physical activity per week, consuming the appropriate quantity and variety of healthy nutrients, regularly practicing mindfulness, limiting multi-tasking, openly discussing emotions and problems with Marco or a friend, and having a good dose of social interactions daily go a long way toward improving your cognitive states (Durmer and Dinges, 2005; Masley et al., 2009; Moore and Malinowski, 2009; Tucker et al., 2010; Khodarahimi, 2018; Honn et al., 2019)."

"I can't do all of that. Where would I find the time!" exclaimed Isabelle.

"I am not suggesting that you do all of that, but any combination of those interventions that works for you personally will make a difference. Some people like to meditate, others don't. Some like to work out, others don't. You can try to find out what works for you. Connecting to your family seems important to you. Maybe you start there."

"OK, I need to think about this, but I think you are right. But let's continue, you mentioned there was more. I am keen to learn about all factors. What is the second group of factors, the cognitive adaptive skills?" asked Isabelle.

"The second group of factors that helps shape the exploration/exploitation balance relates to cognitive skills, which most humans have to differing degrees and which they can extend and strengthen with focus and practice.

"Three cognitive skills seem to be particularly relevant to decision-making: attention control, cognitive flexibility, and empathy. Let's review them in turn.

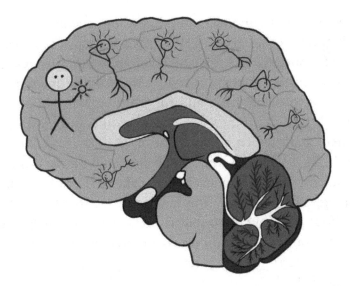

Figure 11.3 Attention control.

"First, take *attention control* (Figure 11.3). This includes the ability to focus, and sustain such focus, evaluate and plan potential alternative courses of action, and choose among them. Laureiro-Martinez (2014) and Laureiro-Martinez et al. (2015) studied these skills under the labels of cognitive control or attention control. These skills are very important as they are in charge of selecting external information and internal information, storing such information in the short-term memory so it can be held in the focus of attention in order to be processed. They are also in charge of thinking in abstract and analogical ways, planning future actions, and initiating or inhibiting actions. The brain circuitries in charge of attention control are somehow like the brain's boss and extend over multiple brain regions, a key one being the most anterior portion of the brain, the prefrontal cortex (PFC).

"The brain networks that underlie attention control are somewhat present in childhood and experience important development over time, maturing only in early adulthood.

"People can train their attention control ability throughout their lifetime (Posner et al., 2014). It is a matter of practice. Repetition of a specific task that involves an attention network can improve attention control; that is, repeatedly performing a task that requires concentration and focus strengthens attention control. People also can improve their attention control with physical movement and exercise and meditation (Posner et al., 2015; Dodich et al., 2019). Just 13 minutes of meditation daily can improve attention control significantly (Tang et al., 2017; Basso et al., 2019; Landsberg, 2023). Further, simply taking time to reflect, that is, 'to think about thinking' (also called metacognition), helps develop attention control skills. Brain scans of individuals with better metacognition suggest that they have more gray matter in the PFC (Fleming, 2014)."

"Interesting. I think attention control is a strength of mine. I've always been good at keeping focus, inhibiting inappropriate actions. . . although lately I admit that sometimes I struggle to concentrate. What's the second cognitive skill that matters in effective decision-making, cognitive flexibility?" asked Isabelle.

"*Cognitive flexibility* is the second cognitive skill. Cognitive flexibility is the ability to change thoughts or actions depending on the environment (Geurts et al., 2009) and to adapt cognitive and behavioral strategies effectively in response to changing tasks or environmental demands (Deák, 2003; Diamond, 2013). A very cognitively flexible person will recognize different elements of a problem and will use their empathy to see a problem from different perspectives (Brusoni and Laureiro-Martinez, 2018)," answered Eve.

"It is a skill, so I guess it can be developed and strengthened, right?" asked Isabelle.

"Yes, that's right," answered Eve. "The skill of cognitive flexibility develops throughout life, but it can decrease with age. Children develop cognitive flexibility by playing games that foster creative thinking and problem solving. Adults can develop it further and maintain it with meditation, yoga, creative activities, or simply learning a completely new skill, like speaking a new language proficiently or playing a musical instrument.

"Recognizing and valuing diversity are, by the way, an important driver of cognitive flexibility (Laureiro-Martinez and Brusoni, 2018). Studies have shown that experiential learning can also improve cognitive flexibility. Forcing individuals to make decisions working together with others, who come from different professional and social environments, helps improve cognitive flexibility (Greene, 2014). Furthermore, methods, such as design thinking, provide an approach that pushes individuals to shift from exploration to exploitation multiple times, hence providing an environment in which they can train their cognitive flexibility abilities (Randhawa et al., 2021) and possibly turn them into habits."

"OK, got that. I think I am good at this. I always found a way around obstacles when I had to. I learned that in my childhood. What about empathy?" asked Isabelle.

Eve continued: "*Empathy* is the third cognitive skill that matters in decision-making. The ability to 'put oneself in other people's shoes' can help people manage the exploration-exploitation dilemma since it enables them to take a wider range of perspectives into account, and thus to gain richer information. Empathy refers to an interaction between two people where one experiences and shares the other's emotional or cognitive states, whether positive or negative, in the knowledge that such states are originating from the other person. People who are more empathetic are better at explaining and predicting other people's behavior, since they can form a clearer forecast of someone's future actions if they understand that person more fully. This means empathetic people can perceive and respond better to their environment, are more flexible in social interactions, and make better decisions in social contexts (Laureiro-Martinez, 2022).

"Empathy manifests in two primary ways: affective and cognitive.

"*Affective* empathy refers to sharing another person's emotions or having an emotional reaction to his or her state. It is linked to compassion or sympathy, a feeling of warmth and concern for other people that often leads to being motivated to help them. Those who experience compassion or sympathy in the face of others' emotions tend to be more supportive, comforting, and helpful.

"For an experience to be characterized as empathic, the person experiencing it must be able to differentiate between his or her own emotions and the emotions and states they share with someone else. People who cannot make this distinction tend to experience empathic distress: a strong, self-oriented aversion to the other person's suffering and the desire to withdraw from the situation to protect themselves from negative feelings. For example, if a colleague is struggling to perform because of personal problems, you are likely to feel sympathy and offer to help. However, if you repeatedly see your colleague suffering and you empathize, sharing their feelings and helping with their tasks, this may eventually lead to empathic distress, accompanied by emotional and physical burnout (Laureiro-Martinez, 2022).

"*Cognitive empathy* or 'Theory of Mind' refers to understanding or being able to mentally simulate what another person thinks and feels without experiencing it yourself. The central characteristics of cognitive empathy are reasoning and inferring about other people's thoughts, emotions, and mental states, without actually experiencing them. People who cannot distinguish between their thoughts and mental states and those of other people tend to project their emotional or mental states onto others, or to allow other people's state of mind to influence their self-appraisal (Laureiro-Martinez, 2022)."

"Interesting. My husband Marco is really good at this, and so is Carlo the chairman. I think Marco is better at emotional empathy, while Carlo is better at cognitive empathy. I didn't know that there were two types of empathy," said Isabelle.

"Yes, there are," said Eve. She continued: "The ability to empathize varies among individuals, so someone can be better at one type of empathy than the other. Both abilities are independent and rely primarily on distinct areas of the brain. Two brain networks are activated differentially for cognitive and affective empathy and being better at one type of empathy does not generally contribute to being better at the other (Laureiro-Martinez, 2022)."

"OK, then Marco probably has both. You are describing empathy as a skill. That implies that it can be developed?" asked Isabelle.

"Yes, correct," answered Eve. "Studies have shown that, as with attention control and cognitive flexibility, empathy develops throughout life and grows with experience. You can build empathy by traveling, meeting new people, making new experiences, or learning a new skill, among other things. People also can develop empathy with deliberate practice (Teding van Berkhout and Malouff, 2016), for example, using deep or empathetic listening and 'profiling' others. Life experiences also matter. For example, if you have never experienced vertigo, it's harder to empathize with someone who is terrified of heights. Or, if you survived cancer, you may have more ability to relate to people who are going through treatment."

"Good, good, all three cognitive skills can be developed through practice. . .," said Isabelle, thinking.

"Indeed!" answered Eve. "Continuous practice is useful in developing attention control, cognitive flexibility, and empathy. As with any other cognitive function, such practice helps train the brain. That's why I believe that experiential training, that is, putting individuals in real-life situations and having them practice those skills, has great potential (Haney et al., 2020) in helping executives, in fact, anyone, become better decision-makers."

"Looking at the figure (Figure 11.2), and deep down under the waterline – which I assume means that they are the least conscious – are cognitive-behavioral inclinations. What are those?" asked Isabelle.

Eve continued, "Cognitive-behavioral inclinations – commonly called character, personality, or values – make up the third set of factors that affect the exploration/exploitation balance. These inclinations may include whether someone tends to take risks, be open-minded (Keller and Weibler, 2015), be curious, seek novelty, or focus on learning (Kauppila and Tempelaar, 2016), as well as whether a person thinks about the future rather than the past or present. Having all those inclinations would make someone more likely to favor exploration.

"Your values matter. If integrity, loyalty, or relationships matter to you, they'll play a more important role in decision-making for instance. Also, the image you have about yourself. The person you want to be or become influences your decision-making," said Eve.

The comment made Isabelle think. Her thoughts went back to the situation at home. She wondered whether, as a wife and a mother, she was acting as the person she wanted to be. The thought made her sad, and angry with herself.

Immersed in her thought and emotions, she stopped paying attention to Eve, who continued: "Cognitive-behavioral inclinations are somewhat fixed and hard to change, and yet they also can serve as a guidepost and inspiration for decisions under uncertainty."

At that point, Eve realized that Isabelle wasn't paying attention anymore. "Are you OK, Isabelle?" she asked.

"Yes, yes,. . . I'm sorry. I was thinking about something that bothers me and that I think I must address. You have given me a lot of food for thought today, also about myself and my family," she answered. Looking at her watch, she said that she had to leave now, but she didn't want to do so without summarizing the conversation: "Individual characteristics at three levels of unconsciousness matter for decision-making effectiveness: cognitive states, cognitive adaptive skills, and cognitive and behavioral inclinations, that is, personality and values.

"Cognitive states can be regulated relatively quickly. Any combination of high-quality sleep, taking several short breaks during the day, performing 2–3 hours of vigorous physical activity per week, healthy nutrition, practicing mindfulness, limiting multitasking, and investing in social interactions, improve decision-making quality rapidly.

"Brain training, that is, regular and continuous practice is required to build the cognitive skills – attention control, cognitive flexibility, and empathy – that help improve decision-making quality. It takes more time and effort, but these skills are learnable.

"Changing cognitive and behavioral inclinations – that is, personality, values, and emotional inclinations – is much harder, but they also influence decision-making a lot."

"Wow, as always, a great synthesis, Isabelle! Helpful to me as well. As you must go, I will send you a note about cognitive-behavioral inclinations. We didn't have much time to discuss them, but they are super important. They are your assets, your gifts, your secret when making tough decisions," said Eve as Isabelle stood up, putting on her coat.

Neurotransmitters: The Biology of Exploit-Explore Decisions

Neurotransmitters, the body's chemical messengers, are a relatively new field of study, and a very interesting one. It appears that in future, neurotransmitters may be another factor to consider in improving decision-making, even though many questions are still open.

The process of using neurotransmitters to influence the performance of neurons is called neuromodulation. In this process neurotransmitters diffuse through areas of the nervous system influencing (or "modulating") the activity of neurons in the brain. Neurotransmitters used as neuromodulators in the central nervous system include dopamine (popularly called the "happiness hormone"), serotonin (the "well-being hormone"), histamine, and norepinephrine or noradrenalin (the "stress hormone").

Physicians use drugs that build on neuromodulation to treat diverse forms of mental disorder, such as ADHD (attention deficit hyperactivity disorder), sleep disorder (narcolepsy), depression, or anxiety disorders. However, healthy individuals sometimes take neuromodulating drugs "off-label," not for their original intended use, to "modulate" their mental state and improve their work behaviors and performance. Neuroenhancers, sometimes called "smart drugs" or nootropics, are pharmaceuticals taken, often off-label, to improve memory, learning, focus, attention, and other cognitive skills (Bloomfield and Dale, 2020).

Neuromodulating drugs are starting to creep into the workplace. In the United States, these drugs are believed to touch all professions, from medics to bankers to military personnel. In the United Kingdom, 1 in 12 adults report taking neuro modulating drugs to gain an intellectual edge, according to a 2018 survey. The rising prevalence of neuromodulating drugs among university students is also well documented. In a recent survey, nearly 1 in 5 students at the University of Cambridge said that they had used neuromodulating substances to improve their performance (Sharp, 2018).

Recent research in neuroscience has focused on the role of neurotransmitters on decisions under uncertainty (Addicott et al., 2014). Research suggests that such decisions are influenced by dopamine, acetylcholine, and noradrenaline. Dopamine is known to generate satisfaction, acetylcholine has a calming effect, and noradrenaline reduces pain and improves energy levels (Schacter et al., 2011). Interestingly, these are the very neurotransmitters present in tobacco addiction. Research on tobacco use has shown that addiction modifies the balance of exploration and exploitation in ways that favor exploitation (Addicott et al., 2014). Addiction is, in essence, the persistent exercise of known harmful behaviors, such as smoking.

The concept of harmful exploitation is interesting. It helps explain the proverbial "what got me here, won't get me there" problem, that is, that we sometimes behave in ways that are harmful to us and others, but even though we know we are causing harm, we can't change our behavior. This would be the case, for example, with an executive who has learned to be successful with a directive, authoritarian leadership style, but who simply can't change his or her style when the situation changes, say, after encountering changes in expected behavioral norms when moving to another company or working with new, diverse team members. The executive may recognize that his or her known leadership style doesn't work. Yet he or she may be unable to change it.

Habits, i.e., automatic behaviors, have many good sides. They help us reduce cognitive load and make decisions faster. However, they can also become "addictions" that prevent us from changing behaviors when change is needed.

But these neurotransmitters aren't only involved in the formation of habits. Studies suggest that dopamine may also modulate the process of exploration. For example, Gershman and Tzovaras (2018) found that people with high levels of prefrontal dopamine tend to be impacted by relative uncertainty in their directed exploration strategies. Also, science associates higher levels of striatal dopamine transmission with a reduction in both directed and random exploration behaviors. Dopamine appears to play an important role in assessing uncertainty when making decisions.

Various studies have also investigated the role of dopamine and noradrenaline on different decision-making strategies (Gershman and Tzovaras, 2018; Dubois et al., 2021). There are effects but much research is still needed to clarify the role of neurotransmitters in different brain regions during different forms of exploration.

However, taken together, all these results suggest that neurotransmitters play an important role in modulating decisions under uncertainty.

We lack long-term clinical studies on the use of neurotransmitters, a typical dilemma for diseases in the central nervous system. Long-term clinical studies on the impact of neuromodulators could help us reach a more thorough understanding of how – and under which conditions – science could suggest using neurotransmitters to improve people's performance in ambidextrous decision-making. Future research would profit from pharmacological studies about the use of different agents. Pharmacological manipulation through agents that block receptors allows for a clearer view of causality than investigating the putative dopamine transmission associated with genetic variation. However, researchers must select the pharmacological agents to test carefully in order to target solely the receptors of interest. Alternatively, researchers could work with carefully chosen control groups using different pharmacological agents to single out dopamine's specific contribution.

Further research is needed to determine how neurotransmitters could be used to mediate human behavior in a targeted manner during exploration and exploitation.

Until then, you can turn to some effective, inexpensive alternatives to neuromodulators: give up burgers and pizza, go for a run, and get some good sleep!

Eve's last comment was intriguing, but Isabelle had to leave and thought she might find out what Eve meant talking about cognitive and behavioral inclinations as gifts when reading her note. "Yes, please do so. I am looking forward to reading them," she said. She hugged Eve and left in a rush. On her way to the office, she realized that her thoughts were consumed by the situation at ATG and at home. For a moment, she realized that she could observe her own thoughts and felt surprised about this. . . perhaps this is what Eve had said about attention control and "thinking about thinking," she thought. Could this be what Eve had called metacognition? Somehow, having seen her own concerned thoughts gave Isabelle some momentary peace.

Key Takeaways

- Your cognitive states, cognitive abilities, and personal inclinations influence dramatically the quality of your decisions.
- Cognitive states are influenced among others by sleep, diet, movement and/or exercise, meditation, social connections, and purpose. You can address many of these factors rapidly. Sometimes, even a few nights of quality sleep and some fresh nutritious food can make a difference.
- You can train cognitive abilities – attention control, cognitive flexibility, and empathy. Regularly learning something new and paying attention to others go a long way.
- Your cognitive and behavioral inclinations – personality, values, reactive tendencies – are harder to change, but investing in gaining self-awareness is key. They are important gifts for decision-making under uncertainty.

Chapter 12

Case 6: Making "Tough" Decisions

**Claudio Feser, David Redaschi,
and Karolin Frankenberger**

Isabelle was wondering how to deal with the take-over bid for ATG, while addressing the situation at home.

Isabelle turned to the Decision Navigator methodology to evaluate three of her options, that is: (1) to resign from ATG and focus on immediate issues at home; (2) to reduce her workload through delegation and asking for help to have time to address the issues at home; or (3) to focus solely on work and address family issues later – which might mean never (Figure 12.1).

After long discussions with Marco, Isabelle decided to share her personal situation with her board chairman Carlo and with the members of the GET.

She had never shared vulnerabilities with anyone, but Marco. "Showing weaknesses is dangerous." A lesson she had learned dearly in her childhood. She had learned to look after herself, not to depend on others. But this time she had no choice.

1. Dilemma	Family or career?							

2. Options on the Exploit-Explore continuum — Exploit → Explore

The seven heuristics	Resign and focus on family?		Delegate and ask for help, and spend time addressing family issues?		Focus on work and address family issues later		Option	
	3. Assumptions	4. Facts	3. Assumptions	4. Facts	3. Assumptions	4. Facts	3. Assumptions	4. Facts
a) Objectives	Save the family	T	Save the family Maintain ATG independence/CEO job	T T	Maintain ATG independence/CEO job	T		
b) Opportunities	There are no opportunities to delegate	F	There are opportunities to delegate/ask for help	R	There are no opportunities to delegate	F		
c) Time	Family requires time now	T	Family requires time now	T	Family can wait	F		
d) Competitive actions and stakeholder expectations	n.a.		n.a.		n.a.			
e) Our values and culture	Family is more important than career	R	Both family and career are very important	R	Career is more important than family	F		
f) Our capabilities	Limited capabilities to deal with the situation. No one she can delegate.	F	Others are capable in managing the situation	T	Limited capabilities. She cannot delegate	F		
g) Our "mood" or prevalent collective cognitive states	Pessimistic, very worried	T	Worried but confident she can pull it off	R	Optimistic driven to save ATG	?		

5. Optimization	None
6. Resolution	Option 2

Figure 12.1 Six-step Decision Navigator for Case 5.

To her surprise, but not Marco's, Carlo and her GET colleagues rallied to help her: "Isabelle, we have your back. We will do
whatever it takes to give you the room and space you need. As long
as you don't give up on ATG and our journey!" said Alessandro,
speaking for the GET.

She hadn't expected that. She never trusted anyone, and now
the whole team was trying to help her.

Hugo suggested that he could lead the take-over defense team
operationally for Isabelle and to report daily to her and Carlo.
Alessandro suggested he could help Hugo get the defense team
up and running, and the rest of the GET team members reorgan-
ized their own activities so they could take over commitments and
obligations – internal and external ones – from Isabelle. It was as if
the chairman and her GET colleagues just had put in place a huge
safety net and she could let herself fall.

She felt a sense of warmth and care, something she had only
experienced with Marco and the girls, and – once she thought
about it – with Eve, so far.

Being able to step away from the acquisition battle gave Isabelle the space and time to take care of Marie and her concerns.

At first, Marie rejected Isabelle's efforts to talk to her. All of her
attempts met with instant temper flare-ups and slammed doors.
Isabelle didn't know how to deal with this deterioration of her
relationship with her daughter, and she felt responsible for it. Faced
with the fact that Marie would not sit down with her or let her
into her room, Isabelle asked Marco to fill her in on all she had
missed – with him, with Annelies and with Marie.

She listened, grateful for his understanding, and apologized to
him again for being so absent from the family, both physically and
mentally – even when her body was at home, her attention was
elsewhere. She told him about everything she was setting aside at
ATG to be more available, and more present, realizing as she talked
that they needed some time for just the two of them as well.

Then on Marco's advice, she went back to Marie's closed door
and made an offer: "Marie, honey, would you let me just listen to

you? I want to hear what you're thinking, not to tell you anything. I need to know where you are. . ."

Marie slowly opened the door. She started to say, "Really, Mom, listening — since when?" but when she saw her mother's pained, pale face, she relented. "OK, Mom, then let's talk."

On Marco's advice, Isabelle tried hard to do as she had promised: not talk or argue, but simply to listen and try to understand what Marie was feeling and why. It was clear that while sustainability was the starting point of Marie's trouble with Isabelle's company, the teen's personal concerns ran deeper. She had problems with her boyfriend, and no one to talk to about them.

When Marie was younger, Isabelle was more than just her mother. Isabelle was Marie's best friend. They could talk about anything, laugh together, and hug often. Marie missed both her mom and her best friend. She was fond of Annelies, when her baby sister wasn't being a tennis diva, and Marco was always there to take care of both, but he was not their mother.

Isabelle also missed Marie. Her job took up so much of her time that she had lost her inner sense of balance. Most nights she slept little and poorly, she ate irregularly and unhealthily, and she had just about stopped running. ATG often absorbed all her thoughts, and she was often tired and testy. She rarely relaxed. She had lost a lot of her connection with her two daughters and somehow with her husband. She longed to rekindle their romance and connection beyond just being commiserating parents.

On Sunday, Marie and Isabelle talked all afternoon about everything. About Marie's boyfriend ("that skunk," Isabelle thought), about Isabelle's job — the challenges she had to face and the pressure she was under — all the things they hadn't talked about for months. They even talked about ATG's business model — about the role of travel in bringing people closer together and opening up perspectives, about Marie's ideas about sustainability, including offering only CO_2-compensated flights, and about ecotourism. When Isabelle wondered aloud if ATG could introduce that as a possible theme for special travel experiences, Marie lit up.

It was the most beautiful afternoon Isabelle had experienced in a long time. She felt reconnected with Marie. They could finally hug and express how much they loved each other. Before they stopped to make pasta primavera for supper – cooking together again at last – they resolved to spend more time together. To start, they arranged to go for a regular Sunday morning jog, followed by breakfast, so they could talk about whatever was on their minds.

Isabelle also made fresh plans with Marco for a regular date night dinner on Wednesdays in town, and resolved to stop working nights and weekends, permanently. She promised Annelies a tennis match every Saturday after Annelies told her with great excitement that her school team was starting to compete across the canton. Annelies outlined her dream: that her tennis skill might eventually earn her a college scholarship in California. As she gazed at her exhilarated 15-year-old, Isabelle could hardly imagine having her daughter live so far away, but she clearly saw Marco's imagination and her own ambition reflected in Annelies' hopes.

And, finally, she also resolved to get healthy again: more sleep, more sports, and regular, nutritious meals. After a couple of months of sticking to that plan, workingout three days a week and getting some rest and recreation – including a romantic week in Tuscany with Marco – Isabelle went back to work, but on a more balanced schedule and with a far more balanced perspective.

She held a few long conversations with individual GET members, and with their encouragement, she asked Kosta to draft a strategy proposal centered around Marie's ideas about ecotourism, including sustainable travel and CO^2-compensated flights. When the full GET saw the proposal, it won their unanimous support, and they decided to put sustainable practices into immediate action. CO_2-compensated travel and the theme of ecotourism became ATG's unique selling points in the following years.

As Isabelle prepared to reengage operationally on the take-over bid – where Hugo had everything in order, as promised – the hostile bidder abruptly withdrew the offer. The bidding company's management and the board of directors had not consulted with its main shareholders, who reacted very angrily to the submission of their hostile, overpriced take-over bid, which offered a 40% premium for control of ATG. The bidder's CEO was forced to resign the following month, and several board members found themselves replaced.

However, the work that Hugo, Carlo, ATG's board, the GET members and the staff did to prepare a defense against the hostile take-over bid proved to be time well spent. It deepened the relationship between the board and the GET, spread more information deeper into ATG's staff ranks, and created a sense of corporate unity.

Isabelle felt emotionally connected with the chairman and her GET colleagues. It was a new emotion she had not experienced before, outside of her family: to be part of something bigger than herself.

An Unexpected Challenge

As she got back to work full-time – but no more nights and weekends – Isabelle looked into how ATG's international expansion was going more than 18 months into its efforts in North America and Asia. After carefully weighing the pros and cons, the GET had decided to go ahead with the US expansion and to conduct a pilot project in Asia, focused on Asia. But a year and a half in, it looked as if the Asia pilot had been the wrong decision.

For the first 12 months, the expansion efforts appeared successful. But then the expansion slowed, though it kept consuming more funds than originally calculated. When ATG published its first-quarter numbers, which made its difficulties in Asia obvious, the share price fell. ATG's business in Asia didn't materially affect the bottom line, but many analysts saw Asia as a very important future travel market, and the expectations embedded in ATG's share price implied a successful expansion into Asia.

Several analysts expressed doubts about the expansion efforts. Critics said that ATG had overestimated the capabilities of its local leaders in Asia and underestimated the challenges and costs of its

China venture. Analysts raised fears that the company's European model could not be transferred one-on-one to Asia, because customers' behavior was so different. Asian travel clients were younger, less interested in experiences, and more interested in low prices and standard greatest-hits tour offerings.

To make matters worse, and to Isabelle's disappointment, authorities in Guangdong were investigating one of Thomas's Asian team members for corruption. They alleged that he had bribed local authorities to speed up the launch of ATG's agency in the city.

Isabelle turned to the GET for an explanation. Neither Hugo, from a finance perspective, nor Frank, who ran foreign sales, nor Alessandro speaking for operations, nor anyone else could explain transparently what problems beset the Asia expansion, though they were all glad to report on why the expansion in America was going well. It was simply not clear why Asia was consuming so many resources. Isabelle sent Thomas an urgent message to call her directly, fearing that his staff member's possible bribery scandal was just the tip of the iceberg, and that the problem could be much bigger. If the bribery allegations were true, his employee had tarnished ATG's reputation.

And well before ATG's internal investigation could bear fruit, analysts began downgrading the stock. The situation was very chaotic. Isabelle was under great pressure. Clinging to her new resolve not to let ATG's problems – or the need to make a lot of decisions without enough information and with ongoing uncertainty – sabotage her overall well-being, she knew she needed to get to the bottom of the situation in China. The relevant GET members had to take accountability for providing full information on the Asia expansion, and fast.

While she was still waiting to hear from Thomas – and she'd put Frank on urgent notice to facilitate that conversation – she received a call from a major shareholder. James "Big Hat Jack" Foster, head of a Texas-based fund known for its values-oriented business and investment practices, expressed great concern about the Asia situation. He demanded an explanation of the corruption allegations, and a quick, forceful response from Isabelle.

"I don't want to add to your pressures, Mrs. Dubois," he said, doubling her stress and speaking with exaggerated slowness – while ignoring the fact that they had been on a first-name basis for years. "But you have 24 hours to find out what is going on here and fix it pronto, or we have to rethink – or maybe withdraw – our investment in ATG."

"You know I'm on it, Jack," she answered calmly. "But with the time differences and the complexity in front of me, 24 hours is a lot to promise. It's already evening here."

"It's only Wednesday morning in Texas," he said, his voice softening nearly imperceptibly. "Isabelle, no fooling, I expect a solution from you by Friday morning. I can give you a full business day, but that's it. And that's not just my deadline – I'm a horse with tight reins: it's coming from my board."

To make matters worse, members of ATG's board were sending very mixed signals to Isabelle and the GET. Some board members were very committed to the China expansion and didn't seem to be bothered about the Guangdong issue. They encouraged Isabelle to press ahead with the program. Other members – including Carlo, the chairman – urged her to stop the expansion and get a handle on the corruption accusations ASAP.

Conny, who abhorred any whiff of alleged misbehavior, and Alison, who was trying to get to the bottom of what happened with Thomas's staffer, wanted to terminate Thomas's contract with ATG, or at least to put him on leave during the investigation. He was responsible for this mess and was simply not in control of the situation. Terminating him would also send a strong, decisive signal to the ATG's board, the markets, and the public, not to mention Big Hat Jack, and would give CFO Hugo and his team time to conduct a more thorough review of the financial flows. Someone on the board suggested having Hugo fly to China to take over the Asian business during the investigation.

The situation was confusing. The US fund deadline was looming. As if that were not enough, the media network "Money Switzerland" asked Isabelle for an interview, or at least for a public statement on the allegations. Isabelle felt that such a statement or interview might be a good way to set the record straight, reassure investors, and regain control of the situation. Open and honest communication could only help, she thought. But she hadn't yet come up with the right thing to say – and neither had Conny's public relations team – or the right action plan to present. She just didn't have enough information.

And the clock was ticking. . .

Questions for Reflection

How can Isabelle reconcile the different and diverging expectations – from investors, different camps on the board, and the public, among others? And how can she protect ATG's reputation. . .

Should Isabelle:

- Follow the advice of the GET and separate from Thomas immediately to send an immediate signal?
- Put Thomas on leave?
- Send Hugo to oversee the Asia operations for the duration of the investigations?
- Wait until all the facts are on the table and only then decide, thus risk alienating a powerful US shareholder?
- Do something else, and, if so, what?

You may want to write down your answer before continuing.

Chapter 13

Preparing to Be Wrong

Claudio Feser, Daniella Laureiro-Martinez, and Stefano Brusoni

To know thyself is the beginning of all wisdom.

—Aristotle

As Isabelle was reflecting on how to address the situation, she remembered Eve's comment about cognitive-behavioral inclinations being gifts, the secret sauce when making tough decisions. She remembered the second note that Eve had shared with her. She remembered reading it and wondered whether there could be some help in there.

She pulled it out of her files and started reading it anew.

To: Isabelle

From: Eve

Subject: note 2 – Know Thyself

Dear Isabelle,

As promised, here comes my second note, as we didn't have time to discuss cognitive and behavioral inclinations in detail last week.

Many of our decisions to optimize the exploit-explore balance are driven by cognitive-behavioral inclinations. Some people may value tradition; they might be conservative, conscientious, and risk-averse, and therefore favor exploitation when optimizing the exploit-explore balance. Others may be more open-minded, curious, and risk-oriented, and they might favor exploration.

Everyone's cognitive-behavioral inclinations consist of a combination of cognitive and behavioral strategies that are determined genetically or developed mostly in early childhood. They are largely unconscious (Kets de Vries, 2006).

In my research, I use three lenses to unearth and better understand these cognitive-behavioral inclinations: personality, values, and reactive emotional tendencies. These concepts are not always distinctive. They don't exist in isolation. For instance, values are emotionally loaded.

These three concepts do offer three, simple, non-mutually exclusive lenses through which we can hypothesize about our own and other people's cognitive and behavioral inclinations. Let's review the three lenses in turn.

Personality

Personality theories are the mainstream approach to understanding cognitive-behavioral inclinations. These theories focus on explaining behaviors that individuals exhibit consistently over time. They predict how humans will react to other people, as well as to stress, crises, and problems (Winne and Gittinger, 1973).

The study of personality probably started with Hippo-crates' ancient "Four Humours" theory. The theory postu-lated that an individual's character or personality was based on the balance of four bodily humors: yellow bile, black bile, phlegm, and blood. In more modern times, over the last 100 years, psychologists have extensively explored the concept of personality. As a result, they developed a myriad of different tools and frameworks to describe it. The most popular include the Myers-Briggs' MBTI and The Big Five personality framework, sometimes described with the acronym OCEAN, which stands for Openness, Consci-entiousness, Extroversion, Agreeableness and Neuroticism (McCrae and John, 1992).

I use another tool, a newer one: the *Temperament and Char-acter Inventory* (TCI). It is an inventory of personality traits (Cloninger et al., 2016). TCI examines seven dimensions of personality. Four are called "temperaments" and three are called "character traits."

Research suggests that temperament is largely fixed, that is, genetically determined. Temperament influences auto-matic, unconscious behavioral responses (Figure 13.1). It has four dimensions that are believed to be visible from the early childhood (Bajraktarov et al., 2017). They are:

- Novelty Seeking (NS): NS is a system of behaviors asso-ciated with activation. It is characterized by a tendency toward enthusiasm, excitement, curiosity, and impulsive-ness. The sub-dimensions of NS are exploratory excit-ability, impulsiveness, extravagance, and disorderliness.
- Harm Avoidance (HA): HA is a system of behaviors associated with inhibition. HA is also associated with cautiousness, tension, irritability, and pessimism. Its sub-dimensions are anticipatory worry, fear of uncertainty, shyness, and fatigability.

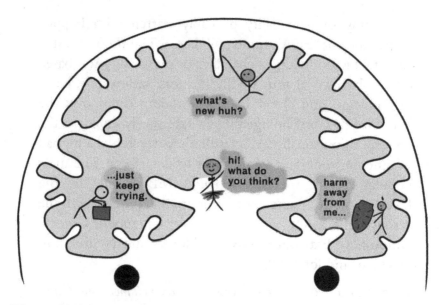

Figure 13.1 Know thy temperament.

- Reward Dependence (RD): RD is a system of behaviors connected to sensitivity for warmth, sensibility, dependence, and conviviality. Sentimentality, openness to warm communication, attachment, and dependence are its sub-divisions.
- Persistence (PS): PS is a system of active behavior despite fatigue and frustration. The sub-dimensions of PS are eagerness of effort, as well as being work-hardened, ambitious, and perfectionistic.

Character's three dimensions are determined more by environment and social factors than by genes. They are (Bajraktarov et al., 2017):

- Self-Directedness (SD): SD refers to the extent to which an individual can define his/her own identity autonomously and is able to solve situations based on his or her goals and values. The sub-dimensions of SD

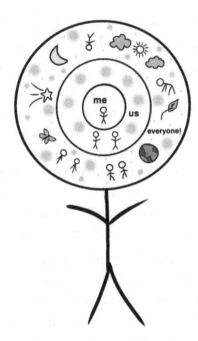

Figure 13.2 Know thy character.

are responsibility, purposefulness, resourcefulness, and self-acceptance.

- Cooperativeness (CO): CO indicates the extent to which individuals are dependent on others in defining their own identity. The sub-dimensions of CO are social acceptance, empathy, compassion, helpfulness, and pure-hearted conscience.
- Self-Transcendence (ST): ST corresponds to how a person identifies with a sense of unity of all the things in the world. The sub-dimensions of ST are self-forgetful, transpersonal, identification, and spiritual acceptance.

Values

Values provide each person with an internal signpost of what is good, desirable, important, and valuable. They reflect a person's perception of what's "right," of what is "important," or what "ought" to be.

Although values relate to norms, they are more abstract and general. Norms regulate behavior in specific situations, while values define what you judge as good or bad. For instance, not interrupting others while they are talking, that is, letting them finish their sentences is a norm, but it reflects the value of respect. Or, putting a dirty mug into the dishwasher at work may be a normative behavior in some companies, but it may reflect the value of cleanliness and respect for your co-workers.

Individuals form and change their values over time. Generally, people shape the "bulk" of their values during three significant periods (Massey, 1973): the imprint period (from birth to age seven), the modeling period (from ages 8 to 13), and the socialization period (from 13 to 21). The culture you operate in may further shape how your values develop.

Values have a strong influence on behavioral tendencies (Rokeach, 1973). For example, say that a man who values diversity goes to work for an organization that treats specific groups, such as minorities, much worse than other employees. He may come to believe that the behaviors he observes in the company are unethical. He may be less committed at work, which may undermine the quality of his work, or he might leave the company altogether. It is likely that if the company had implemented its diversity policies, his attitudes would remain more positive, and he would perform better.

Some values are physiologically determined. People normally consider these values objective. They include values such avoiding physical pain, striving for pleasure, or even striving for survival. Other values are seen as subjective.

They vary among individuals, organizations, and cultures. There are many types of subjective values – moral, ideological (religious, political), social, and so on.

Reactive Emotional Reactions

Over the last 30 years, scientific advances in neuroscience have created significant interest in the science of emotions. Emotions such as joy, fear, anger, and sadness are universal and, interestingly, valid across cultures. For instance, when confronted with danger, people in San Francisco experience the same emotion of fear as people in Tokyo or Kinshasa (Ekman, 2007).

Emotions are believed to be a result of evolution. Charles Darwin believed that many animals, especially mammals, experience emotions in a way that is similar to humans. Emotions serve many purposes. They help us remember, communicate, and connect. They also serve an evolutionary purpose: to aid survival. For instance, sadness is a cry for help; it imposes one person's suffering on others so they will help or come to the rescue. Fear may make you freeze (hide) or flee, and thus protect you from danger. And anger may provide you with the strength and energy to fight someone or something that you perceive as attacking or endangering you (Ekman, 2007).

Emotions play an important role in regulating human behavior. Science widely recognizes that emotions modulate much of our daily decision-making behavior. As we have seen in our discussion on the neuroscientific foundations of decision-making, this happens often in an unconscious way. This is particularly true in situations of tiredness, stress, and pressure – when the amygdala is aroused, and the neocortex is less active. This is when people tend to act less rationally, since their "emotions take over" (Feser, 2011).

For our purposes, we are interested in how emotions influence cognitive-behavioral inclinations, or habitual cognitive processes and behaviors, within the concept of emotional dispositions or reactive tendencies. The concept postulates that – while we all share the same emotions – different people have different tendencies or inclinations when it comes to reacting to their emotions (Davidson, 2012). For instance, some people are more likely to get active under stress, while others may tend to withdraw and become passive.

I use the concept of *Reactive Emotional Tendencies*. This concept originates in the work of the clinical psychologist Karen Horney, who identified coping strategies as reactive patterns on the part of individuals who are exposed to challenges and situations that arouse strong emotions.

Reactive tendencies describe habitual behavior in situation of stress and pressure, for instance. They play a central role in regulating leadership behaviors and decision-making behaviors. Building on Horney's research, Anderson and Adams (2015) identified three main reactive tendencies: Controlling, Protecting, Complying.

We describe them in turn:

- *Controlling*: The Controlling dimension measures the extent to which someone reacts to the emotions provoked by setbacks or challenges with behaviors associated task accomplishment, personal achievement, power, and control (Anderson and Adams, 2015). The behavioral inclinations associated with Controlling include competing; setting exacting standards; striving for perfection; using authority to take charge, exercise influence, and get your own way; exerting tremendous effort and energy to achieve goals; speaking directly and bluntly; pushing yourself and others to win; and taking charge in most situations (Anderson and Adams, 2015).

People with strong controlling tendencies are often perceived by others as being upset, irritated, or angry.

- *Protecting*: This dimension measures the extent to which someone reacts to emotions with behaviors associated with withdrawal, remaining distant, hidden, aloof, cynical, superior, and/or rational (Anderson and Adams, 2015). The behavioral inclinations associated with Protecting include holding back and seeing how situations unfold; identifying what is wrong, illogical, or insufficiently planned; seeing the flaws in other people's thinking, speaking, and actions; and analyzing what is right and what is wrong (Anderson and Adams, 2015). People with strong protecting tendencies are often perceived by others as being frustrated, lonely, disappointed, distant, or sad.

- *Complying*: This dimension measures the extent to which people react to emotions with behaviors that comply with others' expectations rather than acting on their own intentions (Anderson and Adams, 2015). The behavioral inclinations associated with Complying include cautiously managing what you do to stay in others' good graces; being a "do-gooder;" saying "yes" when you may really want to say "no;" calibrating the emotional climate in meetings to see if it is safe to speak; double-checking with authorities before acting; and couching what you say so others will not have a strong emotional response (Anderson and Adams, 2015). People with strong complying tendencies are often perceived by others as being concerned, worrisome, anxious, or alarmed.

Leveraging Cognitive-Behavioral Inclinations

Cognitive-behavioral inclinations are dispositional, that is, mostly genetically determined and developed in early childhood. You can change them, but it takes significant effort and time, and the changes are typically limited.

Given that individuals may systematically over-exploit or over-explore, does this mean that some people just can't be Super Deciders?

No, it doesn't.

A person is not an island. Humans are social creatures who have naturally altruistic, collaborative inclinations (Fehr and Gächter, 2000). When collaborating with others, someone can complement their own deficiencies, but they can also contribute their own gifts and unique characteristics, if they have figured out what those might be. This is knowledge you need.

But let me highlight another aspect relating to cognitive-behavioral inclinations, and that is their role in what I call "tough decisions." The Decision Navigator model creates an approach to decision-making that transforms high stakes "either-or" decisions into step-by-step approaches of developing options, testing assumptions, and refining decisions. It is an experimentation-based, learning-oriented, adaptive, and flexible approach that not only improves the quality of decisions, but it also reduces the risk of making the wrong decision. However, there are situations when multiple alternative options do not exist, or when hypotheses cannot be tested, either because it is too expensive to do so, or because there is no time. Though decisions are decisions that are high risk, there is a real possibility that the decision-maker will be badly wrong.

That's when cognitive-behavioral inclinations come to play, that's when you take decisions based on your values. When making tough decisions, it is important to know what you stand for. If you end up being wrong, at least you are being truthful to yourself and to what you stand for.

When making tough decisions, it is important to know what you stand for. If you end up being wrong, at least you are being truthful to yourself and to what you stand for.

The implication of all of this is "Know Thyself." Know Thyself was a maxim found on the ancient Temple of Apollo in Delphi, in Greece. Over time, various writers and researchers have attributed a different meaning to this maxim, but today it is used as a statement of the need to know yourself.

Knowing yourself means knowing your gifts and dispositional inclinations and using them – not only to work more effectively in teams – but also to make tough decisions, decisions that can't be made with the help of the Decision Navigator.

By now, you know me. I get carried away when talking about this. Please let me (for once) summarize.

Many of our decisions under uncertainty are driven by cognitive-behavioral inclinations. Everyone's cognitive-behavioral inclinations consist of a combination of cognitive and behavioral strategies that are determined genetically or developed mostly in early childhood. They are mostly unconscious.

I use three lenses to unearth and better understand these cognitive-behavioral inclinations: personality, values, and reactive emotional tendencies. These concepts are not always distinctive. They don't exist in isolation. For instance, values are emotionally loaded.

Cognitive-behavioral inclinations are dispositional. You can change them, but it takes significant effort and time, and the changes are typically limited. A more effective approach is to collaborate. When collaborating with others, someone can complement their own deficiencies, but they can also contribute their own gifts and unique characteristics, if they have figured out what those might be. Cognitive-behavioral disposition are also the "go-to factor" when it comes to making tough decisions, decisions where the Decision Navigator is of little use, because the options space is limited or there is no way to test your assumptions.

Knowing yourself means knowing your gifts and how you can leverage your gifts when working with others and when making decisions.

I hope this is helpful.

Warm regards,

Eve

PS I am looking forward to seeing you and finally meeting your family at my wedding. It is going to be great (Swiss weather permitting. . .!)

Isabelle's Reflection on Herself

The note was indeed helpful. It made her think. She started reflecting about herself. Who was she? Who was Isabelle, not the CEO, but the person? What did she stand for?

She reflected on her personality. She was persistent, no doubt. Hard-working, ambitious, and perfectionistic. And she was self-directed. She believed in her ability to solve tough situations based on her goals. That's what she learned to do to survive her childhood.

She cared a lot about others, especially for her family, about success, about hard work, about honesty, about being truthful, and about fairness.

And when it came to emotions, she saw herself clearly having controlling tendencies. She was and had always been ambitious and courageous. She set high expectations, always striving for perfection, always taking risks to win. She was used to taking charge in critical situations, to push herself and others to win. Importantly, under stress, she often felt energized but also irritated or angry.

At first, she didn't exactly like the picture that emerged from her reflection. But then Eve's phrase that she should contribute her gifts, her secret, struck a chord, an important chord, as Isabelle was about to find out.

Key Takeaways

- Sometimes you need to make "tough decisions," "either-or" decisions where it is not possible to widen the option space, or even to test assumptions.
- That's when knowing what you stand for, your values, matters. When deciding based on your values, you are prepared to be wrong. Even if wrong, your decision was the "right thing to do."

Part Five

CONCLUSIONS

Chapter 14

Epilogue

Claudio Feser, David Redaschi, and Karolin Frankenberger

Isabelle faced a difficult situation. Although not a "people pleaser" by nature, she wanted to make sure she met all her various stakeholders' expectations perfectly.

But meeting all expectations is not always possible – and she was trying to please several different, demanding audiences.

Isabelle recalled a lecture on leadership that she attended as part of her Advanced Management Program at Harvard. In the course, Professor Robert Kegan, an author and developmental psychologist, had explained the concept of cognitive complexity. She recalled his statement that leaders get bogged down if they try to meet every demand, including those that conflict. But Kegan also suggested a way out. "Try to meet as many [demands] as you can, but ultimately listen to your own values and inner compass. Leadership is not about making everyone happy. It is about being authentic, using values when making decisions."

She made the connection to the second note Eve had sent. "That's it! My personality, my values, and my emotions are my gifts!" she thought. And she decided to use her gifts.

She knew that it wasn't fair to dismiss Thomas based only on a hypothesis and without any facts. Nor was it fair to fire him just to meet other people's expectations, including board members, investors, and GET members. It took courage, but correctly, at that moment, she pressed the pause button so she could quickly but thoroughly analyze ATG's situation in order to proceed ultimately based on facts. But she also knew that it was her duty to decide, together with the board of directors, and to communicate her decision honestly and transparently.

She called Big Hat Jack, head of the Texas investment fund, and explained the situation. She acknowledged the problem and told him that ATG had immediately started an investigation. She promised that once she had the results, she and ATG's other leaders would decide what to do according to the firm's values and principles. She promised to keep him informed, but she made it clear that one of her values was to be truthful and not to judge on opinions but on facts. Jack listened. He wasn't pleased, but he dropped his bombastic façade and gave her some breathing room. "I hear you, Isabelle," he said, "I'm not happy, you know, but I trust you. We have a lot of money at stake, so figure this out fast."

She took a similar path with the press. She politely declined interviews but promised to follow a principled, values-based approach to informing the public as quickly as possible.

Finally, she asked the board for more time so that Hugo could work through the problems with the Asian team and ATG's meticulous compliance officer Lukas Berney.

Lukas's thorough investigation confirmed that Thomas's staffer in Guangdong had not done anything dishonest. He had behaved properly, but he'd done a poor job of communicating his actions. Furthermore, although the expansion in China required more resources than expected, as Hugo and Thomas predicted, over time its earnings and revenue growth also exceeded forecasts. China became one of ATG's most important, successful markets.

Isabelle's principled and courageous approach to this situation inspired many of those around her: the shareholders, the board of directors, the GET, the entire management team, ATG's investors, the staff in China – and her family.

She also acknowledged a new emotion: she was proud of herself. She felt proud not of what she had outwardly accomplished – since she was accustomed to high achievement – but of her courage and commitment to stick to principles, to her values. She had found her gifts, who she really was and what she stood for.

She felt a deep sense of accomplishment. It wasn't about her accomplishments as a CEO. It was about the feeling of finally being part of the something bigger at ATG, about having regained her family, about having found her little sister Eve, and importantly about having connected to herself.

Inner Peace

Eve's wedding took place in early summer at *Villa Honegg*, a small hotel overseeing Lake Lucerne in Switzerland. The weather was gorgeous, as was the bride. Eve was wearing a beautiful, white, lace wedding dress.

The ceremony took place outdoors on the large terrace of the hotel. It was hot, but the light evening breeze made it just perfect. There were about sixty guests. Besides many friends of Eve and Raul, mostly university colleagues, and Raul's family (Eve had lost her parents when she was 8 years old), Isabelle, Marco, Marie, and Annelies attended the ceremony.

Isabelle was part of the ceremony. Eve had asked Isabelle to be her bridesmaid, a role that she accepted with great honor. She felt honored to be such an important person in Eve's life.

After the ceremony Eve and Raul posed for photos with the photographer, while Isabelle's family mingled with the guests.

Isabelle stood by herself sipping a glass of champagne and enjoying the majestic view of the Alps with their peaks still covered in snow and of the deep blue lake of Lucerne that seemed to be lying at her feet. She reflected on her journey. She felt a deep sense of satisfaction, joy, and peace. For the first time in her life, she felt at peace with the world, with others, and with herself. And she felt that she was no longer alone. She felt connected with Marco, with Marie and Annelies, with Eve, with Carlo and her colleagues at ATG, and importantly with herself.

Eve walked up to her, saying, "What are you doing?"

That's when she noticed that Isabelle was crying.

They hugged.

Chapter 15

Conclusions

**Claudio Feser, Daniella Laureiro-Martinez,
Karolin Frankenberger, and Stefano Brusoni**

This book has summarized advances in management, psychology, and neuroscience in relation to making decisions in dynamic and uncertain situations. And, given that knowledge, it proposes a model for effectively making difficult, high-stakes decision in practice.

The Decision Navigator is a six-steps model of making decisions under uncertainty: identifying the Dilemma (the "either-or" solutions of a problem), widening the Option space, identifying exploit-explore assumptions under which the options are valid, validating the assumptions with facts (Testing), Optimizing the options, and Resolution. The Decision Navigator creates a path for identifying and thinking through multiple options for decision-making, it unearths unconscious assumptions, and it enables fact-based, and optimized decisions.

Applying the model requires you to pause, take time, and put in effort. But the investment of time and attention in mastering the

Decision Navigator model is well worth it. Think of the time and energy it takes to undo a wrong decision, if that is even possible.

The book also describes an approach to managing tensions created by decisions under uncertainty in organizations. The approach – which goes beyond traditional strategy implementation and change management models – is built on strengthening top teams, separating distinct activities, and engaging the members of your organization.

Further, the book stresses the importance of diverse and well-functioning teams both for making decisions and for managing the organizational tensions that decisions under uncertainty produce.

Finally, it identifies the key factors – cognitive states, cognitive skills, and cognitive-behavioral inclinations – that drive individual decision-making performance. Some of these factors can be positively influenced quickly, some require time and practice to master, and some are hard to change. But each one matters, so we've suggested ways you can build on them.

What are the implications of these findings for individuals and organizations?

Implications for Individual Decision-Makers

There are five implications for individuals:

1. Put yourself at the center, to be in the best state to then think and care about others. A healthy diet, sufficient exercise and sleep, time off, meditation, and good relationships are inexpensive ways to ensure better decision-making.

2. Get to know yourself. Introspection and reflection – sometimes with help of a partner, a friend, or a coach – can help improve your understanding of yourself and how to contribute to others. They foster authenticity, collaboration, better decisions, and better leadership.

3. Don't make important decisions alone. Working in teams and debating decisions improve them.

4. Keep a learning mindset and aim for learning new stuff every day. Learning something new, like a fresh skill or a language; participating in new experiences; meeting new people; and most importantly, listening carefully and with an open mind are just a few of the continual activities you can undertake to improve your cognitive abilities.

5. Practice using the Decision Navigator. The Decision Navigator is a research-based approach to decision-making. Applying it proficiently and efficiently requires practice, but doing so will make identifying dilemmas, options, and assumptions straightforward and it will sharpen your critical thinking.

> Don't make important decisions alone, take care of yourself, learn new stuff, get to know yourself, and practice decision-making.

Implications for Organizations

There are also five implications for organizations.

First, create engaging and mentally safe work environments. Cognitive states – feeling safe, connected, engaged, focused – matter at work. It matters for people to have the right conditions to make effective decisions. Employees who aren't getting what they expect from their organizations, who may be disengaged, frustrated, or angry may share their negativity with other people, emotionally infecting them, and bringing down morale in the workplace. Emotions are contagious.

Unfortunately, nowadays most people are not engaged at work. A recent Gallup survey of roughly 67,000 people in the United States found that only 32% of employees are engaged with their work. Gallup measured employees' engagement based on a series of questions such as: Does the employee understand what is expected of them at work? Do their opinions seem to count? Do they have opportunities to do what they do best? Do they have a best friend at work? (Hsu, 2023).

American Gen Zers and young millennials, in particular, are not engaged at work. Those under 35 say that they don't feel cared for or heard in their jobs. Few Gen Zers and young millennials say that they have someone at work who encourages their development. They also find few opportunities to learn and grow (Hsu, 2023). Many US employees across all tenure groups report not feeling connected to their organization's mission or purpose. Also, only about one-quarter of US employees surveyed say that their company cares about their overall well-being (Hsu, 2023).

The situation may be even worse in Europe, where engagement is typically lower than in the United States (Bakos and Jolton, 2022). Interventions that organizations may consider to address these issues include measuring engagement and mental health, making employee engagement and mental health KPIs part of the evaluation of people's leaders, and offering mental health and coaching support, among others.

Second, experiment with cognitive skills training. Organizations can experiment providing more cognitive skills training, broadly, but particularly to employees in positions that require careful decision-making – that is, executives. Despite the continuous and widespread discussion of the need for "21st-century skills," most organizations do not provide the necessary training. In a recent career development survey, only 20% of participants said that their employer was providing training in necessary skills. And, when such skills training was provided, it focused mostly on communication and teamwork (Slocum and Hora, 2020). Another survey of 28,000 US business leaders shows that most organizations focus their leadership development programs on only three areas: coaching skills, communication, and employee engagement (Westfall, 2019).

Even though – due to their experiential nature – organizations are a perfect locus for training the cognitive skills of attention control, cognitive flexibility, and empathy, executive development training programs almost never cover these skills.

That said, there is currently only limited empirical research on doing such training at work. However, there is a large body of "gray literature" in these areas of training, that is, non-peer-reviewed articles and reports written by practitioners (Slocum and Hora, 2020). Empirical research that validates the relevant findings of this gray literature and leverages the extensive experience of professional groups that focus on workplace training could improve the understanding of approaches to cognitive skills training and its impact on decision-making quality and company performance. Experiments could elucidate the long-term effects of targeted skill-building interventions in the workplace. Such research could also motivate more organizations to allocate resources to this important area.

Third, ensure cognitive and behavioral diversity in the senior executive team. The value of diversity is undisputed. Diverse teams and people who value diversity can "see" more options, more innovative possible courses of action, particularly when they face complex problems (Laureiro-Martinez and Brusoni, 2018).

The composition of teams often reflects diverse experiences, thus providing so-called "low-level" diversity, but not psychological or so-called "deep-level" diversity (Schoss et al., 2022). When boards and senior organizational leaders assemble top teams, they would be well served to include an assessment of candidates' cognitive-behavioral inclinations – personality, values, reactive tendencies – and to put more emphasis on ensuring that executive teams include people who represent diverse cognitive-behavioral tendencies. This is especially important in achieving better decision-making, particularly amid uncertainty.

Fourth, use cognitive skills and cognitive-behavioral inclinations as criteria for recruitment and advancement. Skills and cognitive and behavioral inclinations influence the optimization of the exploit-explore balance, but, unlike cognitive states, developing these assets takes time. The requirements of leadership positions differ. Some leadership positions focus on more operational improvement-oriented activities, such as, for instance, running a sales organization that focuses many employees on short-term performance. The most effective individual for such a position might be preferably high in conscientiousness. Some other positions may have a more innovation-oriented focus, for instance, strategic planning or business development. The best leaders for those positions might be those who have strong novelty-seeking characteristics and strong attention control capabilities. Organizations can use assessments of cognitive skills and cognitive-behavioral inclinations as part of recruiting and promoting candidates into positions that require careful decision-making.

Fifth, train executives in using the Decision Navigator and embed it in the performance management system. Results from surveys by the Chief Learning Officer Business Intelligence Board suggest that nearly 95% of organizations plan either to increase or to maintain their current investment in leadership development, a US$366 billion global industry (Westfall, 2019). Even so, most programs don't achieve the desired results (Gurdjian et al., 2014; Feser et al., 2018) since they often fail to embed themselves in the organization's fabric – in its performance management system and corporate culture. As noted, work organizations are the perfect locus for developing the cognitive states, cognitive skills, and cognitive-behavioral inclinations, and for practicing a structured approach of decision-making under uncertainty. High-performance organizations that build on ambitious objectives ("more exploration"), clear accountability, transparency of performance, role modeling and the support of leaders, mentors, and coaches (Kegan et al., 2014) seem ideal for the application of the outlined model of decision-making.

Organizations can improve decision-making by promoting cognitive health, by experimenting with cognitive skills training, and by ensuring not only gender but also cognitive diversity in teams. Furthermore, they can improve decision-making by using both factors that drive decision-making quality, and decision quality itself, in recruitment, performance management, and advancement decisions.

Research by Kegan and Lahey (2016) on creating deliberately developmental organizations seems particularly relevant to us here.

The Big Open Question: AI

What areas of technology and knowledge development may lead to new findings that could help the evolution of how humans make decisions? One area is at the forefront of the discussion: AI.

As we are writing this book, the use of ChatGPT is being discussed intensely in public and academic circles, and a fierce debate has broken out between optimists and pessimists.

Some argue that AI may worsen our ability to make sound decisions. Historian Yuval Noah Harari, for instance, argues that AI's performance in generating reality by manipulating words, sounds, or images could trick us into making poorly informed political decisions and thus undermine democracy. (*The Economist*, 2023). One example of generated reality are deepfakes. In June 2022, several mayors of European capitals were misled by a deepfake of their counterpart Vitali Klitschko, the mayor of Kyiv. The deepfake Klitschko tried to convince Western European politicians that supporting Ukraine and hence a prolonged war would lead to more immigration and criminality in Western Europe.

Some others even argue that artificial intelligence can replace human judgment and decision-making altogether. They cite that this has been already partly done quite successfully in a number of areas, such as identifying and prioritizing restaurants for health inspections, or identifying teenagers at highest risk for committing a crime (Satopää et al., 2021).

The discussion reminds one of the "Luddites," an expression that describes people who are concerned and fear new technologies. The expression has its origin in the nineteenth-century labor movement that mobilized workers to destroy machines that made the skilled craftsmen in the textile industry obsolete. The Luddites were British artisans who had spent years learning their craft. They feared that the textile machines were destroying their livelihood and existence. Therefore, some of them broke into factories and smashed textile machines (Andrews, 2019).

Despite the fears of the Luddites, technological advances over the past two centuries have increased life expectancy, reduced work hours, mostly eliminated child labor, and created prosperity. Technological advances have eliminated many menial, repetitive, and harmful workplace activities. The activities humans pursue in the workplace have become more complex, more varied, and more interesting.

It is true, however, that the process to reach these benefits was long and painful. It will remain so. Some of the ideas proposed in this book, and the Decision Navigator, will hopefully help senior leaders identify the trade-offs involved in the myriad of decisions they will have to take to lead the current technology-enabled transformation of organizations. While we remain (occasionally with some effort) optimistic about the role that technology plays in society, we are also mindful that its benefits, particularly in the short term, may not be equally distributed.

In 1967, when computers were a new thing, and it still was a matter of debate whether companies should have one, let alone individuals (the PC was only invented in 1974), Peter Drucker wrote in 1967:

We are beginning to realize that the computer makes no decisions; it only carries out orders. It's a total moron, and therein lies its strength. It forces us to think, to set the criteria. The stupider the tool, the brighter the master has to be – and this is dumbest tool we have ever had. All it can do is say either zero or one, but it can do that awfully fast. It doesn't get tired, and it doesn't charge overtime. It extends our capacity more than any tool we have had for a long time, because of all the really unskilled jobs it can do. By taking over these jobs, it allows us – in fact, it compels us – to think through what we are doing.

It may be premature to call AI a moron. Advances in research and in applying AI in many domains are happening at breathtaking speed. AI is likely to significantly shape the workplace and our lives at work and beyond in the coming years, and much is still unclear.

That said, there are reasons to believe that artificial intelligence might augment but will never fully replace human judgment and decision-making under uncertainty. In Chapter 3, we discussed the Gittins index – the only available general rule for making decisions under uncertainty. We highlighted the three conditions under which the Gittins index provides a valid algorithm for decision-making under uncertainty: (1) it applies when making decisions from a finite number of options; (2) when it delivers the rewards of each option with unknown but fixed probabilities; and (3) when the decision-maker can discount the value of each option's rewards over time. AI may augment a decision-maker's ability to discount rewards exponentially over time, but it might never be able to select a strategy from an infinitive number of options with unknown rewards and with unknown probabilities.

We hypothesize that AI may be helpful in increasing the exploration radius, i.e., widening the option space, of decision-makers, in uncovering unconscious assumptions (or systematic biases), and in testing them with facts. AI may yet help us become better decision-makers, but not deciding for us.

But the truth is that at this time we do not know how, and we have no way to test our hypothesis. Progress and time will elucidate how artificial intelligence can, in a targeted way, support, improve, and maybe even replace human decision-making.

That said, we know one thing for sure: our perceptions are already today shaped by AI-powered traditional and social media.

AI-powered information providers – whether traditional or social media – constantly feed us with information that may confirm our tendencies and biases, thus creating echo-chambers, undermining real debates, and leading to poor choices whether in organizations or beyond. Examples abound where AI has tried to trick leaders or voters to make poor decisions. The risks are real, but we believe that the proposed Decision Navigator can help alleviate those risks. By augmenting experience-based biases with a "scientific experi- mentation" approach, the proposed model fosters critical thinking and may help to effectively function in the world shaped by AI we are living in.

The Decision Navigator may prove to be useful for everyone, not just for leaders of organizations.

Building a Better Future

The brain relies on biases to reduce cognitive effort. In novel situa- tions, in situations of uncertainty, biases can lead to poor decisions, and poor decisions in organizations and in life can be expensive and sometimes fatal.

But working together with others, taking the time and making the effort to think through important decisions, and making them in a scientific, fact-based way can make a difference. Teams and the Decision Navigator can make a difference. They create super decisions.

And working on yourselves, on your mental states, on your cog- nitive skills and inclinations, can make you become a Super Decider.

Who we marry, how we raise our kids, how we choose to con- tribute to others, how we exercise our rights to vote and to partici- pate in the democratic process are important decisions made under uncertainty.

As a Super Decider, you can shape the world and build a bet- ter future.

Notes

Prologue

1. A description of the ATG and its numbers can be found in Appendix 1

Chapter 1

1. Brier scores measure the accuracy of predictions. They are equal to the mean squared error, that is, the difference between a predicted probability of an outcome and the actual outcome. For example, if a forecaster predicted an event with 80% probability, and the event actually happened (which is scored as 1), the forecaster's Brier score would equal $(0.8 - 1)^2$, or 0.04. If the event hadn't happened (which is scored as 0) the forecaster's Brier score would equal $(0.8 - 0)^2$, or 0.64.

Chapter 3

1. https://www.merriam-webster.com/dictionary/ambidextrous
2. https://corporate.exxonmobil.com/about-us/who-we-are/our-guiding-principles (accessed March 30, 2023).
3. https://about.meta.com/company-info/ (accessed March 30, 2023).

Appendixes

Appendix 1 – Description of Alpina Travel Group (ATG)
Appendix 2 – Curriculum Vitae, Isabelle Dubois
Appendix 3 – Case 1: The Economy
Appendix 4 – Case 1: The Travel Market
Appendix 5 – Case 1: The Financial Situation
Appendix 6 – Case 2: Digital Trends in the Travel Industry
Appendix 7 – Case 2: Competition Review
Appendix 8 – Case 2: Trends and SWOT Analysis
Appendix 9 – Case 3: International Expansion Data
Appendix 10 – Case 4: ATG Employee Survey

Appendix 1 – Description of Alpina Travel Group (ATG)

At year of appointment of Isabelle as CEO.

Description:	ATG is a medium-sized, independent tour operator. ATG has grown continuously since it was founded and enjoys an excellent reputation as a specialist in planning, designing and coordinating travel.
Headquarters of the company:	Zurich
Chief Executive Officer (CEO):	Isabelle Dubois
Chairman of the Board of Directors:	Carlo Proconi
Group Executive Team (GET):	Hugo Werner (CFO)
	Frank de Vries (Chief Sales Officer International)
	Conny Keller (Chief Sales Officer Switzerland and Chief Marketing Officer)
	Alessandro Rossi (Chief Information and Operations Officer)
	Alison Brown (Chief Human Resource Officer)
Number of customers:	Roughly 2.5 million.
Revenues:	CHF 1.3 billion
Number of employees:	Roughly 1,800 globally.
Infrastructure:	280 Agencies and 3 hotels.
Sales:	Own agencies as well as roughly 7,000 partner agencies in Switzerland, Germany, Austria, The Netherlands, Belgium, France, and the United States.

Holiday/ destination areas:	Balearic Islands, Canary Islands, Andalusia, Turkey, Israel, Egypt, Tunisia, Portugal, Bulgaria, Greece, Croatia, Montenegro, Italy, Malta, Cyprus and Cape Verde as well as the long-distance destinations of the Caribbean, Mexico, Thailand, Sri Lanka, Bali, the Maldives, Mauritius, and United Arab Emirates, and North America (US Rockies, Florida, Alaska, Canada). Germany, Austria, the Netherlands, Belgium, Poland and Switzerland.
Hotel and cruise partners:	More than 5,000 hotels in more than 60 European holiday destinations and long-haul destinations. Including almost all well-known hotel chains worldwide. ATG also offers cruise combination trips with AIDA, Costa Cruises, and TUI Cruises.
Flight partners:	ATG offers around 6,500 weekly departures with all well-known airlines from almost all European commercial airports in the summer season.

Appendix 2 – Curriculum Vitae, Isabelle Dubois

Professional career	
Present	ATG, Zurich, Switzerland Chief Executive Officer
Prior 8 years	The Travel Group, Copenhagen, Denmark Vice-President Marketing and Sales
Prior 2 years	The Travel Group, Copenhagen, Denmark Head of Marketing
Prior 3 years	ATG, Zurich, Switzerland Head Customer Service
Prior 3 years	ATG, Zurich, Switzerland Head of Controlling
Prior 2 years	ATG, Zurich, Switzerland Team Leader Finance & Controlling
Prior 1 year	ATG, Zurich, Switzerland Finance Analyst
Education	
6 weeks	Advanced Management Program, Harvard, Boston, USA
2 years	Executive MBA ETH and University of St. Gallen, Zurich and St. Gallen, Switzerland
5 years	Master's in finance and accounting, University of Zurich, Zurich, Switzerland
Personal information	
Family:	Married to Booker-nominated author Marco Dubois. Mother of Marie Isadora Dubois, and Annelies Elsa Dubois.
Interests:	Travel, languages, geography, history, photography, running

Appendix 3 – Case 1: The Economy

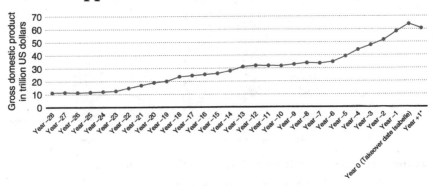

Appendix 3.1   World gross domestic product (GDP) in current prices up to year 0 (takeover date of Isabelle) with forecast for year +1 (in trillion US dollars).

Notes: Worldwide ★ Forecast for year + 1.

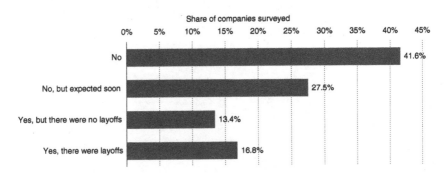

Appendix 3.2   Has the recession already had an impact on your workforce?

Notes: Europe, 4,219 companies; SMEs with fewer than 500 employees.

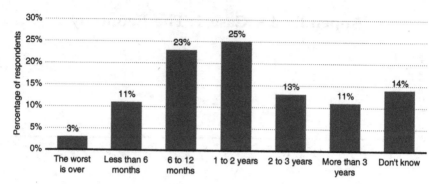

Appendix 3.3   How long do you think the recession will last?

Notes: Europe, age 15–65 years; 1102 respondents.

Appendix 4 – Case 1: The Travel Market

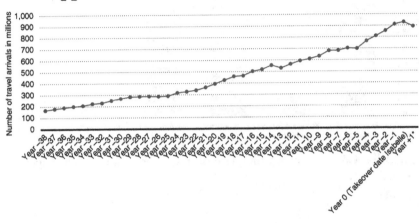

Appendix 4.1 Worldwide tourism volume by number of travel arrivals in years –38 to year 0 (takeover date of Isabelle) with forecast for year +1 (in millions).

Notes: Worldwide ★ Forecast for year + 1.

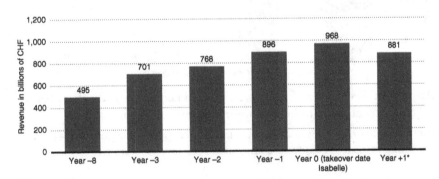

Appendix 4.2 Global tourism revenue from year –8 to year 0 (takeover date of Isabelle) with forecast for year + 1 (in CHF billion).

Notes: Worldwide ★ Forecast for year + 1.

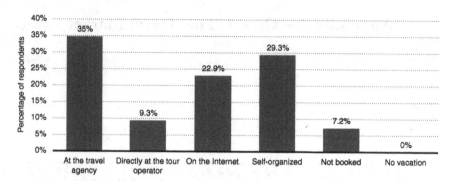

Appendix 4.3 Survey on the place of travel booking (e.g. travel agency, internet).

Note: EU.

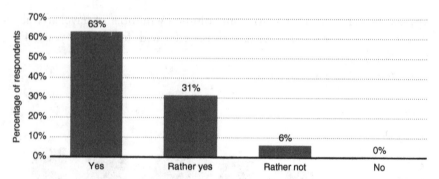

Appendix 4.4 Rate of price increase, bed tax, air tax and other charges. Do you expect travel to become more expensive in year +1?

Notes: EU, 2010, 252 respondents, decision–makers (managing directors, sales and marketing managers, etc.) from companies in the tourism industry.

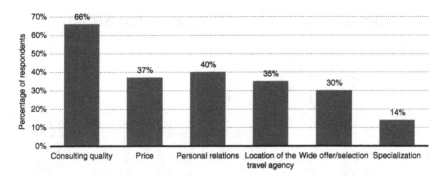

Appendix 4.5 What is important for you when choosing a travel agency? Selected criteria of the Swiss for the choice of a travel agency in the year 0 (takeover time of Isabelle).

Notes: 1024 respondents.

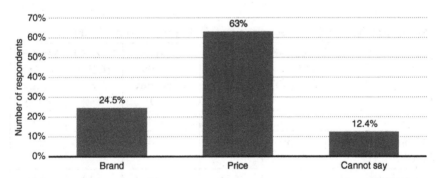

Appendix 4.6 When booking a trip, do you pay more attention to the brand or the tour operator or more to the price? Brand awareness, price awareness when booking a trip in year 0 (takeover time of Isabelle).

Note: Europe.

Appendix 5 – Case 1: The Financial Situation

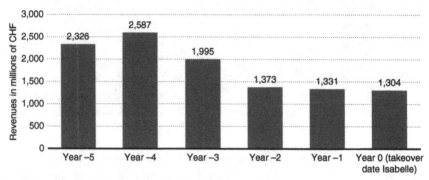

Appendix 5.1 ATG revenues from year -5 to year 0 (takeover time of Isabelle).

Appendix 5.2 Income statement of ATG (in millions of CHF).

	Year -2 (Mayer is CEO)	Year -1 (Mayer is CEO)	Year 0 (Isabelle becomes CEO)	Year +1 (CFO fore-cast)	Year +2 (CFO fore-cast)
Revenues	1373	1331	1304	1199	1152
Gross operating profit	259	260	254	222	225
Distribution costs	241	141	139	143	141
Contribution margin 1	**118**	**119**	**115**	**79**	**84**
Marketing/ Customer Service/Ops	35	35	36	37	35
Contribution margin 2	**83**	**84**	**79**	**42**	**49**
Central Services (HR, IT, Finance)	28	28	29	29	29

(Continued)

(Continued)

	Year -2 (Mayer is CEO)	Year -1 (Mayer is CEO)	Year 0 (Isabelle becomes CEO)	Year +1 (CFO fore-cast)	Year +2 (CFO fore-cast)
Contribution margin 3	55	56	50	13	20
Depreciation	23	23	23	24	24
Extraordinary items	0	0	0	0	0
Earnings before interest and tax	32	33	27	-11	-4
Interest	1	1	11	1	1
Taxes	9	8	7	-2	-1
Net profit	22	24	19	-10	-4

Appendix 5.3 Balance flow and cash flow statement, ATG (in millions of CHF).

Balance sheet	Year -2 (Mayer is CEO)	Year -1 (Mayer is CEO)	Year 0 (Isabelle becomes CEO)	Year + 1 (CFO fore-cast)	Year + 2 (CFO fore-cast)
Current assets	218	211	207	190	182
Property and equipment	349	347	345	343	345
Assets	567	558	551	533	525
Current liabilities	361	351	343	315	303
Long-term liabilities	33	32	26	45	53
Equity	173	175	181	173	189
Liabilities	567	558	552	534	525
Cash flow statement					

(Continued)

(Continued)

Balance sheet	Year –2 (Mayer is CEO)	Year –1 (Mayer is CEO)	Year 0 (Isabelle becomes CEO)	Year + 1 (CFO fore-cast)	Year + 2 (CFO fore-cast)
Net profit	22	24	19	–10	–4
+ Depreciation	23	23	23	24	24
–Increase current assets	0	7	4	17	8
+ Increase current liabilities	0	–10	–8	–28	–12
= Operating free cash flow	**45**	**44**	**38**	**3**	**16**
Investments	–24	–21	–20	–22	–22
Long-term liabilities	0	–1	–6	+19	=8
Cash flow before dividends	**21**	**22**	**12**	**0**	**2**
Dividends	20	–16	–11	0	0

Appendix 5.4 Distribution of ATG agencies by contribution margin, location, and age.

Deciles	Contribution margin 1 (%)	% in Switzerland	Average age years	Agencies <3 years of age
1	23	53	33	0
2	20	44	26	0
3	18	70	25	5
4	17	26	31	0
5	17	70	15	9
6	12	53	31	10
7	9	35	12	42
8	2	18	4	85
9	–10	18	18	11
10	–18	9	12	7

Appendix 6 – Case 2: Digital Trends in the Travel Industry

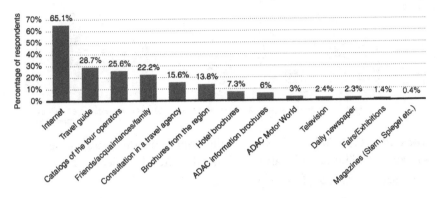

Appendix 6.1 Sources of information used for independent vacation planning.

Notes: EU, approx. 4000 private households.

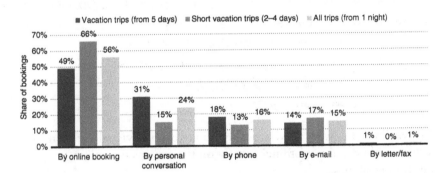

Appendix 6.2 Distribution of Europeans' vacation trips by duration and booking method.

Notes: Europe, age 14 or older; n = 6207 respondents.

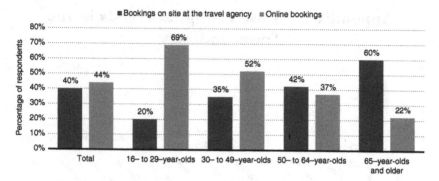

Appendix 6.3 Where do you usually book individual vacation services? Survey on the booking location of individual travel services.

Notes: age 16 and older, 1007 respondents.

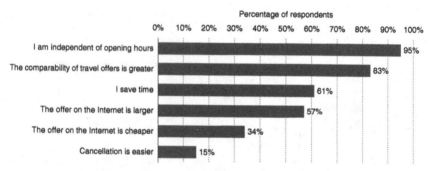

Appendix 6.4 Why do you usually book your individual vacation services online and not offline? Survey on the reasons for online vacation bookings.

Notes: Europe, 16 and older, 399 respondents.

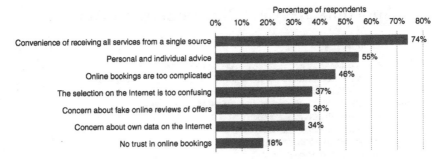

Appendix 6.5 Why do you usually book your individual vacation services not on the internet? Survey on the reasons for offline travel bookings.

Notes: Europe, 16 and older, 1007 respondents.

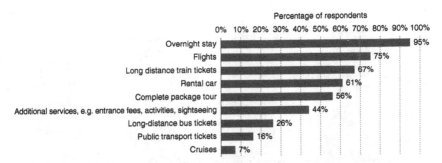

Appendix 6.6 What travel and vacation services have you already purchased or booked on the internet? Survey of bookings of travel services on the internet.

Notes: Europe, 16 and older, 399 online bookers.

Appendix 7 – Case 2: Competition Review

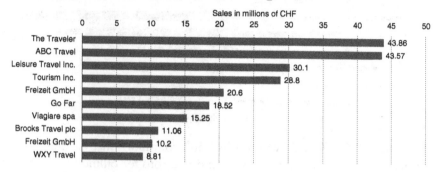

Appendix 7.1 The largest tour operators in Europe Year 0 (takeover date of Isabelle) by revenue (in millions of CHF).

Notes: EU.

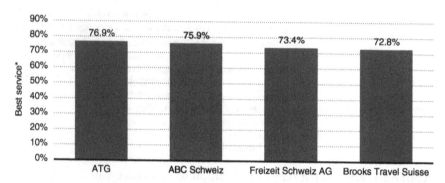

Appendix 7.2 Ranking of tour operators in Switzerland with the best service in Year 0 (takeover date of Isabelle).

Notes: Switzerland, age 14 and older, 300 customers (depending on industry), representative top 5.

Appendix 8 – Case 2: Trends and SWOT Analysis

Online Marketplace. It's no secret that planning and booking tourism services has gone digital. Marketplaces like Booking.com are quickly displacing travel agencies and tour operators with physical infrastructure.

Digital Enabling of Travel. Travel is becoming increasingly digitized. From QR codes and facial recognition software at airports to wifi and robots in hotels and location-based services in cities, technology is being used everywhere to make travel easier, more enjoyable and more efficient. Credit: Possessed Photography/UnSplash

VR Experiences. People want to have unique and exciting experiences when they travel. But it's also true that many people want to experience things without actually experiencing them. This is where the power of virtual reality comes into play. Virtual reality allows people to experience simulations and games of all kinds. This is especially interesting for travelers who want to have a unique pre-trip experience before leaving for a faraway destination. Credit: Rawpixel.com/Adobe Stock Photos

Mobile First! The travel experience is becoming increasingly digital and mobile. The cell phone is a constant companion for every well-connected tourist. Thanks to its numerous functions, travelers use it both to make phone calls and to surf the various social networks and take beautiful and memorable photos. Thus, about 68% of tourists use their mobile device to search for information instead of using a computer or tablet; on the other hand, for 42% of respondents, the smartphone is indispensable to share their experiences on social profiles; finally, 38% use it to leave comments and reviews on specific applications and websites (statista.com).

Gaming. When visiting a city, there is a new activity that is becoming more and more successful: Indoor Virtual Reality. Whether escape games or laser tags, the gamification trend is growing very fast and is now almost a must for city breaks. Credit: Imaginechina Limited / Alamy Stock Photo

Appendix 8.1   Current trends in the travel industry 1.

Experiential Tourism. People are no longer looking for conventional travel experiences. Instead, they would rather pay for vacations that offer once-in-a-lifetime experiences that they will remember forever. These don't have to be great experiences, just memorable or unique ones. Airbnb promotes its "experiences" almost as heavily as it does accommodations. Through Airbnb's website, you can find all kinds of experiences in almost any city in the world. Credit: mannmayvinze/Shutterstock

Ecotourism. It's understandable that more people than ever are concerned about the environment and the impact of their travel plans on it. People are concerned about the CO_2 emissions they create and how they can travel in a more environmentally friendly way. People are looking for ethical options, and this applies to all sectors of the tourism industry. A small example of this is the increasing demand for electric-powered rental cars. Credit: Rupesh Sali/Shutterstock

Local cultural experiences. In the age of social media, authenticity is more important than ever, and that's what many tourists are now demanding. That's why many people give preference to local cultural experiences. They want to see, feel, taste and smell local culture up close, rather than staying in an exclusive area designed just for tourists. Nowadays, far fewer people want a generic travel experience. Credit: Steven Rio/Shutterstock

Personalization. Nowadays, everything is becoming more and more individualized because people want this kind of experience. The travel and tourism industry has not remained unaffected by these changes. People want a travel experience that matches their ideas, priorities, and needs, and they expect travel companies to provide this. Credit: Helena Lopes/Pexels

Leisure Travel = Bleisure Travel. The upscale travel industry is increasingly focused on business clients. Many top companies use travel and group vacations to provide shared experiences and build team spirit. The combination of business and leisure travel has become known as "bleisure" travel. It is typically a higher-end form of travel used by some of the largest companies in the world. As a result, they must be tailored to meet the needs of business customers while providing the leisure aspect of the travel experience. Credit: Muhammedkazeez/Shutterstock

Appendix 8.2 Current trends in the travel industry 2.

	Segment size	Growth	Relevance US	Relevance EU	Relevance Asia	Competence ATG
Online marketplace	+++++	++++	+++++	+++++	+++++	+
Digital Enabling Travel	++	++++	+++	+++	+++++	+
VR Experience	+	+++++	+++	+++	+++++	+
Mobile First!	++++	+++++	++++	+++	+++++	+
Gaming	+	+++++	+++	++	+++++	+
Experience tourism	+++	+++++	++++	++++	++	+++
Ecotourism	++	+++++	+++	+++++	+	+
Local cultural experiences	+	+++	+++	+++++	+	++
Personalization	++	+++	++++	+++++	+	+++++
Leisure Travel	++++	++++	+++++	+++	++	++

Appendix 8.3 Current trends in the travel industry: size and growth of submarkets/services.

STRENGTHS	OPPORTUNITIES
• Traditional company with a very good national reputation • Competitive advantage in planning, designing and coordinating trips (consulting) • Extensive product range • Large agencies network/strong presence in Europe	• Travel is an attractive growth market in the long term, both in established and emerging markets • Increasing affluency and demand for travel experiences in Asia, LatAm, and Africa • Consolidation of the industry • Several trends that match Inuk's capabilities • Inclusion of technology
WEAKNESSES	**RISKS**
• Analysts describe the company as rigid – it has changed little over the many years • Dependence on Europe and the DACH region • No market traction of B2B business • Revenue stagnating at below average level growth • Mid-sized tour operator in Europe (top 12) • Low profitability	• Emergence of digital competitors • Global economy in recession • Decline in travel market • Changing customer needs • Intense competition with many participants

Appendix 8.4 SWOT analysis of ATG in year 0 (takeover date of Isabelle).

Appendix 9 – Case 3: International Expansion Data

Appendix 9.1 Data on planned expansion to North America or Asia (in thousands of CHF)

Year	Free cash flow for invest-ment in North America	Free cash flow for investment in Asia	Discount rate (%)
1 (current date)	-1504	-2967	
2	341	711	
3	580	987	12
4	735	1546	
5	903	2307	

Appendix 10 – Case 4: ATG Employee Survey

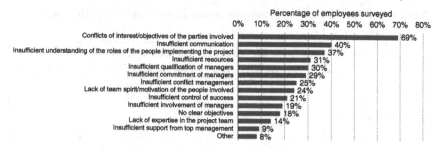

Appendix 10.1 General assessment of the employees about the most important difficulties and problems in the transformation process at ATG.
Notes: ATG, 301 respondents, employees.

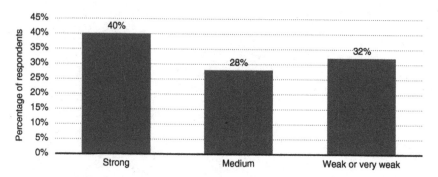

Appendix 10.2 How strongly do you feel connected to your employer?
Notes: ATG, 261 employees surveyed.

References

Addicott, M.A., Pearson, J.M., Froeliger, B., Platt, M.L., and McClernon, F.J. (2014). Smoking automaticity and tolerance moderate brain activation during explore–exploit behavior. *Psychiatry Research: Neuroimaging*, 224(3), 254–261. https://doi.org/10.1016/j.pscychresns.2014.10.014

Almaatouq, A., Alsobay, M., Yin, M., and Watts, D. J. (2021). Task complexity moderates group synergy. *PNAS*, 118(36). https://doi.org/10.1073/pnas.2101062118

Anderson, R.J. and Adams, W.A. (2015). *Mastering Leadership: An Integrated Framework for Breakthrough Performance and Extraordinary Business Results*. Hoboken, NJ: Wiley.

Andrews, E. (2019). Who were the Luddites? https://www.history.com/news/who-were-the-luddites

Ashkenas, R. (2013). Change management needs to change. *Harvard Business Review*, April 16.

Bajraktarov, S., Novotni, A., Arsova, S., Gudeva-Nikovska, D., and Vujovik, V. (2017). Character and temperament dimensions in subjects with depressive disorder: Impact of the affective state on their expression. *Open Access Macedonian Journal of Medical Science*, 5(1), 64–67. https://doi.org/10.3889/oamjms.2017.022

Bakos, R., and Jolton, J. (2022). Stability is an illusion – take a closer look. Global trends in employee engagement 2022. *Kincentric*. www.kincentric.com/-/media/kincentric/2022/GTEE/Global_Trends_in_Employee_Engagement_2022.pdf

Balcetis, E. and Dunning, D. (2010). Wishful seeing: More desired objects are seen as closer. *Psychological Science*, ;21(1), 147–152. https://doi.org/10.1177/0956797609356283

Barba, V. (2019). Kite gets freedom to fly after separation from Gilead, *Bio Pharma Reporter*, May 8. https://www.biopharma-reporter.com/article/2019/05/08/gilead-separates-kite-pharma (accessed June 6, 2023).

Basford, T., and Schaninger, B. (2016). The four building blocks of change. Four key actions influence employee mind-sets and behavior. *McKinsey Quarterly*, April.

Basso, J.C., McHale, A., Ende, V., Oberlin, D.J., Suzuki, W.A. (2019). Brief, daily meditation enhances attention, memory, mood, and emotional regulation in non-experienced meditators. *Behavioral Brain Research*, 356, 208–220. https://doi:10.1016/j.bbr.2018.08.023

Bechara, A. (2005). Decision making, impulse control and loss of willpower to resist drugs: A neurocognitive perspective. *Nature Neuroscience*, 8(11), 1458–1463. https://doi.org/10.1038/nn1584

Beer, M., and Nohria, N. (2000). Cracking the code of change. *Harvard Business Review*. 78(3), 133–141, 216.

Beinhocker, E.D. (2006). *The Origino Of Wealth: Evolution, Complexity, and the Radical Remaking of Economics*. Boston: Harvard Business School Press.

Birkinshaw, J., Zimmermann, A., and Raisch, S. (2016). How do firms adapt to discontinuous change? Bridging the dynamic capabilities and ambidexterity perspectives. *California Management Review*, 58(4), 36–58. https://doi.org/10.1525/cmr.2016.58.4.36

Bloomfield, B.P., and Dale, K. (2020). Limitless? Imaginaries of cognitive enhancement and the labouring body. *History of the Human Sciences*, 33(5), 37–63. https://doi.org/10.1177/0952695119888995

Bolte-Taylor, J. (2008). *My Stroke of Insight*. London: Hodder and Stoughton.

Brauer, M., and Laamanen, T. (2014). Workforce downsizing and firm performance: An organizational routine perspective. *Journal of Management Studies*, 51. https://doi.org/10.1111/joms.12074

Brown, K.M., Hoye, R., and Nicholson, M. (2012). Self-esteem, self-efficacy, and social connectedness as mediators of the relationship between volunteering and well-being, *Journal of Social Service Research*, 38(4), 468–483, https://doi.org/10.1080/0148 8376.2012.687706

Brusoni, S., and Laureiro-Martinez, D. (2018). Cognitive flexibility and adaptive decision-making: Evidence from a laboratory study of expert decision makers. *Strategic Management Journal*, January 18. https://doi.org/10.1002/smj.2774

Brusoni, S., Laureiro-Martínez, D., Canessa, N., and Zollo, M. (2020). Exploring exploration: The role of affective states as forces that hinder change. *Industrial and Corporate Change*, 29(1), 207–223. https://doi.org/10.1093/icc/dtz070

Brusoni, S., Feser, C., and Laureiro-Martinez, D. (2023). The neuroscience of decision making under uncertainty. Chapter submitted.

Calabretta, G., Gemser, G., and Wijnberg, N.M. (2017). The interplay between intuition and rationality in strategic decision making: A paradox perspective. *Organization Studies*, 38(3–4), 365–401. https://doi.org/10.1177/0170840616655483

Camuffo, A., Cordova, A., Gambardella, A., and Spina, C. (2020). A scientific approach to entrepreneurial decision making: Evidence from a randomized control trial. *Management Science*, 66(2), 564–586. https://doi.org/10.1287/mnsc.2018.3249

Carmeli, A. (2008). Top management team behavioral integration and the performance of service organizations. *Group and Organization Management*, 33(6), 712–735. https://doi.org/10.1177/1059601108325696

Carmeli, A., and Halevi, M.Y. (2009). How top management team behavioral integration and behavioral complexity enable organizational ambidexterity: The moderating role of contextual ambidexterity. *The Leadership Quarterly*, 20(2), 207–218. https://doi.org/10.1016/j.leaqua.2009.01.011

Cattell, R.B. (1987). *Intelligence: Its Structure, Growth, and Action.* Amsterdam: North-Holland.

Chee, M.W.L., and Chuah, L.Y.M. (2008). Functional neuroimaging insights into how sleep and sleep deprivation affect memory and cognition. *Current Opinion in Neurology*, 21(4), 417–423. https://doi.org/10.1097/WCO.0bref3e3283052cf7

Cloninger, C.R. (1994). *The Temperament and Character Inventory (TCI): A Guide to Its Development and Use.* St. Louis, MO: Center for Psychobiology of Personality, Washington University.

Cloninger, C.R., Svrakic, D.M., and Przybeck, T.R. (1993). A psychobiological model of temperament and character. *Archives of General Psychiatry*, 50(12), 975–990. https://doi.org/10.1001/archpsyc.1993.01820240059008

Cockburn, J., Man, V., Cunningham, W., and O'Doherty, J.P. (2021). Novelty and uncertainty interact to regulate the balance between exploration and exploitation in the human brain. *Neuroscience.* https://doi.org/10.1101/2021.10.13.464279

Cohen, J.D., McClure, S.M., and Yu, A.J. (2007). Should I stay or should I go? How the human brain manages the trade-off between exploitation and exploration. *Philosophical Transactions of the Royal Society B: Biological Sciences*, 362(1481), 933–942. https://doi.org/10.1098/rstb.2007.2098

Cole, S., Balcetis, E., and Zhang, S. (2013). Visual perception and regulatory conflict: Motivation and physiology influence distance perception. *Journal of Experimental Psychology: General*, 142(1), 18–22. https://doi.org/10.1037/a0027882

Comaford, C. (2015). Achieve your goals faster: The latest neuroscience of goal attainment. *Forbes*, November 22.

Congleton, C., Hölzel, B.K., and Lazar, S.W. (2015). Mindfulness can literally change your brain. *Harvard Business Review*, January 8.

Dane, E., and Pratt, M.G. (2007). Exploring intuition and its role in managerial decision making. *Academy of Management Review*, 32(1). https://doi.org/10.5465/amr.2007.23463682

Davidson, R.J. (2012). *The Emotional Life of Your Brain: How Its Unique Patterns Affect the Way You Think, Feel, and Live, and How You Can Change Them*. New York: Hudson Street Press.

Deák, G.O. (2003). The development of cognitive flexibility and language abilities. In R.V. Kail (Ed.), *Advances in Child Development and Behavior*, vol. 31. New York: Academic Press, pp. 271–327.

Descartes, R. (2018). *Discourse on the Method*. SMK Books.

De Smet, A., Jost, G., and Weiss, L. (2019). Three keys to faster, better decisions. *McKinsey Quarterly*, May.

Diamond, A. (2013). Executive functions. *Annual Review of Psychology*, 64: 135–168. https://doi.org/10.1146/annurev-psych-113011-143750

Dodich, A., Zollo, M., Crespi, C., Cappa, S.F., Laureiro Martinez, D., Falini, A., and Canessa, N. (2019). Short-term Sahaja Yoga meditation training modulates brain structure and spontaneous activity in the executive control network. *Brain and Behavior*, 9(1), e01159. https://doi.org/10.1002/brb3.1159

Drucker, P.F. (1967). The manager and the moron. *McKinsey Quarterly*, December 1.

Dubois, M., Habicht, J., Michely, J., Moran, R., Dolan, R.J., and Hauser, T.U. (2021). Human complex exploration strategies are enriched by noradrenaline-modulated heuristics. *ELife*, 10, e59907. https://doi.org/10.7554/eLife.59907

Duhigg, C. (2016). What Google learned from its quest to build the perfect team. *The New York Times*. February 25. https://www.nytimes.com/2016/02/28/magazine/what-google-learned-from-its-quest-to-build-the-perfect-team.html

Durmer, J.S., and Dinges, D.F. (2005). Neurocognitive consequences of sleep deprivation. *Seminars in Neurology*, 25(01), 117–129. https://doi.org/10.1055/s-2005-867080

Dweck, C.S. (2006). *Mindset: The New Psychology of Success*. New York: Ballantine Books.

Edmondson, A. (1999). Psychological safety and learning behavior in work teams. *Administrative Science Quarterly*, 44(2), 350–383. https://doi.org/10.2307/2666999

Ekman, P. (2007). *Emotions Revealed: Recognizing Faces and Feelings to Improve Communication and Emotional Life.* New York: St. John's Press.

Ewenstein, B., Smith, W., and Sologar, A. (2015). Changing change management. *McKinsey Digital,* July.

Fehr, E., and Falk, A. (2002). Psychological foundations of incentives. *European Economic Review,* 46, 687–724.

Fehr, E., and Gächter, S. (2000). Cooperation and punishment in public good experiments. *American Economic Review,* 90(4), 980–994. https://doi.org/10.1257/aer.90.4.980

Feser, C. (2011). *Serial Innovators: Firms That Change the World.* Hoboken, NJ: John Wiley and Sons, Inc.

Feser, C. (2016). *When Execution Isn't Enough: Decoding Inspirational Leadership.* Hoboken, NJ: John Wiley and Sons, Inc.

Feser, C., Rennie, M., and Nielsen, N.C. (2018). *Leadership at Scale. Better Leaders, Better Results.* London: Nicholas Brealey Publishing.

Fisher, M., and Keil, F.C. (2018). The binary bias: A systematic distortion in the integration of information. *Psychological Science,* 29(11), 1846–1858. https://doi.org/10.1177/0956797618792256

Fleming, S.M. (2014). The power of reflection. *Scientific American Mind,* 25(5), 30–37. https://doi.org/10.1038/scientificamericanmind0914-30

Gershman, S.J., and Tzovaras, B.G. (2018). Dopaminergic genes are associated with both directed and random exploration. *Neuropsychologia,* 120, 97–104. https://doi.org/10.1016/j.neuropsychologia.2018.10.009

Geurts, H.M., Corbett, B., and Solomon, M. (2009). The paradox of cognitive flexibility in autism. *Trends in Cognitive Sciences.* 13(2), 74–82. https://doi.org/10.1016/j.tics.2008.11.006.

Gibson, C.B., and Birkinshaw, J. (2004). The antecedents, consequences, and mediating role of organizational ambidexterity. *Academy of Management Journal,* 47(2), 209–226. https://doi.org/10.2307/20159573

Gilovich, T., Griffin, D., and Kahneman, D. (2002) *Heuristics and Biases: The Psychology of Intuitive Judgment*. New York: Cambridge University Press.

Gist, M.E. (1987). Self-efficacy: Implications for organizational behavior and human resource management. *The Academy of Management Review*, 12(3), 472. https://doi.org/10.2307/258514

Gittins, J.C. (1979). Bandit processes and dynamic allocation indices. *Journal of the Royal Statistical Society, Series B*, 41, 148–177.

Gittins, J.C. and Jones, D.M. (1974). A dynamic allocation index for the sequential design of experiments. In J. Gans (Ed.), *Progress in Statistics*. Amsterdam, The Netherlands: North-Holland, pp. 241–266.

Glöckner, A., and Witteman, C. (2010). Beyond dual-process models: A categorisation of processes underlying intuitive judgement and decision making. *Thinking and Reasoning*, 16(1), 1–25. https://doi.org/10.1080/13546780903395748

Gneezy, U., Meier, S., and Rey-Biel, P. (2011). When and why incentives (don't) work to modify behavior. *Journal of Economic Perspectives*, 25(4), 191–210.

Grant, A. (2021). *Think Again: The Power of Knowing What You Don't Know*. London: W.H. Allen.

Greene, J. (2014). *Moral Tribes: Emotion, Reason, and the Gap Between Us and Them*. New York: Penguin Books.

Gurdjian, P., Halbeisen, T., and Lane, K. (2014). Why leadership-development programs fail. *McKinsey Quarterly*, January 1.

Hambrick, D.C. (1994). Top management groups: A conceptual integration and reconsideration of the "team" label. *Research in Organizational Behavior*, 16, 171.

Hambrick, D.C. (1998). Corporate coherence and the top management team. In D.C. Hambrick, D.A. Nadler, and M.L. Tushman (Eds.), *Navigating Change: How Ceos, Top Teams, and Boards Steer Transformation*. Boston, MA: Harvard Business School Press, pp. 123–140.

Haney, A.B., Pope, J., and Arden, Z. (2020). Making it personal: Developing sustainability leaders in business. *Organization and Environment*, 33(2), 155–174. https://doi.org/10.1177/1086026618806201

Harrison, E.F. (1996). A process perspective on strategic decision making. *Management Decision*, 34(1), 46–53. https://doi.org/10.1108/00251749610106972

Hayward, J.W., and Varela, F.J. (1992). *Gentle Bridges: Conversations with the Dalai Lama on the Science of the Mind.* Boston: Shambhala.

He, Z.-L., and Wong, P.-K. (2004). Exploration vs. exploitation: An empirical test of the ambidexterity hypothesis. *Organization Science*, 15(4), 481–494. https://doi.org/10.1287/orsc.1040.0078

Heath, C., and Heath, D. (2013). *Decisive: How to Make Better Choices in Life and Work.* New York: Currency.

Hill, S.A., and Birkinshaw, J. (2014). Ambidexterity and survival in corporate venture units. *Journal of Management*, 40(7), 1899–1931. https://doi.org/10.1177/0149206312445925

Hoffman, B.J., Woehr, D.J., Maldagen-Youngjohn, R., and Lyons, B.D. (2011). Great man or great myth? A quantitative review of the relationship between individual differences and leader effectiveness. *Journal of Occupational and Organizational Psychology*, 84(2), 347–381. https://doi.org/10.1348/096317909X485207

Honn, K.A., Hinson, J.M., Whitney, P., and Van Dongen, H.P. (2019). Cognitive flexibility: A distinct element of performance impairment due to sleep deprivation. *Accident Analysis Prevention*, 126: 191–197. https://doi.org/10.1016/j.aap.2018.02.013

Hsu, A. (2023). America, we have a problem. People aren't feeling engaged with their work, NPR, January 25. https://www.npr.org/2023/01/25/1150816271/employee-engagement-gallup-survey-workers-hybrid-remote

Janssen, C., Segers, E., McQueen, J. M., and Verhoeven, L. (2015). Lexical specificity training effects in second language learners: Lexical specificity training in L2 learners. *Language Learning*, 65(2), 358–389. https://doi.org/10.1111/lang.12102

Junni, P., Sarala, R.M., Taras, V., and Tarba, S.Y. (2013). Organizational ambidexterity and performance: A meta-analysis. *Academy of Management Perspectives*, 27(4), 299–312. https://doi.org/10.5465/amp.2012.0015

Kahneman, D. (2002). Maps of bounded rationality: A perspective on intuitive judgment and choice. Nobel Prize Lecture, December 8, p. 455.

Kahneman, D. (2012). *Thinking, Fast and Slow*. New York: Penguin.

Kahneman, D., and Tversky, A. (Eds.). (2000). *Choices, Values, and Frames*. Cambridge: Cambridge University Press.

Kauppila, O.-P., and Tempelaar, M.P. (2016). The social-cognitive underpinnings of employees' ambidextrous behaviour and the supportive role of group managers' leadership: The underpinnings of employees' ambidextrous behaviour. *Journal of Management Studies*, 53(6), 1019–1044. https://doi.org/10.1111/joms.12192

Kayser, A.S., Mitchell, J.M., Weinstein, D., and Frank, MJ. (2015). Dopamine, locus of control, and the exploration-exploitation tradeoff. *Neuropsychopharmacology*, 40(2), 454–462. https://doi.org/10.1038/npp.2014.193

Kegan, R., and Lahey, L.L. (2016). *An Everyone Culture: Becoming a Deliberately Developmental Organization*. Boston, MA: Harvard Business Review Press.

Kegan, R., Lahey, L., Fleming, A., and Miller, M. (2014). Making business personal. *Harvard Business Review*, April.

Keller, T., and Weibler, J. (2015). What it takes and costs to be an ambidextrous manager: Linking leadership and cognitive strain to balancing exploration and exploitation. *Journal of Leadership and Organizational Studies*, 22(1), 54–71. https://doi.org/10.1177/1548051814524598

Kets de Vries, M.F.R. (2006). *The Leader on the Couch: A Clinical Approach to Changing People and Organizations*. San Francisco: Jossey-Bass.

Khodarahimi, S. (2018). Self-reported nutritional status, executive functions, and cognitive flexibility in adults. *Journal of Mind and*

Medical Sciences, 5(2), Article 11. https://doi.org/10.22543/7674 .52.P210217

Killgore, W.D.S. (2015). Sleep deprivation and behavioral risk-taking. In: R.R. Watson (Ed.), *Modulation of Sleep by Obesity, Diabetes, Age, and Diet*. New York: Academic Press, pp. 279–287. https://doi.org/10.1016/B978-0-12-420168-2.00030-2.

Kleinsinger, F. (2018). The unmet challenge of medication non-adherence. *The Permanente Journal*, 22: 18-033. https://doi .org/10.7812/TPP/18-033

Kolbe, L.M., Bossink, B., and de Man, A.-P. (2020). Contingent use of rational, intuitive and political decision-making in R&D. *Management Decision*, 58(6), 997–1020. https://doi.org/10.1108/ MD-02-2019-0261

Kopalle, P.K., Kuusela, H., and Lehmann, D.R. (2023). The role of intuition in CEO acquisition decisions, *Journal of Business Research*, 167. https://doi.org/10.1016/j.jbusres.2023.114139.

Kounios, J., Fleck, J.I., Green, D.L., Payne, L., Stevenson, J.L., Bowden, E.M., and Jung-Beeman, M. (2008). The origins of insight in resting-state brain activity. *Neuropsychologia*, 46(1), 281–291. https://doi.org/10.1016/j.neuropsychologia.2007.07.013.

Kruger, J., and Dunning, D. (1999). Unskilled and unaware of it: How difficulties in recognizing one's own incompetence lead to inflated self-assessments. *Journal of Personality and Social Psychology*, 77(6), 1121–1134. https://doi.org/10.1037/0022-3514.77.6.1121

Landsberg, M. (2023). *The Power of the Dao. Seven Essential Habits for Living in Flow, Fulfillment and Resilience*. New York: LID Publishing.

Latham, G.P., and Locke, E.A. (2006). Enhancing the benefits and overcoming the pitfalls of goal setting. *Organizational Dynamics*, 35(4), 332–340. https://doi.org/10.1016/j.orgdyn.2006.08.008

Laureiro-Martinez, D. (2014). Cognitive control capabilities, routinization propensity, and decision-making performance. *Organization Science*, 25(4), 1111–1133.

Laureiro-Martinez, D. (2022). *Self-Assessment Report. Technology and Innovation Management*. Zürich: ETH Zürich.

Laureiro-Martínez, D., and Brusoni, S. (2018). Cognitive flexibility and adaptive decision-making: Evidence from a laboratory study of expert decision makers. *Strategic Management Journal*, 39(4), 1031–1058. https://doi.org/10.1002/smj.2774

Laureiro-Martínez, D., Brusoni, S., Canessa, N., and Zollo, M. (2015). Understanding the exploration-exploitation dilemma: An fMRI study of attention control and decision-making performance: Understanding the exploration-exploitation dilemma. *Strategic Management Journal*, 36(3), 319–338. https://doi.org/10.1002/smj.2221

Laureiro-Martínez, D., Brusoni, S., and Zollo, M. (2010). The neuroscientific foundations of the exploration–exploitation dilemma. *Journal of Neuroscience, Psychology, and Economics*, 3(2), 95–115. https://doi.org/10.1037/a0018495

Laureiro-Martínez, D., Canessa, N., Brusoni, S., Zollo, M., Hare, T., Alemanno, F., and Cappa, S.F. (2014). Frontopolar cortex and decision-making efficiency: Comparing brain activity of experts with different professional background during an exploration-exploitation task. *Frontiers in Human Neuroscience*, 7, 927.

Lawson, E., and Price, C. (2003). The psychology of change management, *McKinsey Quarterly*, August.

Lick, D.J., Alter, A.L., and Freeman, J.B. (2018). Superior pattern detectors efficiently learn, activate, apply, and update social stereotypes. *Journal of Experimental Psychology: General*, 147(2), 209–227. https://doi.org/10.1037/xge0000349

Linden, D.J. (2008). *The Accidental Mind: How Brain Evolution Has Given Us Love, Memory, Dreams, and God* (1st ed.). Cambridge, MA: Belknap Press.

Liu, L., Oroz Artigas, S., Ulrich, A., Tardu, T., Mohr, P.N.C, Wilms, B., Koletzko, B., Schmid, S.M., and Park, S.Q. (2021). Eating to dare: Nutrition impacts human risky decision and related brain function, *NeuroImage*, 233. https://doi.org/10.1016/j.neuroimage.2021.117951

Lubatkin, M.H., Simsek, Z., Ling, Y., and Veiga, J.F. (2006). Ambidexterity and performance in small-to medium-sized firms: The pivotal role of top management team behavioral integration. *Journal of Management*, 32(5), 646–672. https://doi.org/10.1177/0149 206306290712

Macnamara, B.N., and Burgoyne, A.P. (2023). Do growth mindset interventions impact students' academic achievement? A systematic review and meta-analysis with recommendations for best practices. *Psychological Bulletin,* 149(3–4), 133–173. https://doi.org/10.1037/bul0000352

Mandolesi, L., Polverino, A., Montuori, S., Foti, F., Ferraioli, G., Sorrentino, P., and Sorrentino, G. (2018). Effects of physical exercise on cognitive functioning and wellbeing: Biological and psychological benefits. *Frontiers in Psychology*, 9, 509. https://doi.org/10.3389/fpsyg.2018.00509

Manly, J. et al. (2023). Reaching new heights in uncertain times: Most innovative companies in 2023. Report. BCG, May 23, 2023.

March, J.G. (1991). Exploration and exploitation in organizational learning. *Organization Science*, 2(1), 71–87. https://doi.org/10.1287/orsc.2.1.71

Masley, S., Roetzheim, R., and Gualtieri, T. (2009). Aerobic exercise enhances cognitive flexibility. *Journal of Clinical Psychology in Medical Settings*, 16(2), 186–193. http://doi.org/10.1007/s10880-009-9159-6

Massey, M. (1973). *The People Puzzle. Understanding Yyourself and Others*. New York: Brady.

Matthews, G. (2007). The impact of commitment, accountability, and written goals on goal achievement. Psychology, Faculty Presentations. 3. https://scholar.dominican.edu/psychology-faculty-conference-presentations/3 (accessed August, 28, 2023).

McCrae, R.R., and John, O.P. (1992). An introduction to the five-factor model and its applications. *Journal of Personality*, 60, 175–215. http://dx.doi.org/10.1111/j.1467-6494.1992.tb00970.x

Mellers, B., Stone, E., Atanasov, P., Rohrbaugh, N., Metz, S.E., Ungar, L., Bishop, M.M., Horowitz, M., Merkle, E., and Tetlock, P. (2015a). The psychology of intelligence analysis: Drivers of prediction accuracy in world politics. *Journal of Experimental Psychology: Applied*, 21(1), 1–14. https://doi.org/10.1037/xap0000040

Mellers, B., Stone, E., Murray, T., Minster, A., Rohrbaugh, N., Bishop, M., Chen, E., Baker, J., Hou, Y., Horowitz, M., Ungar, L., and Tetlock, P. (2015b). Identifying and cultivating super-forecasters as a method of improving probabilistic predictions. *Perspectives on Psychological Science*, 10(3), 267–281. http ://doi .org/10.1177/1745691615577794

Moore, A., and Malinowski, P. (2009). Meditation, mindfulness and cognitive flexibility. *Consciousness and Cognition*, 18(1), 176–186. http://doi.org/10.1016/j.concog.2008.12.008

Newell, A., and Simon, H.A. (1972). *Human Problem Solving*. Englewood Cliffs, NJ: Prentice-Hall.

O Reilly, C.A., and Tushman, M.L. (2004). The ambidextrous organization. *Harvard Business Review*, 82(4), 74–83.

O'Reilly, C.A., and Tushman, M.L. (2008). Ambidexterity as a dynamic capability: Resolving the innovator's dilemma. *Research in Organizational Behavior*, 28, 185–206. https://doi.org/10.1016/j.riob.2008.06.002

Parker-Pope, T. (2014). Better ways to learn. *New York Times*, October 6.

Peterson, S.J., and Luthans, F. (2006). The impact of financial and nonfinancial incentives on business-unit outcomes over time. *Journal of Applied Psychology*, 91(1), 156–165.

Pilkington, P.D., Windsor, T.D., and Crisp, D.A. (2012). Volunteering and subjective well-being in midlife and older adults: the role of supportive social networks. *Journal of Gerontology, Series B, Psychological Sciences and Social Sciences*, 67(2), 249–260. https://doi.org/10.1093/geronb/gbr154

Posner, M.I., Rothbart, M.K., Sheese, B.E., and Voelker, P. (2014). Developing attention: behavioral and brain. *Advances in Neuroscience*. https://doi.org/10.1155/2014/405094

Posner, M.I., Rothbart, M.K., and Tang, Y.-Y. (2015). Enhancing attention through training. *Current Opinion in Behavioral Sciences*, 4, 1–5. https://doi.org/10.1016/j.cobeha.2014.12.008

Post, S.G. (2014). It's good to be good: 2014 biennial scientific report on health, happiness, longevity, and helping others. *International Journal of Person Centered Medicine*, 2, 1–53.

Raichle, M.E., and Gusnard, D.A. (2002). Appraising the brain's energy budget. *PNAS*, 99(16), 10237–10239. https://doi.org/10.1073/pnas.172399499

Raisch, S., and Birkinshaw, J. (2008). Organizational ambidexterity: Antecedents, outcomes, and moderators. *Journal of Management*, 34(3), 375–409. https://doi.org/10.1177/0149206308316058

Randhawa, K., Nikolova, N., Ahuja, S., and Schweitzer, J. (2021). Design thinking implementation for innovation: An organization's journey to ambidexterity. *Journal of Product Innovation Management*, 38(6), 668–700. https://doi.org/10.1111/jpim.12599

Rock, D., and Schwartz, J. (2006). The neuroscience of leadership. *Strategy Business*, 43, 72–82.

Rokeach, M. (1973). *The Nature of Human Values*. New York: The Free Press.

Sana, F., Weston, T., and Cepeda, N.J. (2013). Laptop multitasking hinders classroom learning for both users and nearby peers. *Computers and Education*, 62, 24–31. https://doi.org/10.1016/j.compedu.2012.10.003

Satopää, V.A., Salikhov, M., Tetlock, P.E., and Mellers, B. (2021). Bias, information, noise: The BIN model of forecasting. Paper submitted to *Management Science*.

Savage, L.J. (1954). *Foundations of Statistics*. New York: Wiley.

Schacter, D., Gilbert, D., Wegner, D., and Hood, B. (2011). *Psychology*. European Edition. Basingstoke: Palgrave Macmillan.

Schirrmeister, E., Göhring, A., and Warnke, P. (2020). Psychological biases and heuristics in the context of foresight and scenario processes. *Futures and Foresight Science*. https://doi.org/10.1002/ffo2.31

Schoemaker, P.J.H., and Tetlock, P.E. (2016). Superforecasting: How to upgrade your company's judgment: How to dramatically improve your company's prediction capability. *Harvard Business Review*, May.

Schoss, S., Urbig, D., Brettel, M., et al. (2022). Deep-level diversity in entrepreneurial teams and the mediating role of conflicts on team efficacy and satisfaction. *International Entrepreneurship and Management Journal*, 18, 1173–1203. https://doi.org/10.1007/s11365-020-00654-1

Schulze, P., Heinemann, F., and Abedin, A. (2008). Balancing exploitation and exploration. *Academy of Management Proceedings*, 2008(1), 1–6. https://doi.org/10.5465/ambpp.2008.33622934

Schunk, D.H., and Pajares, F. (2002). The development of academic self-efficacy. In: *Development of Achievement Motivation*. Oxford: Elsevier, pp. 15–31. https://doi.org/10.1016/B978-012750053-9/50003-6

Sharot, T. (2017). *The Influential Mind: What the Brain Reveals About Our Power to Change Others*. New York: Henry Holt and Company.

Sharp, R. (2018). The rise of performance-enhancing drugs. *HR Magazine*, November 7.

Simon, H.A. (1979). Rational decision making in business organizations. *The American Economic Review*, 69(4), 493-513.

Slocum, S., and Hora, M.T. (2020). Workplace training and cognitive, intra- and interpersonal skills: A literature review. Center for Research on College-Workforce Transitions (CCWT), University of Wisconsin Madison.

Stajkovic, A.D., and Luthans, F. (1997). A meta-analysis of the effects of organizational behavior modification on task performance, 1975–1995. *Academy of Management Journal*, 40(5), 1122–1149.

Tang, Y.Y., Tang, Y., Tang, R., and Lewis-Peacock, J.A. (2017). Brief mental training reorganizes large-scale brain networks. *Frontiers in Systems Neuroscience*, 11. https://doi.org/10.3389/fnsys-2017.00006

Tarba, S.Y., Jansen, J.J.P., Mom, T.J.M., Raisch, S., and Lawton, T.C. (2020). A microfoundational perspective of organizational ambidexterity: Critical review and research directions. *Long Range Planning*, 53(6), 102048. https://doi.org/10.1016/j.lrp.2020.102048

Teding van Berkhout, E., and Malouff, J.M. (2016). The efficacy of empathy training: A meta-analysis of randomized controlled trials. *Journal of Counseling Psychology*, 63(1), 32–41. https://doi.org/10.1037/cou0000093

Tetlock, P.E., and Gardner, D. (2016). *Superforecasting: The Art and Science of Prediction*. New York: Crown Publishing.

Thaler, R.H., and Sunstein, C.R. (2008). *Nudge: Improving Decisions about Health, Wealth and Happiness*. New Haven, CT: Yale University Press.

The Economist (2023). Yuval Noah Harari argues that AI has hacked the operating system of human civilisation. April 28.

Tomov, M.S., Truong, V.Q., Hundia, R.A., and Gershman, S.J. (2020). Dissociable neural correlates of uncertainty underlie different exploration strategies. *Nature Communications*, 11(1), 2371. https://doi.org/10.1038/s41467-020-15766-z

Tomporowski, P.D., Davis, C.L., Miller, P.H., and Naglieri, J.A. (2008). Exercise and children's intelligence, cognition, and academic achievement. *Educational Psychology Review*, 20(2), 111–131. https://doi.org/10.1007/s10648-007-9057-0

Toulmin, S.E. (2003). *The Uses of Argument*. Cambridge: Cambridge University Press.

Tucker, A.M., Whitney, P., Belenky, G., Hinson, J.M., and Van Dongen, H.P. (2010). Effects of sleep deprivation on dissociated components of executive functioning. *Sleep*, 33(1), 47–57. https://doi.org/10.1093/sleep/33.1.47

Turner, M. (1996). *The Literary Mind: The Origins of Thought and Language*. Oxford: Oxford University Press.

Tushman, M.L., and O'Reilly III, C.A. (1996). Ambidextrous organizations: Managing evolutionary and revolutionary change. *California Management Review*, 38(4), 8–29.

Tversky, A., and Kahneman, D. (1974). Heuristics and biases. *Science*, New Series, 185(4157), 1124–1131.

Tzu, L. (2016). *Tao Te Ching*. CreateSpace Independent Publishing Platform.

Unsworth, N., Fukuda, K., Awh, E., and Vogel, E.K. (2014). Working memory and fluid intelligence: Capacity, attention control, and secondary memory retrieval. *Cognitive Psychology*, 71, 1–26. https://doi.org/10.1016/j.cogpsych.2014.01.003

Volz, K.G., and Gigerenzer, G. (2012). Cognitive processes in decisions under risk are not the same as in decisions under uncertainty. *Frontiers in Neuroscience*, 6. https://doi.org/10.3389/fnins.2012.00105

Weiss, H.M., and Cropanzano, R. (1996). Affective events theory: A theoretical discussion of the structure, causes and consequences of affective experiences at work. In: B.M. Staw and L.L. Cummings (Eds.), *Research in Organizational Behavior: An Annual Series of Analytical Essays and Critical Reviews*, Vol. 18, Oxford: Elsevier Science/JAI Press, pp. 1–74.

Westfall, C. (2019). Leadership development is a $366 billion industry: Here's why most programs don't work. *Fortune*, June 20. www.forbes.com/sites/chriswestfall/2019/06/20/leadership-development-why-most-programs-dont-work/?sh=1570df6761de

Wiehler, A., Branzoli, F., Adanyeguh, I., Mochel, F., and Pessiglione, M. (2022). A neuro-metabolic account of why daylong cognitive work alters the control of economic decisions. *Current Biology*, 32(16), 3564–3575. https://doi.org/10.1016/j.cub.2022.07.01

Winne, J.F., and Gittinger, J.W. (1973). An introduction to the Personality Assessment System. Journal of Community *Psychology*, 1(2), 99–163. https://doi.org/10.1002/1520-6629(197304)1:2<99::AID-JCOP2290010202>3.0.CO;2-U

Woolley, A.W., Chabris, C.F., Pentland, A., Hashmi, N., and Malone, T.W. (2010). Evidence for a collective intelligence factor in the performance of human groups. *Science*, *330*(6004), 686–688. https://doi.org/10.1126/science.1193147

Yukl, G., Seifert, C.F., and Chavez, C. (2008). Validation of the Extended Influence Behavior Questionnaire. *The Leadership Quarterly*, 19(5), 609–621.

Zaccaro, S.J., Gilbert, J.A., Thor, K.K., and Mumford, M.D. (1991). Leadership and social intelligence: Linking social perspectiveness and behavioral flexibility to leader effectiveness. *The Leadership Quarterly*, 2(4), 317–342. https://doi.org/10.1016/1048-9843(91)90018-W

About the Authors

Ana Procopio-Schön serves as a Senior Learning and Development Manager at ETH Zurich, where she manages executive education initiatives and custom programs for companies. With a very international career, Ana has brought her expertise to roles as a lecturer and research associate in higher education, as well as a project manager in both IT and the tourism industry. Ana's educational background includes a distinguished Ph.D. in Management and Economics, complemented by a master's degree in Entrepreneurship and Innovation.

Claudio Feser is a Senior Partner Emeritus and a Senior Advisor of McKinsey & Company, Inc. He served as a management consultant at McKinsey for nearly three decades, leading among others the Greek and the Swiss offices of McKinsey, and the firm's global leadership development practice. He was also a member of the Shareholder Council, McKinsey's global Board of Directors. He currently serves as chairman and member of several company boards. Further, he is a member of the Executive Education Committee and of the Senate Committee for Continuing Education of the University of St. Gallen. He is also an educator and lecturer. He lectures on innovation, individual and corporate adaptation, and leadership at both the University of St. Gallen and ETH Zurich, Switzerland. He has authored or co-authored three books – *Leadership at Scale: Better Leadership, Better Results*; *When Execution Isn't Enough: Decoding Inspirational Leadership*; *Serial Innovators: Firms that Change the World* – and several articles and teaching cases on company adaptation, innovation, strategy, and leadership.

Daniella Laureiro-Martinez works at ETH Zurich, in the Technology and Innovation Management Group. Within this group, she leads the COLAB, an internationally recognized research group focused on cognition, learning, and adaptive behavior. The group studies how individuals change and adapt, and how they lead organizations in adjusting to change and generating innovation. In her previous research, Daniella has delved into understanding the cognitive factors influencing decision-making and problem-solving in situations involving trade-offs, such as those between exploration and exploitation, profit and social outcomes, or different temporal horizons. Daniella prefers empirical studies and data – the more, the better – and does not shy away from combining methods and approaches depending on the question. She has often used think-aloud studies, behavioral experiments, neuropsychological tasks, and functional Magnetic Resonance Imaging (fMRI). Her research has been published in top peer-reviewed scientific journals in management, psychology, and cognitive neuroscience. Together with her colleagues, they have shown in different organizational settings that the brain networks and cognitive abilities related to cognitive control (such as attention control and cognitive flexibility) play an important role in shifting the type of thinking processes needed in a new situation, which in many cases leads to better performance. Her current research has two main goals. One is to find ways to improve the abilities related to attention and cognitive control and thus the decision-makers' learning and performance. A second goal is to expand the focus on decision-making to better understand the individual abilities and external factors that play a role in the earlier stages of problem solving. Daniella co-developed and teaches a variety of courses related to innovation, creativity, and leadership. All her courses build on her ongoing research and have a strong focus on participants increasing their self-knowledge and on developing transferability of the learned skills into their daily work and life routines. She holds a Ph.D. in Management (Strategy and Innovation) from Bocconi University. Prior to entering academia, she worked as a researcher and a business and government consultant in areas related to small businesses development in Latin America.

David Redaschi is currently a Ph.D. student at the Institute of Management & Strategy (IoMS) at the University of St. Gallen (HSG) and a visiting Ph.D. student at Harvard Business School (HBS). In his Ph.D., he specializes in business models, especially in their design and innovation. Before joining academia, he successfully founded and exited his platform startup. David holds an M.A. (with honors) in Business Management from the University of St. Gallen (HSG) and a B.A. in Business and Economics from the University of Basel, Switzerland.

Karolin Frankenberger is a full Professor of Strategic Management and Innovation at the University of St. Gallen, Switzerland, where she is also the Dean of the Executive School of Management, Technology, and Law. Prior to her academic career, Karolin worked for seven years at McKinsey & Company. Her research, which focuses on the topics of business transformation, ecosystems, business model innovation, and the circular economy has won several prestigious awards and appears regularly in top-tier academic and practitioner-oriented journals, such as *Harvard Business Review* and the *Academy of Management Journal*. Her co-authored book, *The Business Model Navigator* has become an international bestseller and is known as a standard reference in business model innovation literature. Karolin has also founded a spin-off, is an internationally renowned keynote speaker and supports company leaders from numerous industries worldwide in their strategy and innovation challenges. Karolin holds a Ph.D. with highest distinction from the University of St. Gallen, Switzerland, and was a visiting scholar/ faculty at Harvard Business School, University of Connecticut, and SGI-HSG in Singapore. She and her husband are parents to two children.

Stefano Brusoni (DPhil, University of Sussex) is Professor of Technology and Innovation Management and Vice Rector for Continuing Education at ETH Zurich, Switzerland. He studies how leaders in established organizations reconcile the conflicting expectations of business and society. His work aims at understanding how to develop organizations and leaders, in both the profit and non-profit space, who can reconcile such conflicts through innovation. He has published in journals such as *Strategic Management Journal*; *Administrative Science Quarterly*; *Organization Science*; *Academy of Management Journal*; and many others. He is Senior Editor of *Organization Science*. He is also a founder and entrepreneur, currently active in the EdTech space (www.sparkademy.com).

Index

acronym for model 115
addiction 180, 181
affective empathy 175-6, 177
agile teams 140
AI 221-4
ambidexterity 43, 51, 52, 138-9
   contextual 139, 140, 141
   structural 139
   temporal 139, 140-1
ambitiousness of goals 37, 38, 40
amygdala 75-6, 146, 201
anxiety disorders 179
Apple Macintosh 140
Aristotle 195
attention control 172-4, 177, 178-9, 182, 183, 218
attention deficit hyperactivity disorder (ADHD) 179
automatic behaviors 181
automatic limbic system 80-1

Balcetis, Emily 38-9
Bayesian decision theory 4
behavioral change 145-6, 148, 151-2
behavioral integration 143
behavioral patterns 12
biases see cognitive biases
Big Five personality framework 197
binary bias 31, 32-3
binary reward systems 33
Boston Consulting Group 48
brain
   contextual 139, 140, 141
   biases, overcoming 82-4
   "Either/Or" categories 32-3
   mammalian brain 77-9
   neural architecture 33
   predictive neural circuits, 6-7
   structure 73-4
   synaptic organization 33
   training 178-9
brainstem 74-5

Brier scores 8-9, 11
Browne, Sir Thomas 43
burnout 171

Camuffo, Arnaldo 116, 118
capabilities 6, 96, 102, 103, 130,
    148, 190, 220
  organizational 46, 51
cash-flow optimization program 63
cerebellum 75
cerebral cortex 77
character traits 177-8, 197
ChatGPT xiv, xvii, 221
choices 26, 30, 51, 52, 224
coaching skills 218
cognitive abilities 12, 36, 183, 217
cognitive-adaptive skills 169, 172-3, 178
cognitive and behavioral diversity 219
cognitive-behavioral disposition 205-6
cognitive-behavioral inclinations 169,
    177-8, 196, 216, 219-20
  leveraging 203-6
cognitive biases 16, 72-3, 81, 83
  harm to decision-making
    performance 91
  reduction of cognitive load 91-2
cognitive control 173
cognitive empathy 176-7
cognitive fatigue 78, 79
cognitive flexibility 172-3, 174-5, 177,
    178-9, 183, 218
cognitive health 220
cognitive load 170-1
  biases reducing 91-2
  reducing 146
cognitive skills 216, 219-20
  training 217, 220
cognitive states 41-2, 169-70, 172, 178,
    183, 216, 220
collective intelligence (CI) 15, 144
communication 150, 218
compassion 176

confident humility 122-4
confirmation biases 8
conservative personality 41
contextual ambidexterity 139, 140, 141
cooperativeness 199
coping strategies 202
cortisol 170
cost-reduction program 63
critical reasoning 86
cross-unit collaboration 149
crystallized intelligence 12
customer loyalty 129, 159

Darwin, Charles 201
Decision-Making Canvas see Decision
    Navigator
decision-making-model 119, 122
Decision Navigator 88, 122, 125
Decision Navigator, four-step 47, 52, 53
  with solution for Case 1 61
Decision Navigator, five-step 92, 93
  with solution for Case 2 98, 100
  with solution for Case 3 110
Decision Navigator, six-step
    125, 126, 215
  with solution for Case 3 114-15
  for Case 4 158
  for Case 5 186
decision rules see heuristics
decisions trees 5
decisions under certainty 4
decisions under risk 4
decisions under uncertainty, defined 5, 6,
    13, 17, 18
deductive problem solving 118
deepfakes 221
deep-level diversity 219
de-personalize assumptions 85
depression 171, 179
Descartes, René: Discourse on the
    Method 3, 69
design thinking 175

diet 170, 172, 183
Diogenes Laertius: Lives of the
    Philosophers 107
dispositional traits 13
diversity 142-3
dopamine 33, 179, 180, 181, 182
Drucker, Peter 222
Dunning, David 123
Dunning-Kruger effect 123-4
Dweck, Carol: Mindset: The New
    Psychology of Success 15

Edison, Thomas 123
either-or decisions 34, 52, 204, 207
emotions 76, 78, 79, 80, 175-6, 201-3
empathy 15, 172-3, 174, 178-9, 183,
    218
  affective 175-6, 177
  cognitive 176-7
employee engagement 218
employees, changing behaviour 147-8
entrepreneurial energy 130
Excite xiv
exercise 170, 174, 183
exits 116-17
exploit, definition 49
exploit-explore balance 36, 42, 48
exploit-explore continuum 33, 83
exploit-explore dilemmas 31, 49, 51, 52
exploit-explore optimization, heuristics
    of 44-6, 52
exploitation 31, 196
exploitation-oriented activities 35,
    43, 44, 137
exploitation routines 80-1
exploitation strategies 146-7. 148-9
exploration 31, 196
exploration-oriented activities 35,
    137-8, 148-9
exploration-oriented initiatives 43
explore, definition 51
ExxonMobil Corporation
    (Exxon) 48-9, 50

Facebook xiv
faith 12
financial incentives 148-9
fluid intelligence 12
forecasts, frequency of updating 13
Freud, Sigmund: iceberg picture 169

Gambardella, Alfonso 116, 118
general intelligence 14
Gilead 140
Gittins index 35, 36, 223
glutamate 78
goals
  ambitiousness of 37, 38, 40
  importance of 39
  mood 41-2
  opportunities 40
  performance achievement 38
  personality and values 41
  rewards 148
  skills 41
  social context 40-1
  time 40
  visualizing 39
  writing down 39
Good Judgment Project (GJP) 7-8
Google xiv
  20% time' rule 40
Grant, Adam 122
growth 159
growth mindset 15-16
gut feelings 120-1

Harari, Yuval Noah xvii, 221
harm avoidance 197
harmful exploitation 180
hemispheres 77
Heraclitus 135
heuristics 5, 6, 13, 16, 17, 18
    seven 36-7, 44, 46, 47, 50, 51, 52, 69,
        83-4, 109, 112-13, 115

high-stakes decisions xvi, xviii, 204, 215
hippocampus 75, 76, 146, 170
Hippocrates: "Four Humours"
    theory 197
histamine 179
homeostasis 75
Horney, Karen 202
hostile bid 163
Human Resources (HR) 22
hypothalamus 75

incentives 148
individual decision-makers 216-17
individual intelligence 144
inductive problem solving 118
Instagram xiv
insula 146
integrity 178
intelligence 12, 16
intelligence tests 14
intuition 120-1
inverted U 43

Kahneman, Daniel 72
kanban sessions 140
Kegan, Robert 211
Kennedy, John F. 150
Kite Pharma 140
Klitschko, Vitali xvii, 221
Know Thyself 205
Kodak xiv
Kruger, Justin 123

Lao Tzu: Tao Te Ching 29
large language model (LLM)
    technology xiv
large worlds 5
leadership repertoire 151
lean production method 140

limbic system 75-6, 77, 146
low-level diversity 219
loyalty 178
Luddites 221-2

medial prefrontal cortex (MPFC) 39
medication nonadherence 145-6
meditation 172, 174, 183
Mellers, Barbara 7-8, 11
mergers and acquisitions (M&A) 163
Meta Platforms, Inc. 48, 49, 50
metacognition 174, 182
Microsoft xiv
mindfulness 172
minimum viable product (MVP) 87, 116
mission statement 150
moods 41-21
multi-armed bandit (MAB) test 167-9
Multiple R 14
multi-tasking 172
Myers-Briggs: MBTI 197

narcolepsy 179
neocortex 77, 78-9, 146, 201
net promoter scores (NPS) 129
neuro-enhancers 180
neuromodulating drugs 179=80
neuromodulation 179
neurotransmitters 33, 179-82
non-financial incentives 149
non-sequitur reasoning 86
noradrenaline 179, 180, 181
norepinephrine see noradrenaline
Novelty Seeking (NS) 197

OCEAN (Openness, Conscientiousness,
    Extroversion, Agreeableness and
    Neuroticism) 197
OpenAI xiv

operational performance 43
optimization algorithm 112-13
option space 83, 92
organizational tensions 136-7, 151-3, 216
organizations, implications for 217-21
overconfidence 8

performance
    cognitive 91, 169, 170, 171
    company 43, 219
    culture of 59, 149
    decision-making 91, 168, 169, 182, 216
    operational 43
    strategic 43
    team 10
performance-oriented culture 59, 149
persistence (PS) 198
personal inclinations 183
personality 177-8, 196-9, 205, 219
personality traits 11-12
physical activity per week, 172
pivots 117
predictions
    ability to make 14
    debating with others 14
    forecasting accuracy 14
prefrontal cortex (PFC) 79, 170, 173
prefrontal dopamine 181
prejudices see cognitive biases
private equity (PE) 20
probabilistic theory 4
profitability 159
Project Management Office (PMO) 130
prototype 87, 116

qualitative market research 87

reactive emotional tendencies 196,
    201-3, 205, 219
relative uncertainty 82, 90

return on equity (ROE) 20
reward dependence (RD) 198
risk-averse people 41
risk-oriented people 41
role modeling 149-50
Rubik's cube 34

satisficers 36
Savage, Leonard 4, 5
scenario planning 5
scientific experimentation
    approach xvii, 224
scientific thinking, impact on
    entrepreneurial
    decision-making 117
self-awareness 183
self-directedness 198-9
self-transcendence 199
serotonin 179
Simon, Herbert 36
situational factors 12-13
skunk works 139-40
sleep 170, 172, 179, 183
small worlds 4
smart drugs 180
social media 48
Socrates 107
start-ups 117
statistics 5
stereotypes see cognitive biases
stories, use of, to illustrate values and
    ideals 150
strategic intent 137
strategic performance 43
strategic planning process 140
striatal dopamine transmission 181
striatum 76, 78, 80
structural ambidexterity 139
structural separation 141-2
sub-optimal options 92
superforecasters, 8, 11, 12, 13, 14
SWOT analysis 63

sympathy 176
systolic blood pressure (SBP) 39

T experiment 70-1
takeaways 18, 52, 92, 125, 153, 183, 207
take-over bid 163
targets 148
team diversity 15, 144, 219, 220
team dynamics 143, 144
teamness 144
Temperament and Character
    Inventory (TCI) 197
temperaments 197
temporal ambidexterity 139, 140-1
tensions, organizational 136-7, 138, 141-2
Tetlock, Philip 7
thalamus 75
Theory of Mind 176-7
thinking about thinking 182
thinking in options 82-3
time 10, 40, 151
Tolstoy, Leo 165

tough decisions xviii, 179, 185-93, 195,
    204-6, 207
transformation programs 148-50

uncertainty bonus 82, 83
unconscious biases 72

values 177-8, 196, 199-201, 205,
    219
virtual reality 48

Wooley, Anita 15
work-life balance 153

Yahoo xiv

Zuckerberg, Mark 49